WAR *and* PEACE

in the

MAJID KHADDURI

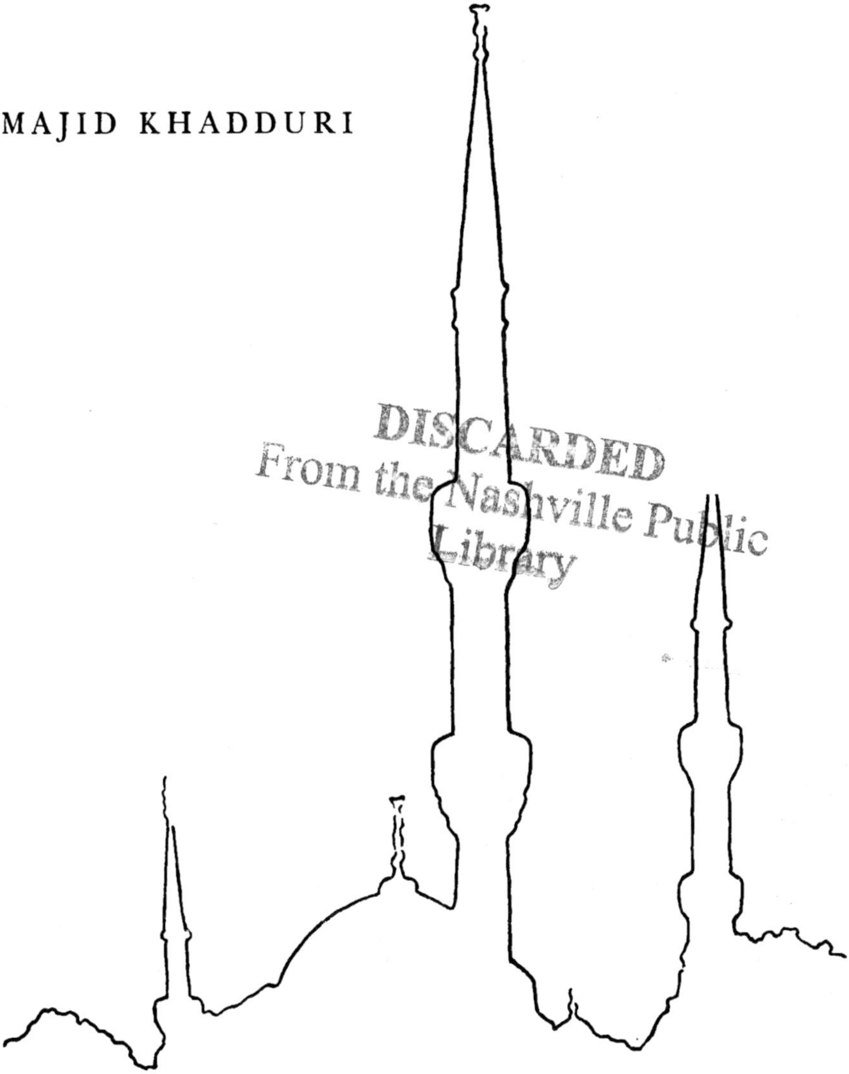

THE LAWBOOK EXCHANGE, LTD.
Clark, New Jersey

ISBN-13: 9781584776956 (hardcover)
ISBN-13: 9781616190484 (paperback)

Lawbook Exchange edition 2006, 2010

THE LAWBOOK EXCHANGE, LTD.
33 Terminal Avenue
Clark, New Jersey 07066-1321

Please see our website for a selection of our other publications and fine facsimile reprints of classic works of legal history:
www.lawbookexchange.com

Library of Congress Cataloging-in-Publication Data

Khadduri, Majid, 1908-
War and peace in the law of Islam / Khadduri, Majid.
p. cm.
Originally published: Baltimore : Johns Hopkins Press, [1955]
Includes bibliographical references and index.
ISBN-13: 978-1-58477-695-6 (alk. paper)
ISBN-10: 1-58477-695-1 (alk. paper)
1. International law (Islamic law) 2. War (Islamic law) 3. Jihad. I. Title.
KB260.K53 2006
340.5'9--dc22 2006003089

WAR AND PEACE IN THE LAW OF ISLAM

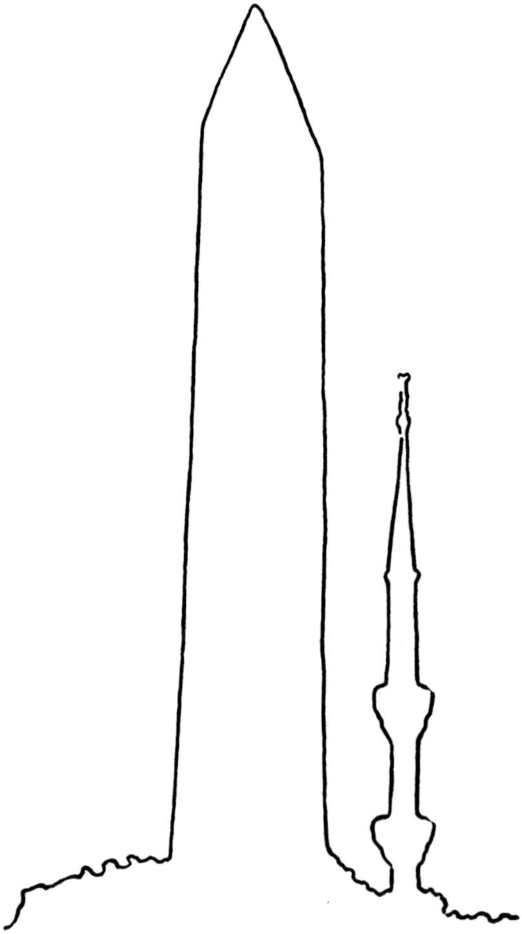

WAR *and* **PEACE**
in the Law of **ISLAM**

MAJID KHADDURI

The Johns Hopkins Press *Baltimore*

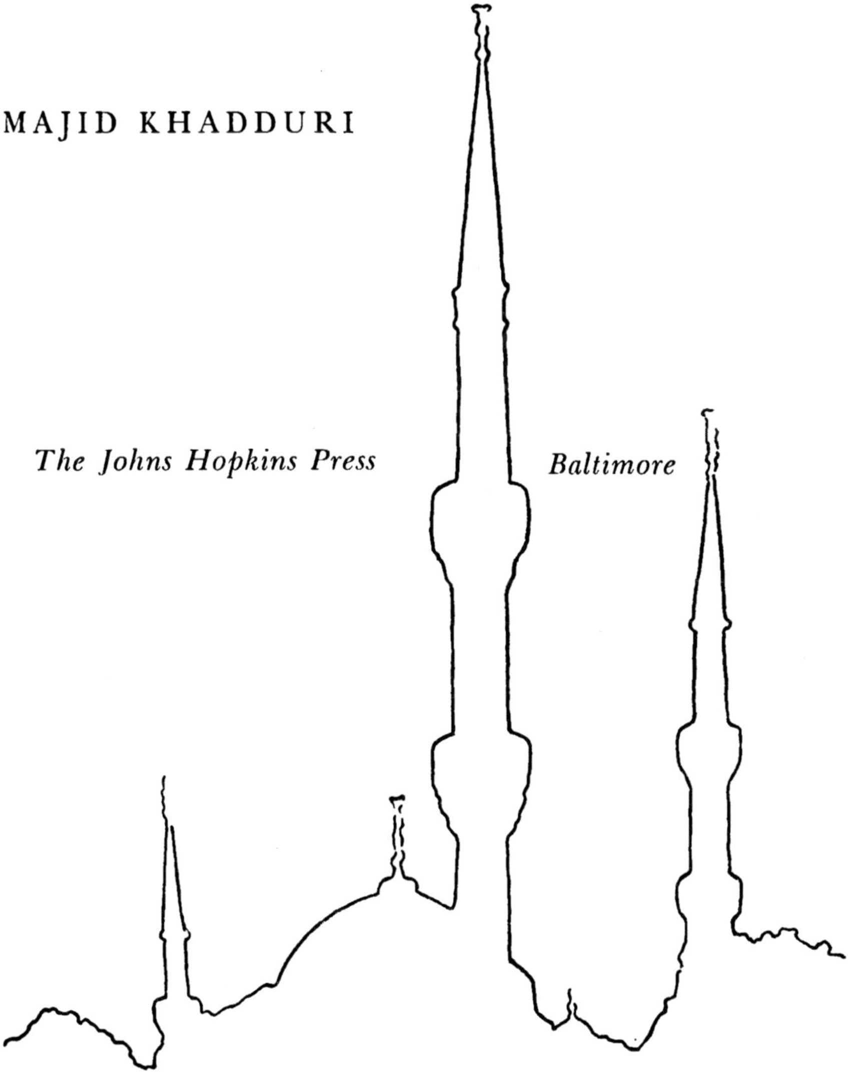

Distributed in Great Britain by Geoffrey Cumberlege:
Oxford University Press, London

Printed in U.S.A. by the William Byrd Press,
Richmond, Virginia

Library of Congress Catalog Card No. 55–8427

TO QUINCY WRIGHT

with esteem and affection

PREFACE

The entry of ten Muslim states into the United Nations and its agencies is a significant phenomenon in view of the radical differences between the traditional Muslim law of nations and the principles embodied in the United Nations Charter. Islam, emerging in the seventh century as a conquering nation with world domination as its ultimate aim, refused to recognize legal systems other than its own. It was willing to enter into temporary treaty relations with other states, pending consummation of its world mission. The "temporary" period endured for several centuries, and it proved itself more permanent than originally contemplated. It was in this fashion that Islam, undergoing many changes in its legal structure, came to reconcile itself to modern conditions of life; the various nations professing this religion today are participating in promoting stable world order and international co-operation.

It is the aim of the present study to reconstruct the classical legal theory of Islam, as well as the principles and the rules governing Islam's relations with non-Muslim countries. Since any discussion of the classical theory and practice would merely indicate the radical differences that existed between the Muslim and the modern laws of nations, a concluding chapter has been added which discusses the fundamental changes that the Muslim law of nations had undergone and how it adapted itself to peaceful coexistence with rival legal systems.

The first edition of this work, published in England in

1941, confined itself to a study of the principles and practices in early Islam. The present edition seeks not only to formulate from the diverse original documents a consistent legal theory and practice of Islam's relations with other nations throughout the centuries but also to discuss the efforts in recent times aimed at adapting Islam to the principles and purposes of the modern community of nations. Certain parts of the first and second chapters which appeared originally in *Islamic Culture, The Muslim World* and *The George Washington Law Review,* have been revised for inclusion in the present volume.

The writer wishes to express his appreciation for the suggestions he has received since the publication of the first edition. A number of critics have read the work after its revision was completed. Professor Joseph Schacht, of the University of Leiden, read the first three chapters, Sir Hamilton Gibb, of the University of Oxford, the fifth chapter, Professor Philip K. Hitti, of Princeton University, the first and seventeenth chapters, Dean Philip W. Thayer, of the School of Advanced International Studies of the Johns Hopkins University, the third and final chapters, Professor Leo Strauss, of the University of Chicago, the first and fifth chapters, and Emil Lang, the seventeenth and final chapters. The writer wishes in particular to express his thanks for the invaluable assistance given him by Quincy Wright, Edwin E. Calverley and Arthur Jeffery, who read the entire work, and to William M. Carson and Jamal Sa'd, who prepared the Index. The author alone is responsible for the views expressed in the volume as well as for any errors which might have remained uncorrected.

Majid Khadduri

CONTENTS

BOOK I

FUNDAMENTAL CONCEPTS OF MUSLIM LAW

"There is in fact a true law namely right reason, which is in accordance with nature, applies to all men and is unchangeable and eternal. . . . It will not lay down one rule at Rome and another at Athens, nor will it be one rule today and another tomorrow. But there will be one law eternal and unchangeable binding all times and upon all peoples." Cicero.

"Knowest thou not that it is God unto whom belongeth the sovereignty of the heavens and earth . . . ?" Qur'ān II, 110.

CHAPTER I

THEORY OF THE STATE

Society and the State

Muslim thinkers, after the fashion of their Greek predecessors, took it for granted that by nature "man is a social animal": he can live only as a member of society. No individual, except God—Allāhu aḥad—can live alone; men were created to live together.[1] To Muslim thinkers, from the Prophet Muḥammad (A.D. 632) to Ibn Khaldūn (A.D. 1406), the individual's rights and obligations were always defined in terms of (though subordinate to) the community's interests. In the Tradition, Muḥammad is reported to have conceived of the Muslim community as "a single hand, like a compact wall whose bricks support each other," and in the Qur'ān it is often referred to as

[1] No one has stated this more finely than Aristotle: "The man who is isolated . . . is no part of the city, and must therefore be either a beast or a god." *Politics,* Book I, p. 6 (Ernest Barker's translation).

a distinct "nation" (umma) or a "brotherhood," bound by common obligations to a superior divine authority.[2] The conception of the umma or brotherhood constituted the basis of the Islamic community in whose membership alone the believer obtains prosperity in this world and salvation in the next. In his compact with the people of Madīna (A.D. 623) Muḥammad defined his Muslim community as "an umma in distinction from the rest of the people"[3] in which all loyalties, tribal or otherwise, were superseded by the Muslim brotherhood. "The protection of Allah," stated Muḥammad in another provision of the treaty, "is one [and is equally] extended to the humblest of the believers." No social distinction was imposed upon the members of the brotherhood; for, although Allah "created you of male and female, and made you races and tribes," He recognized no differences among them save on the basis of "piety" and "godfearing."[4] In this conception of the umma was also implied the idea of the state, but this political concept will be considered later.

Whether founded on filial, customary, or religious ties, the history of early societies shows that greater emphasis seemed to have been attached to the group; the individual counted for little by himself, owing to his weakness and inability either to provide a livelihood or to protect himself against outsiders. Only through the family, clan or *civitas,* to which the individual belonged, could he claim the right to protection by means of custom or social mores. Al-Fārābī (A.D. 870-950), in discussing his model state, stressed the necessity of a society in which the individual could attain physical and moral satisfaction.

"By his very nature," said al-Fārābī, "man is not equipped to

[2] Qur'ān, III, 106 (Hereafter the Qur'ān will be referred to as "Q").

[3] For the text of the treaty, see pp. 206-9, below.

[4] Q. XLIX, 13: ". . . the most honourable of you in the sight of God is the most pious of you."

attain all that is necessary for his needs without the help of others. . . . If man is ever to achieve the perfection of his nature, he must belong to society (qawm) and cooperate with his fellowmen. . . ."[5]

Not only is Society regarded as indispensable for the survival of man, but also inherent in it is the concept of authority. Society, that is, cannot survive without authority. Indeed the Islamic conception of umma presupposes the existence of a set of divine commands, endowed by a Supreme Legislator, constituting its "fundamental law" or "constitution." This is regarded as absolutely necessary since society without authority was impossible; for, though man is a social animal by nature, he is not a well-behaving animal. Has not Allah himself declared "Men are the enemies of each other?"[6] Has He not stated "were it not for God [causing] the restraint of one man [by means] of another, the earth would have been corrupted"?[7] The restraint upon man's social relations was enforced by authority and regulated by law; the latter was to show the beaten track to be trodden (and indeed the very term sharī'a gives us this meaning) and the former as sanction for the enforcement of law. The philosopher-historian Ibn Khaldūn (A.D. 1332-1406), summing up this conception of society and state (to which he himself made no mean contribution), said:

> Human society is necessary . . . the reason being that man has been created in such a manner that he cannot sustain life without food. Each individual's capacity for acquiring food, however, falls short of his need;

[5] Abū Naṣr al-Fārābī, *Risāla fī Arā' Ahl al-Madīna al-Fāḍila,* ed. Friedrich Dieterici (Leiden, 1895), p. 53. In another treatise al-Fārābī goes on to argue that not only man but certain species of the animal and plant kingdoms cannot sustain life without living together in groups (jamā'a). See Fārābī's *Kitāb al-Siyāsāt al-Madaniyya* (Hyderabad, A.H. 1346), pp. 38-9.

[6] Q. XX, 121.

[7] Q. II, 252.

> . . . it is therefore necessary to unite his efforts with those of his fellow men in order that by cooperation they will produce food sufficient for many times their number. [Further], each individual needs the help of his fellow men for defense purposes; for, as God gave to each animal an organ of self-defense . . , to man he gave the mind and the hand which, in the service of the mind, can apply itself to the crafts and produce tools which take the place of animal's organs of defense. . . . [Thus] unless he cooperates with others, he cannot obtain the food necessary for life, nor can he obtain the weapons necessary for defense, without which he will fall a prey to the beasts and his species will perish. Cooperation, however, secures food for life and weapons for defense, thus fulfilling God's will of preserving the species. Thus society is necessary for mankind, without which it cannot exist. . . .
>
> Human society having been achieved . . . then arises the need for restraining each man from another owing to his animal propensities for aggression and oppression. The weapons with which men defended themselves against wild beasts obviously cannot serve as a restraint, since each man can make equal use of them. There must exist accordingly a restraining force . . . which must be sought from one man who will be entrusted with power and authority so that no longer will an individual be attacked by another. This is what is implied in the term *mulk* (sovereignty or statehood) which exists by nature in man and is necessary for his existence.[8]

While it would seem that there is no originality in the Islamic conception of society, Muslim thinkers have stressed the necessity of attaching to the concept of society the corollary concept of the state which is regarded as an essential prerequisite for society. Not that the state preceded society, but that the latter's existence is dependent on the former. The state necessarily had arisen as a result of the aggressive and evil propensities of man; for, if these disruptive elements were left unrestrained, society would be ruined. This is, of course, the idea ascribed several centuries later to Hobbes who based his social-contract theory on the assumption of the evil nature of man which made it imperative that he should surrender part of his individual

[8] Ibn Khaldūn, *Al-Muqaddima,* ed. Quatremère (Paris, 1858), Vol. I, pp. 68-72.

liberty to a superior authority. The contribution of Islamic political theory, accordingly, lies not only in advancing a theory ascribed later to Hobbes, but that the latter, in merely analyzing man's instinct psychologically, failed to show the sociological implications in the relations between man and society which Ibn Khaldūn had grasped three centuries before him.[9]

This is not to suggest, however, that Islam from the very beginning made a clear distinction between society and state. In the early Islamic conception society and the state meant the thing; indeed the term state is not to be found in the Qur'ān, nor was it in vogue in Muḥammad's time. The Qur'ān merely refers to organized authority, which belongs to God (as the source of governing authority) forming part of the state; while society, whether it engulfed the state or constituted certain aspects of it, was the creation of man's needs to fulfill certain social functions.[10]

The Juridical Basis of the State

In the Islamic conception the world was at first created to be inhabited not by one, but by a variety of peoples, each endowed

[9] Aristotle may have preceded both Ibn Khaldūn and Hobbes in making several references to these ideas (*Politics,* I, Chapter 2), but Ibn Khaldūn and Hobbes worked out more elaborate theories of society in which the sociological (Ibn Khaldūn) and the psychological (Hobbes) factors were analyzed.

[10] When the term *dawla* (now equivalent to "state") came into vogue in the early 'Abbāsid period, it was at first applied to the new regime established by revolution, as opposed to the regime of the Umayyads (see Ṭabarī, *Ta'rīkh,* ed. M.J. de Geoje [15 vols.; Leiden, 1879-1901], Series III, Vol. I, pp. 85, 115.) but the concepts of authority and government were necessarily implied. As the 'Abbāsid regime became permanently established, the emphasis was gradually changed from revolution to organized authority.

with its own divine order. To each people Allah sent a Prophet, communicating the divine law, which constituted a covenant between Him and that people. The world before Muḥammad, therefore, was not conceived of as a unified but as a composite community (a pluralistic world), each people to conform to their own covenant and to submit to their own Prophet. But these peoples, one after the other, have broken their covenants and distorted the teachings of their Prophets. Warnings of evil consequences have often been made, but to no avail. It became necessary accordingly to make a last effort and Allah decided to send Muḥammad, the last of His Prophets (referred to in the Qur'ān as the "seal of the Prophets")[11] who was to repair and reconstruct the world into a monistic order. Muḥammad warned first his people and then called all others to accept his mission. Thus Muḥammad's teachings (embodied in the term "Islam") were to constitute the final and definitive religion to all people.

It follows accordingly that Muḥammad's mission might be regarded as an evidence of Allah's desire to renew His earlier covenant (or covenants) with mankind and that those who responded to Muḥammad's call became God's true believers. Hence the term "Islam," which means "surrender" or "submission" to Allah's will,[12] reflects the nature of the relations between Allah as governor and His people, the believers, as governed.[13] Thus the foundation of the Islamic social polity was made on the basis of a compact of agreement, being understood that this agreement was by no means one between two equals. It was rather a compact of submission, which reflects

[11] Q. XXXIII, 40. See Edwin E. Calverley, "Mohammad, Seal of the Prophets?" *The Moslem World,* Vol. XXVI (1936), pp. 79-82.

[12] Q. II, 127, 130; III, 77-8.

[13] The term 'ibād Allah may be used as equivalent to the term "governed" or "subjects."

the nature of Allah's covenant with man. Not only is this true in terms of theology, but also in terms of Islamic law; for the very basis of a contract in Islamic law is merely a formal proposal made by one party and acceptance by the other. And this seems to be exactly how Muḥammad approached his people: Islam was proposed by Muḥammad to each individual and the latter submitted to the divine will for his own welfare in this world and salvation in the next. For every later member of the Islamic community, whether native-born or converted, the individual basis of submission was recognized on the basis of *pactum tacitum*.

Was the Islamic state based on a single-contract theory or two-contracts? By one-contract theory the people gather together to form a society. According to al-Fārābī and Hobbes, the isolated individuals agreed on a universal contract of submission to a ruler who is vested at once with exclusive power. The double or two-contract theory assumes that once a society is formed by one contract, a king is enthroned by another contract to rule in accordance with certain conditions and limitations on his authority.[14] To which of these two categories does the Islamic state belong? The Hebrew covenant, in terms of Biblical political theory, was more like a single-contract establishing God's absolute sovereignty.[15] In the case of the Islamic state there seems to be no difference between the apostolic state of Muḥammad and the caliphial state of his successors.

[14] Otto von Gierke calls the single-contract *Gesellschaftsvertrag* (*pacte d'association*), which establishes the state as a political society, and the second contract *Herrschaftsvertrag* (*pacte de gouvernement*) which creates the state in a sense of a government. See Gierke, *Natural Law and the Theory of Society*, tr. Ernest Barker (Cambridge, 1934), Vol. I, pp. 48, 107-8.

[15] "The distinctive thing about the Hebrew Covenant," says Paul Ramsey, "was God's transcendence over it, not democratic ratification or constitutional contracting" (Paul Ramsey, "Elements of Biblical Political Theory," *The Journal of Religion*, Vol. XXIX (1949), p. 265.)

Both, it is true, regarded Allah as the supreme, though not the direct, ruler of the state. Under Muḥammad not only the executive, but also the legislative and judicial functions of Allah were united. Muḥammad, as the mouthpiece of Allah, had monopolized all the powers of Caesar. In more precise terms we may argue that only the possession of sovereignty resided with Allah, while its exercise was delegated to Muḥammad who, as vicegerent of Allah, was instructed to rule with justice.[16] Allah, accordingly, was the titular head of the state and its source of governing authority; Muḥammad was its head of government.

The apostolic state, however, may be said to have undergone a change after Muḥammad's death. The last of the Prophets died without providing a rule for his immediate succession. Was the contract with Allah, accordingly, broken since his representative on earth had passed away? The Islamic community was divided on this issue, one section arguing that it owed allegiance to Allah, not to Muḥammad himself, and that the situation would resolve itself merely to the selection of a successor who would be entrusted with the execution of the divine commands which were still binding upon the Muslims. Another section of the community, the nomads, who were accumstomed to the tribal tradition of owing allegiance to the very person of the chief, argued that their allegiance to Muḥammad came to an end with his death and they defied the new authority of Madīna.

The outcome of this controversy, in the settlement of which force played an important part, was a compromise between the two points of view establishing a new rule. The position of Muḥammad as the executive head of the governing authority was filled by a caliph (successor to Muḥammad) but not his prophetic function of communicating and promulgating the

[16] Q. XXXVIII, 25.

divine law. The caliph declared that he was merely to administer and enforce the divine law. Thus it was not only that the legislative and executive powers were separated, but also, at least in theory, divine legislation came to an end. The judicial function of the caliph was reduced merely to the interpretation of the law rather than to make new law. To what extent had this new arrangement changed the contractual basis of the Islamic state?

In the single-contract theory, it will be remembered, the people are regarded as a passive party; the election of a successor to Muḥammad by leading Muslims had obviously introduced the "popular" factor in the selection of the executive head of the government.[17] A new contract seems, therefore, to have been added to the first; a contract between the Muslim community on the one hand, and the caliph, who was enthroned for the purpose of enforcing the divine law, on the other. Thus the second contract supplemented the first, since it renewed the people's allegiance to Allah as well as requiring the caliph to carry out all the obligations which he and the people had accepted under their primary contract with Allah.

The question may be asked: to whom was the caliph made responsible—to Allah or to the people? In the double-contract

[17] Our use of the term "popular" factor in the election of the caliph should be qualified by the fact that in practice the caliph was almost always enthroned by a limited number of the people. The jurists have distinguished between the bay'a of ahl al-ḥallwa'l-'aqd and the general bay'a. It would seem that the two might be regarded, from the viewpoint of "popular" election, as supplementary to each other; the former meant the selection or nomination of the caliph—which by no means could be regarded as a final step in theory—and the other, by merely giving a formal or tacit homage, conforms or ratifies the action of the people's representatives (ahl al-ḥallwa'l-'aqd). See al-'Abbās ibn Aḥmad al-Ḥasanī, *Tatimmat al-Rawḍ al-Naḍīr Sharḥ Majmū' al-Fiqh al-Kabīr* (Cairo, A.H. 1349), pp. 17-9.

theory, the ruler is enthroned on the basis of certain conditions and limitations to his power. The caliph's powers were derived from and limited by the divine law; only his appointment was made by the people. It follows, accordingly, that the caliph who could enjoy as much power as Muḥammad (except his prophetic or legislative powers) was responsible to the people only insofar as his faithfulness was concerned in the enforcement of the divine law. But was the caliph to be dethroned if he violated his obligations? The Muslim jurist-theologians were divided on this point. Al-Māwardī (A.D. 974-1058), who worked out in detail the qualifications and functions of the ideal caliph, argued that if the caliph did not fulfill, or was incapacitated from fulfilling, his duties, he had no right to remain a caliph.[18] But al-Māwardī failed to indicate how the caliph was to be dethroned through proper legal channels. Only the Khawārij, it seems, had openly advocated the principle of revolution. To them the caliphate was a purely democratic institution, based on a second-contract theory, which empowers the electorate to depose or put to death a caliph who violated his duties.[19] In contrast to this school of thought, al-Ash'arī (died A.D. 935) not only denied any right of popular revolution but also emphasized the caliph's full claim to obedience even if he had disregarded or violated his duties. Al-Ash'arī said:

[18] See Māwardī, *Kitāb al-Aḥkām al-Sulṭāniyya*, ed. Enger (Bonn, 1853), pp. 25-32. For an analysis of Māwardī's theory of the caliphate, see H. A. R. Gibb, "Al-Māwardī's theory of the Khilāfa," *Islamic Culture*, Vol. XI (July, 1937), pp. 291-302.

[19] For the Khārijī theory of the caliphate, see Sir Thomas Arnold, *The Caliphate* (Oxford, 1924) pp. 188-9; William Thomson, "Kharijitism and Kharijites," in *The Macdonald Presentation Volume* (Princeton, 1933), pp. 373-89; Elie A. Sālim, *The Khawārij Theory and Institutions* (thesis, 1953, the Library of the School of Advanced International Studies of The Johns Hopkins University).

> We uphold the prayer for the welfare of the *imāms* [caliphs] of the Muslims and the confession of their imāmate; and we maintain the error of those who approve of the uprising against them whenever it appeared that they have abandoned the right; and we believe in the denial of an armed uprising against them and abstinence from fighting in civil war.[20]

The tendency among the later Muslim publicists was to exalt the position of the caliph and justify his authority on the grounds of fear of disorder and anarchy. Some publicists went so far as to justify the authority of any ruler who could effectively maintain order, regardless of his piousness or injustice. The justification for this acquiescence has been sought by references in the Qur'ān warning against fitna (strife or civil war).[21] The jurists, in their arguments against rebellion repeated again and again that tyranny and impiousness is better than anarchy.[22] Perhaps there is no better citation in favor of an established ruler's claim to obedience than that of Badr al-Dīn ibn Jamā'a (died A.D. 1333) who, in stating the modes of possessing authority, said:

> If, in the absence of an *imām,* someone assumes power by force, even if he were unqualified and assumes it without *bay'a,* his imāmate becomes binding and obedience to him is necessary in order to maintain the unity of the Muslims. That he may be unjust, vicious, or lacking in knowledge is of no consequence. If the imāmate of force were challenged by another who replaces it by force, the latter becomes the recognized *imām* in view of the fact that this action is consistent with Muslim interests and maintenance of Islam's unity, in accordance with an utterance of ibn 'Umar who said: "We are on the side of the victor."[23]

[20] Ash'arī, *Kitāb al-Ibāna* (Hyderabad, 2nd ed., 1948), p. 9. Nasafī (died A.H. 537), another supporter of Orthodoxy, said: "The *imām* is not to be removed for evil-doing," See Nasafī's *Creed* and Taftāzānī's *Commentary,* tr. E. E. Elder (New York, 1950), p. 150.

[21] Q. II, 187; 214.

[22] See Taftāzānī's *Commentary* on Nasafī's *Creed, op. cit.,* p. 150-1.

[23] Ibn Jamā'a, *Taḥrīr al-Aḥkām fī Tadbīr Ahl al-Islām* in *Islamica* (Leipzig, 1934), Bd. VI, p. 357.

A Divine Universal Nomocracy

The category of statehood in which the temporal and the spiritual powers were united (and these were derived from an ultimate divine source) has often been mistakenly called a theocracy. Certain writers have gone so far as to argue that all religious states were, even though authority was divided into the religious and temporal (but on the assumption that the latter was to be sanctioned by the former), theocracies.[24] A distinction, however, must be made between an authority which is directly derived from and exercised by God, and an authority which is derived from a divine code endowed by God but enforced by His vicegerent (or by a secular ruler) which is equally binding upon the latter and the people. This distinction between the incidence and exercise of authority shows that the term theocracy would be inconsistent with our foregoing discourse on the nature of the Islamic state.

To what category of statehood, therefore, should the Islamic state belong? The state may be called monarchical or oligarchical (in the Aristotelian sense) if its ultimate authority is entrusted, by reason or force, to one or the few; it is democratic, if ultimate authority is regarded as flowing from and by the consent of the people. The State is theocratic, as defined by Ryder Smith, if it "claims to be governed by a god or gods."[25] The *Oxford Dictionary* defines it as "a form of government in

[24] See J. C. Bluntschli, *Allgemeine Staatslehre* (Stuttgart, 1875), pp. 390, 397-399; Fritz Kern, *Kingship and Law in the Middle Ages,* tr. S. B. Chrines (Oxford, 1939), pp. 27-34. For the conception of Islamic theocracy, see J. Wellhausen, *The Arab Kingdom and its Fall,* tr. M. G. Weir (Calcutta, 1927), pp. 5, 8; T. W. Arnold, *The Preaching of Islam* (London, 3rd ed., 1935), p. 32; Muḥammad Ḥamīdullah, *Muslim Conduct of the State* (Lahore, 2nd ed., 1945), pp. 74, 180.

[25] C. Ryder Smith, "Theocracy," *Encyclopaedia of Religion and Ethics,* Vol. XII, pp. 287-9. See also Georg Jellinek, *Allgemeine Staatslehre* (Berlin, 3rd ed., 1919), p. 289.

which God (or deity) is recognized as the king or immediate ruler." The term theocracy was coined by Flavius Josephus (*circa* A.D. 37-100) to characterize the type of the Israelite State which existed in the first century of the Christian era. Josephus said:

> . . . there are innumerable differences in the particular customs and laws that are among all mankind, which a man may briefly reduce under the following heads: some legislators have permitted their governments to be under monarchies, others put them under oligarchies, and others under a republican form; but our legislator had no regard to any of these forms, but he ordained our government to be what, by a strained expression, may be termed a Theocracy, by ascribing the authority and the power to God, and by persuading all the people to have a regard to him, as the author of all things. . . .[26]

Wellhausen, who approves of Josephus' terminology and has applied it to the Arab state, maintains that Jewish theocracy existed only in theory, that is an ideal representation of the Israelite state at the time of Jewish decline.[27] Christianity, which originally was not associated with politics,[28] gradually developed the tradition that every power possessing authority in the state ought to be recognized as a divinely ordained authority.[29] When the state formally adopted Christianity the

[26] Josephus, *Works,* tr. William Whiston (London, 1875), Vol. II, pp. 547-8.

[27] J. Wellhausen, *Prolegomena to the History of Israel,* tr. R. F. Black and A. Menzies (Edinburgh, 1885), p. 411.

[28] This is based on Christ's statement: "My kingdom is not of this World" (John XVIII, 36). "His Kingdom," said Tellenbach, "was a supernatural power working in the World, and remaining for all others a matter of hope and expectation. Out of Christ's attitude to the World arose among the early Christians a tendency to withdraw from temporal affairs and to concentrate on the Kingdom of Heaven" (Gerd Tellenbach, *Church, State and Christian Society at the Time of the Investiture Contest,* tr. R. F. Bennett (Oxford, 1940), p. 25).

[29] Matt. XVII, 21: "Render to Caesar the things that are Caesar's and to God, the things that are God's." See also Fritz Kern, *op. cit.,* p. 27.

sanction of the Church became necessary for political authority, and the aim of the state had become to put God's law into practice. At that stage Christianity and the state had become so closely associated with one another that the Christian religion had become the *Respublica Christiana*.[30]

It is to be noted that in Judaism, Christianity, and Islam God never had been regarded as the immediate ruler of his subjects; only his representatives (vicegerents) on earth were the real executives. Hence the divine law (or a sacred code), regarded as the source of governing authority, was the essential feature in the process of control under these systems. The Law, it will be recalled, precedes the state: it provides the basis of the state. It is therefore not God, but God's law which really governs; and, as such, the State should be called nomocracy, not theocracy. The *Oxford Dictionary* defines nomocracy as "a system of government based on a legal code; the rule of law in a community." Since the Israelite, Christian and Islamic states were based on divine legal orders, it follows that their systems might be called divine nomocracies.

Was the Islamic state a national or universal nomocracy? At the basis of this argument is the issue whether the appeal of Muḥammad was to the Arabs alone or to the world at large. While scholars still differ on this point,[31] it would seem that since the state was the instrument to enforce God's new covenant, replacing all others, both Islam and the Islamic state, therefore, were necessarily designed for the world and not for the Arabs alone.[32] Some of the Qur'ānic injunctions may have emphasized certain Arab characteristics (and indeed Muḥam-

[30] The principal Biblical verses for the so-called theocratic idea in Christianity are: Mark IX, 35: X, 42; Matt. XX, 26 sq; Luke XXII, 26.

[31] For a summary of this controversy, see T. W. Arnold, *The Preaching of Islam* (London 3rd ed., 1935), pp. 4-7.

[32] See p. 14, above.

mad's urgent problems often forced him to compromise with Arab traditions), but the legal prerequisites for a universal state were already recognized in the Qur'ān, such as equality of all races before God and the common allegiance of all believers to one head of the state.

Islam, like Christianity, emerged in a society dominated by parochial traditions and local particularisms, and since both had arisen in protest to these conditions, they adopted universal concepts and values current in the Hellenistic world; for the trend since Alexander the Great advocated his ideas of the "unity of mankind," began gradually to turn from parochial to universal concepts. The Stoics carried further Alexander's ideas and expressed their philosophy in terms of universal values. The Romans translated Alexander's ideas and the Stoic philosophy into an organized system of life. Under the impact of these ideas both Christianity and Islam developed. Thus Islam was bound to be a universal religion and, after the Arab conquests, it became completely Hellenized. The Jewish state, which appeared and developed before these values were ever accepted, was naturally parochial and the Jews were regarded as God's chosen people; their state, therefore, was national, not a universal state.

The universal nomocracy of Islam, like the *Respublica Christiana* in the West, assumed that mankind constituted one supra-national community, bound by one law and governed by one ruler. For it was held, as stated in a Qur'ānic injunction, that "If there were two gods, the universe would be ruined."[33] The nature of such a state is entirely exclusive; it does not recognize, by definition, the co-existence of a second universal state. While Islam tolerated Christianity and Judaism as religions, Islamdom and Christendom, as two universal states, could not peacefully coexist.

[33] Q. XXI, 23.

The Islamic nomocracy, however, in contrast to the *Respublica Christiana,* presented, in its legal theory at least, a real unity between church and state. Thus the Islamic State spared itself the internal conflict between the two which was so characteristic in medieval Europe between the pope and the emperor. The caliph, as head of Islam, stood in some respects for both pope and emperor, whose chief functions were the universalization of Islam and the enforcement of the divine law.[34]

[34] The Pope, however, possesses the power of promulgating new theological doctrines which the caliph did not have. For a comparison between the papacy and the caliphate, see Sir Thomas W. Arnold, *The Caliphate* Chap. I; and D. B. MacDonald, "The Caliphate," *The Moslem World,* Vol. VII, (1917), pp. 349-57.

"Verily, we have revealed to thee the Book with the Truth in order that thou mayest judge between men by means of what God hath shown thee. . . ." Qur'ān IV, 106.

CHAPTER II

NATURE AND SOURCES OF LAW

Customary Law and Islamic Law

Muslim jurists have maintained that since Islamic law was a divinely ordained system, they scarcely had anything to do with pre-Islamic law. Some went so far as to assert that Islam cancelled all the legal systems that preceded it since the Qur'ān provided a detailed account of "everything."[1] Others, especially the Mālikī and Ḥanafī jurists, recognized only those pre-Islamic rules and practices as valid which were not expressly abrogated by divine legislation. While the latter school of thought saw no harm in accepting certain pre-Islamic legal principles,[2] the

[1] See Q. XVI, 91: "We have revealed to you a Book explaining everything;" and Q. VI, 38: ". . . We have neglected nothing in the Book."

[2] See Sarakhsī, *al-Mabsūṭ* (Cairo, 1913), Vol. XV, pp. 171-172; Pazdawī, *Kashf al-Asrār* (Istanbūl, A.H. 1307), Vol. III, pp. 212-7; Cf. Ghazzālī, *al-Mustaṣfa* (Cairo, 1937), Vol. I, pp. 132-5.

other school repudiated the validity of all pre-Islamic doctrines, unless, for the purpose of showing that no inconsistency exists between the two schools, the term "cancellation" was construed, as Ibn Khaldūn stated, to mean "substitution," without giving any value judgment of the validity of pre-Islamic legal systems.[3] No school, however, gives an adequate explanation of the origin and development of Islamic law, much less of the relations of law to Arab society. There is ample evidence to show, however, that Islamic law evolved from Arab customary law and that, after the expansion of the Islamic state, Islam absorbed the local custom and practices of the conquered territories no less than other religious systems had done.

The pre-Islamic law of Arabia was embodied in a system of customary law, comprising legal and moral principles, known as the sunna. The sunna grew out of the custom of the forefathers and its enforcement by practice established its legal validity. Since the structure of pre-Islamic Arab society, even in the relatively large cities of Makka and Madīna, had not become completely urban, the character of customary law of the settled population did not essentially differ from that of the tribal population. Apart from the small Christian and Jewish colonies which had their own religious laws, the majority of the Arabs were idolaters; the sunna, accordingly, was pagan in character, based on what a nomadic or semi-nomadic society would need or honor.

The most distinctive feature of this society was the lack of political unity, a characteristic feature in all tribal organizations. The sayyid, or chief of the tribe, was usually selected on

[3] "The Shar'," said Ibn Khaldūn, "prohibited the consideration of other Heavenly Books than the Qur'ān. The Prophet said: 'do not accept nor refute the views of the People of the Book; say to them: We believe in what is revealed to us and to you; our Lord and yours is one' " (Ibn Khaldūn, *Al-Muqaddima,* ed. Quatermère (Paris, 1858), Vol. II, p. 387.

the basis of seniority, nobility, and reputation for wisdom. His authority rested more on the confidence and respect of his fellow-tribesmen than on the power of the loose machinery of his government. The chief's most important function was to make decisions on the basis of custom, enforced by tribal public opinion. But the chief had no authority to issue orders which exceeded the customary law, for he was the executive, not the legislative, head of the tribe. The chief also represented his tribe in its relations with other tribes, backed in his diplomatic actions by the full powers of his tribesmen.

It follows that the sunna, the common law of a primitive social order, developed in a loose political organization to supplement the benign authority of the chief—it also often ran counter to his authority in such cases as the dakhāla (asylum)—as well as to temper the austere desert life which provides but meager resources for living. Thus, such customary practices as hospitality, dakhāla and najda developed to provide food, asylum, and assistance to helpless desert travelers. The loose—in certain places even the absence of—authority of the chief was augmented by such severe practices as the vendetta (*tha'r*) and the cutting off of the hand of the thief, in order in the former case to prevent crimes against the person by retaliation and in the latter to protect private property in a society whose little respect for property right was too tempting to theft. In spite of some strict customs regulating sex relations, the male enjoyed almost free and licentious rights in marriage, such as unrestricted polygamy, mut'a (temporary marriage) and divorce. The male was permitted to marry the female of the next of kin, such as his stepmother and the wife's sisters.[4] Above all, idolatry had become such an integral part of the customary law that so-

[4] For a discussion of sex relations in pre-Islamic Arabia and in early Islam, see W. Robertson Smith, *Kinship and Marriage in Early Arabia*, ed. S. A. Cook (London, 1907); and Gertrude Stern, *Marriage in Early Islam* (London, 1939).

cial and economic functions were regulated in terms of religious duties, such as the ḥajj and other religious ceremonies. Even the kāhin, like the Greek oracle, performed a social-economic function prescribed by religion.

The rise of Islam, though it did not aim at displacing the prevailing sunna, had far-reaching effects on it. That Muḥammad's aim was at the outset not to alter or violate the established sunna is demonstrated not only by his own personal conduct in conforming to it (a conduct which probably earned him the title of amīn, or trustworthy), but also by his insistence, especially in the Makkan period, that his mission was merely to warn people against idolatry and to preach the oneness of God. Muḥammad's opponents argued, however—not without good reason—that he had violated the sunna; for, despite his reiteration that he merely intended to replace false idols by Allah, the repudiation of idolatry itself implied the violation of the sunna, since idolatry was part of the customary law of the land. Law and religion were so closely interwoven in primitive societies that an attack on religion would constitute a violation of law. Thus Muḥammad's call to abandon idolatry in favor of the Deity inevitably resulted in the establishment of the supremacy of God's law over "idolatrous" law even though customary law was not abolished in toto. The sunna persisted, however, in substance if not in form, as a basic source of legislation.[5]

Nature of Islamic Law

Islam, probably more than any other religion, has the character of a jural order which regulates the life and thoughts of the believer according to an ideal set of revelations communicated to Muḥammad, the last of the Prophets. Thus Islam

[5] Cf. Aḥmad Fahīm Abū Sana, *Al-'Urf wa'l-'Āda fī Ra'y al-Fuqahā'* (Cairo, 1949), pp. 29-32.

established its own order of right and wrong, embodying its own justice, as the correct and valid one. In order to give a rational justification for this jural order Islam, like other religions, asserted that its ideal system proceeded from a divine source embodying God's will and justice. The need for a rational justification of this assumption is so great that man often seeks to satisfy it with mere self-conviction.[6]

In the Islamic legal theory only God, as the source of ultimate authority, has knowledge of the perfect law. This law which is represented in the Jewish and Christian religions as the expression of the will of God, or as God's direct creation, was raised a step higher by the Muslim jurist-theologians—at least after Orthodoxy had triumphed over the rationalist Mu'tazilites—to be on the same level as God: the divine law, originally embodied in the Qur'ān, co-existed with God Himself in a heavenly book which, from the Orthodox Muslim viewpoint, may be called the law of nature.[7] In the same way as natural law was regarded in the West as the ideal legal order consisting of the general maxims of right and justice, so Islamic law was in the eyes of the Muslims the ideal legal system. As a divine law it was regarded as the perfect, eternal and just law, designed for all time and characterized by universal application to all men. The ideal life was the life in strict conformity with this law.

In the Muslim legal theory, the divine law preceded both society and state; the latter existed for the very purpose of enforcing the law. But if the state failed to enforce the law—

[6] Cf. Hans Kelsen, *General Theory of Law and State* (Cambridge, Mass., 1946), p. 8.

[7] The original version of the Qur'ān is thought of as a book preserved in heaven (Q. LXXXV, 22). See Richard Bell, *Introduction to the Qur'ān* (Edinburgh, 1953), p. 37. See also 'Abd al-Qāhir al-Baghdādī, *Kitāb Uṣūl al-Dīn* (Istanbūl, 1928), Vol. I, pp. 106, 108; and al-Asha'rī, *Kitāb al-Ibāna 'an Uṣūl al-Diyāna* (Hyderabad, 2nd ed., A.H. 1367) pp. 19-35.

in such a case the state obviously forfeits its *raison d'être*—the believer still remained under the obligation to observe the law even in the absence of any one to enforce it. The sanction of the law, which is distinct from the validity of the law, need not exist. For the object of the law is to provide for the believer the right path (Sharī'a), or the standard life, regardless of the existence of the proper authority charged with its enforcement. The Muslim jurists, however, agreed—except the Khārijī sect—that in theory the Muslim community must at all times recognize at its head an imām (or caliph), charged with the enforcement of the law, and that the community falls in error if it fails to enthrone one. "He who dies without an imām," Muḥammad is reported to have said, "dies the death of a pagan." But if the imām himself fails to enforce the law, the Muslims are still bound to observe the law regardless of whether the imām, by the very fact that he failed to fulfill his duties, ceased to be the head of the Muslim community or not.

The law comprises devotional obligations to God as well as rules regulating the relations among fellow-believers. If the believer consummates his obedience to the law he realizes his ultimate objective in life, namely, the achievement of salvation. This fulfillment of the law would constitute his happy life—hard as it may seem—by giving him an inner satisfaction that his next life would be assured in Heaven.

The law existed independently of man's own existence. Just as the norms of natural law exist in nature, to be discovered by reason, so the norms of Islamic law were discovered by (or revealed to, in the Islamic conception), Allah's Apostle. The substance of this law, which existed in its perfect and most complete form only in the Mother Book (i.e. nature) was communicated to the Prophet Muḥammad piecemeal, each verse at its proper occasion, and pieced together two decades after Muḥammad's death in a book known as the Qur'ān. Thus the

Qur'ān represents the earthly record of the Mother Book, the embodiment of a universal law or the law of nature.[8]

The divine law represents an effort to rationalize a world in which the Prophet Muḥammad found chaos and conflict while his aspiration was order. The law provided guidance not only in establishing an ordered society, but also in distinguishing what is called ḥusn (beauty)—hence to be followed—and qubḥ (ugly)—which should be avoided—or, in Western terminology, distinguishing between the "good" and "evil." The divine law is a system of obligations (farā'iḍ) which help to show the right "path" (sharī'a) to be traveled by the believer during his life-sojourn in order to achieve salvation. This "path," however, narrow as it may seem, has given the believer several choices between the strictly enjoined (farḍ) and the strictly forbidden (ḥarām). For between these two extremes the believer has the liberty of fulfilling certain recommended actions (mandūb) and of refraining (makrūh, objectionable) from others, but neither is the latter forbidden nor the former obligatory. Further, between the recommended and objectionable, there is the category of jā'iz to which the law is indifferent and the believer has full freedom of action. For instance, the daily prayers or the fasting of the month of Ramaḍān are farḍ; pork, wine, and adultery are ḥarām; any additional prayer or the emancipation of a slave are mandūb; but the flesh of the hyena or divorcing the wife during the period of menstruation are makrūh. All

[8] It is contended that in the same way as the Old and the New Testaments are the Hebraic and Syriac records of God's commands, the Qur'ān represents the Arabic version of them. (Q. IV, 162; XII, 1; XX, 112; XLII, 2). See 'Adb al-Qāhir al-Baghdādī, *Uṣūl al-Dīn* (Istanbūl, 1928), Vol. I, p. 108; and Arthur Jeffery, *The Qur'ān as Scripture* (New York, 1952). For the possibility of the Qur'ān might have been revealed in another language, see Qur'ān, XLI, 42-43. Cf. Abū Isḥāq al-Shāṭibī, *al-Muwāfaqāt fī Uṣūl al-Fiqh* (Cairo, n.d.), Vol. II, pp. 64-6.

other activities which do not fall within these categories are jā'iz. Sale, for instance, or any other contractual arrangements which are not prohibited, are jā'iz. As is provided in a Qur'ānic injunction: "God hath allowed selling and forbidden usury" (Q. II, 276).[9]

The Muslim jurist-theologians assert that the basic principle of law is liberty; but this principle is qualified by another, that human nature is essentially weak and can easily be led astray unless guided by divine wisdom. Hence the divine law, revealed to the Prophet Muḥammad as a set of all-embracing commands, is both authoritarian and totalitarian in nature. For it includes dogma as well as social and political principles; these are combined to constitute an indivisible unity. Law thus has the character of a religious obligation; at the same time it provides a political sanction of religion.

Three fundamental characteristics of the law may be stated, on which the classical Muslim jurist-theologians seem to have agreed. The first is its permanent validity, regardless of place and time. Believers, even if they resided outside the territory of Islam, were bound by the law. For the law was revealed to bind the believers as individuals, not as territorial groups. Secondly, the law takes into consideration primarily the common interests of the community and its ethical standard, the personal interests of the individual believers are protected only insofar as they conform to the common interests of Islam.[10] Not infrequently the interests of the individual were sacrificed for the sake of protecting the common interests of the community. For the law laid emphasis on mediation among individuals rather than on the regulation of their conflicts of interests.

[9] See Āmidī, *al-Iḥkām fī Uṣūl al-Aḥkām* (Cairo, A.H. 1347), Vol. I, pp. 50-65; Pazdawī, Vol. I, pp. 100ff; Ghazzālī, Vol. I, pp. 42-53.

[10] Cf. Sir Henry Maine, *Ancient Law* (World's Classics edition), pp. 101, 138-41.

Thirdly, the law must be observed with sincerity and good faith. In Islam, as in ancient Rome, the law regards the principle of *bona fides* to be the underlying basis of the believer's private and public conduct. Faithlessness, duplicity, and dissimulation have been repudiated as inconsistent with the objectives of the law in normal circumstances; the law permits relaxation of certain strict rules only under extenuating and exceptional circumstances such as when the believer's own life should be subjected to extreme peril or he is threatened with death. This relaxation of the law is permitted under the general principle of moderation, by virtue of which the believer may keep a balance between his obligations under the law and the circumstances permitting their fulfillment. Fasting during the month of Ramaḍan, for instance, is compulsory upon all believers; but this rule, qualified by the principle of moderation, permits the postponement of fasting while the believer is traveling (if his journey exceeds three days) and exempts the sick from fasting so long as he is unable to fulfill the obligation; but the nonfulfillment of an obligation, or even failure to observe the law, does not necessarily imply the supremacy of the believer's interests over the law. For the law, as the ideal divine system, sets the standards to which the believer has to conform; he may not alter or adapt the law to fit his own interests or convenience.[11]

Sources of Law

The Muslim community, after Muḥammad's death, inherited a legal order comprising the Islamic *jus naturale* and the Arabian *jus gentium.* Since the prophetic function was not bequeathed by Muḥammad to his successors, divine legislation came to an end at a time when the Islamic state was about to

[11] See Abū Isḥāq al-Shāṭibī, *Al-Mūwāfaqāt fī Uṣūl al-Fiqh* (Cairo, n.d.), Vol. II, p. 8; and Suyūṭī, *al-Ashbāh wa'l-Nazā'ir* (Cairo, 1938), pp. 7-50.

embark on expansion outside Arabia. Thus the Muslim community was bound to fall back on customary law, which had supplied substance for some divine legislation, in conformity with the Arabian way of life.

The development of Islamic law would have been less complex and the difference among the jurists probably less considerable and confusing if the Muslim community had remained confined to Arabia. The newly conquered territories of Syria, Iraq, Persia, and Egypt presented legal problems which were not easy to solve by the norms of a law that had developed in Arabia. The early caliphs and their jurisconsults inevitably had to resort to personal opinion (ra'y) to supplement divine legislation and customary law. Traditions ascribed to Muḥammad permitting the use of ra'y as a source of law were cited;[12] but a more authentic evidence of the use of reason in early Islam is to be found in Caliph 'Umar's instructions to Abū Mūsa al-Ash'arī (qāḍī of Baṣra) in which the Caliph stated three sources to be used in legal decisions, namely, the Qur'ān, the prevailing sunna (al-sunna al-muttaba'a) and reason.[13] This

[12] The so-called Mu'ādh ibn Jabal's tradition runs as follows: The Prophet Muḥammad sent Mu'ādh as a judge to take charge of legal affairs in al-Yaman, and asked him on what he would base his legal decisions. "On the Qur'ān," Mu'ādh replied. "But if that contains nothing for the purpose?" asked Muḥammad. "Then upon your tradition," answered Mu'ādh. "But if that also fails you?," asked Muḥammad. "Then I will follow my own opinion," said Mu'ādh. And the Prophet Muḥammad approved his purpose. See Ibn Sa'd, *Kitāb al-Ṭabaqāt al-Kabīr,* ed. Sachau (Leiden, 1917), Part II, Vol. II, pp. 107-8, 120.

[13] Doubt has been raised as to the authenticity of 'Umar's letter to Abū Mūsa owing to variations in the text as reported by various authorities. Abū Yūsuf, one of the earliest authorities, refers to the contents of the letter in brief, which indicates that such instructions were likely to have been given (Abū Yūsuf, *Kitāb al-Kharāj,* p. 117). For a critical study of the text and translation of this document, see D. S. Margoliouth, "Omar's Instructions to the Kadi," *Journal of the Royal Asiatic Society* (April, 1910),

document possesses an additional significance in the use of the term sunna, which bears witness that in the early Islamic period the term still meant the Arabian customary law (*jus gentium*) and that it had not yet acquired the technical sense of Muḥammadan traditions (sunna of the Prophet.)

In the conquered territories of Syria and Iraq the term sunna was indiscriminately used to mean not only the sunna of the Prophet, but also (āthār) or traditions from the Prophet's companions and successors (tābi'ūn) as well as local custom. If there were no Qur'ānic rule or sunna, resort was made to ra'y. But ra'y proved to be so controversial a source of law that it was soon abandoned.[14] It was attacked on the grounds that it permitted legislation by man. The jurists, accordingly, had to find other means in which reason was used to supplement the Qur'ān and sunna.[15]

In Iraq, Abū Ḥanīfa (A.D. 699-768) distinguished himself as the chief advocate of analogy (qiyās) as a source of law, whenever specific Qur'ānic verse or tradition was lacking. His use of traditions was so consciously selective—especially those coming from companions and successors—that his knowledge of traditions seemed palpably lacking to his contemporary critics.[16] Abū Ḥanīfa's reply to those critics was that he always

pp. 307-326. Cf. E. Tyan, *Histoire de l'organisation judiciaire en pays d'Islam* (Paris, 1938), Vol. I, pp. 106-113.

[14] According to Ibn al-Muqaffa', writing during the caliphate of Al-Manṣūr (A.H. 136-158), no one but the caliph has the right to use ra'y in matters of military and civil administration and generally on all matters on which there were no traditions (āthār). See Ibn al-Muqaffa', *Risāla fī al-Ṣaḥāba* in *Rasā'il al-Bulaghā'*, ed. Kurd 'Alī (3rd ed., Cairo, 1946), pp. 121-2.

[15] See Edwin E. Calverley, "The Fundamental Structure of Islam," *The Moslem World*, Vol. XXIX 9L939), pp. 373-4.

[16] Khaṭīb al-Baghdādī, *Ta'rīkh Baghdād* (Cairo, 1931), Vol. 13, pp. 415-6, 420-1.

depended on traditions (āthār) in his analogical method, making no use of ra'y (personal opinion),[17] but in fact his analogical reasoning and preferential choice of traditions necessarily carried with it personal opinion. In case there were two traditions bearing on the same subject, Abū Ḥanīfa's choice is known as istiḥsān—a procedure in which Abū Ḥanīfa chose the traditions which he thought would be least harmful.[18] Most damaging of the criticisms levelled at Abū Ḥanīfa's method was his use of casuistry (al-ḥiyal al-shar'iyya).[19] While the ḥiyal were intended to temper the strictness of, or offset the evil consequences created by, certain rules and practices, they were, however, often abused—especially by later Ḥanafī jurisconsults—for the purpose of evading the law.

Abū Ḥanīfa's liberal use of analogical reasoning reflected the need of a new social environment for the development of a system of law which had originated in Arabia before its area of validity was widened by the rapid expansion of the Islamic state. Although Abū Ḥanīfa and his disciples were more outspoken in the use of independent opinion, their critics in Iraq and Syria, such as Ibn Abū Layla and al-Awzā'ī, were not less influenced by their social environment than Abū Ḥanīfa. Zufar went, perhaps, beyond the limits of analogy set by his master, but Abū Yūsuf (died, A.D. 799) and in particular Muḥammad ibn al-Ḥasan al-Shaybānī (died A.D. 805) were more conservative in the use of analogical reasoning.

In Madīna Mālik ibn Anas (A.D. 718–96) had the reputation

[17] Muwaffaq al-Makkī, *Manāqib . . . Abū Ḥanīfa* (Hyderabad, A.H. 1321), Vol. I, pp. 77-8; cf. Al-Khaṭīb al-Baghdādī, *Ta'rīkh Baghdād,* Vol. 13, p. 390.

[18] Abū Muzzafar 'Īsa, *Kitāb al-Radd 'Ala al-Khaṭīb al-Baghdādī* (Cairo, 1932), pp. 79, 102.

[19] Khaṭīb al-Baghdādī, *Ta'rīkh Baghdād,* Vol. 13, pp. 403-4, 408-9. For an exposition of the Ḥanafī system of al-ḥiyal, see Shaybānī, *Kitāb al-Makhārij fī al-Ḥiyal,* ed. Joseph Schacht (Leipzig, 1930).

of making use of traditions of the Prophet and his Companions to a larger extent than his Iraqi contemporaries, but in fact those traditions were no less mixed with local traditions than elsewhere. Mālik and the jurist-theologian of Madīna claimed that their city was the home of true Muḥammadan traditions and therefore their school was designated as the School of ḥadīth (traditions). It is reported that Mālik compiled his law-book, *al-Muwaṭṭa'*, from several thousand ḥadīths which he submitted for approval to seventy jurist-theologians.[20] In this digest the ḥadīths comprised not only the Muḥammadan traditions but also the local sunna and the practice of the Madīnan jurists, which was regarded as constituting the true Muḥammadan tradition.

Mālik's procedure in selecting the body of ḥadīths acceptable to recognized jurists of Madīna introduced a new procedure, which was probably invented by him, namely, the ijmā' (consensus). This was in contrast to the Iraqi jurists who often disagreed with each other. To Mālik the agreement of the Madīna jurists on a rule of law based on ḥadīth (which may have been a local custom embodied in ḥadīth, or by a ḥadīth, lacking in genuineness, circulated to sanction it) constituted law. The ijmā' was a weapon with which the Ḥijāzī attacked the Iraqi jurists (especially the Ḥanafīs) on the ground that they had departed from the sunna of the Prophet. Further, Mālik developed the principle of istiṣlāḥ, on the basis of which he gave legal opinion designed to serve the common interests and welfare of the community. This procedure was derived from the idea of the consent of the community and may be regarded as a form of consensus.

The ijmā' was not accepted without opposition, for it was feared that it might constitute legislation by man. The jurists, however, modifying Mālik's conception of ijmā' to include all

[20] See Suyūṭī, *Kitāb Tazyyīn al-Mamālik* (Cairo, A.H. 1325), pp. 42-3.

the leading scholars (mujtahids), saw the value of agreement and approved of the procedure. This was justified by a ḥadīth ascribed to the Prophet Muḥammad to the effect that "my people shall never be unanimous in error," and a vague Qur'ānic verse: "follow . . . the way of the believers."[21] Moreover, the Prophet said "the learned are the heirs of the prophets"—they are therefore the ones who can interpret the Book.

The jurists of Iraq objected to the narrow Mālikī conception of ijmā' and contended that other provinces of the Islamic world were as capable of arriving at an ijmā' as the Madīnan jurists, though in practice they betrayed similar local prejudices to those of the Madīnans. More constructive criticism of local ijmā' was reserved for Shāfi'ī (A.D. 768-820), the first and probably the greatest Muslim systematic legal theorist, who widened the conception of ijmā' and, although he did not completely repudiate the doctrine of the ijmā' of the scholars, advocated in the final revision of his doctrine the consensus of the community at large. He saw in the doctrine of ijmā' the safest legislative authority.

In trying to achieve a consistent legal theory, Shāfi'ī accepted the unquestionable authority of the Qur'ān, but he rejected the sunna as a source of law unless the sunna was an authentic Muḥammadan tradition. In this he tried to narrow the use of sunna merely to utterances reported on the authority of the Prophet Muḥammad.[22] He attached more significance to the unanimous consensus of the community in arriving at a rule of law than to a sunna ascribed to a questionable source (often invented by certain vested interests) or based on local practice. He also tried to limit the use of analogy to questions

[21] Q. IV, 115.

[22] See J. Schacht, *The Origins of Muhammadan Jurisprudence* (Oxford, 1950). Shāfi'īs legal system is to be found in his collected writings entitled *Kitāb al-Umm* (Cairo, A.H. 1321-5), 7 volumes.

of detail when there was no relevant text in the Qur'ān, no sunna, or no consensus. Analogy, he maintained, cannot supersede the other three sources of law, but rather it must be superseded by them. Neither should it be based on a special or exceptional case; analogy must conform to the general spirit of the law. In taking this attitude Shāfi'ī established a balance between those who used analogy extensively and those who rejected it as a source of law.

Shāfi'ī's doctrine of the ijmā' as the consensus of the community was short-lived, for not only was it opposed by other schools, but was even qualified by his own followers. Al-Ghazzālī, who supported Shāfi'ī's insistence on unanimous agreement, confined unanimity to fundamentals, and left matters of detail to "agreement of the scholars."[23] Ibn al-Humām (died A.H. 861), in trying to reconcile the Ḥanafī with the Shāfi'ī doctrines, offered a formula which reduced ijmā' to agreement of the scholars in one generation, but saw no need for the expiry of the generation (as others contended) before an ijmā' could be reached.[24]

The fundamental weakness in Shāfi'ī's doctrine of universal agreement was procedural, namely, the lack of an adequate method which would provide means for the community to arrive at an ijmā'. Indeed, the whole doctrine of ijmā', whether based on the consent of the community or the scholars' agreement, suffered from this procedural defect. Its critics, especially Al-Nazzām, a Mu'tazilite, attacked it mainly because of the difficulty of securing agreement among scholars who were scattered far and wide throughout the Islamic empire. Some of the jurists offered a corrective by arguing that if a few scholars reached an agreement and no objection was raised by others (ijmā' al-sukūt), or if the majority agreed and only a few raised

[23] Ghazzālī, *al-Mustaṣfa fī Uṣūl al-Fiqh* (Cairo, 1937), Vol. I, pp. 115-21.
[24] Ibn al-Humām, *al-Taḥrīr* (Cairo, A.H. 1351), pp. 399, 401.

an objection, agreement becomes binding upon the community.[25] While this narrowed the possibilities of disagreement, the process itself remained undefined. No precise definition of the ijmā' were ever given nor the qualification of a scholar ever agreed upon by the jurist-theologians.

Schools of Law

The controversy over the "sources" of law arose from the termination of revelation—Muḥammad's chief Prophetic function—without providing a rule for further legislation. A more serious issue that had arisen revolved on the question of succession, because Muḥammad's sudden death left the matter undecided. These two lacunae in Muḥammad's jural heritage profoundly affected the political and legal development of the Islamic state—the one created the greatest schism in Islam, and the other, confusion and diversity in the legal system.

All the jurist-theologians agreed that the Qur'ān, embodying the infallible revelations, was an unquestionable source of law. But here agreement ended, since the Qur'ān provided no clear guidance for further legislation. As a result, the controversy that followed was essentially one concerning the sources, rather than the substance, of legislation. The character of this controversy was not, strictly speaking, legal; at bottom it was theological, since an inquiry into what would constitute an authoritative supplement to the Qur'ānic revelations is a doctrinal, not a legal matter.

The confusion and diversity in the initial stages of the development of Islamic law were opposed by the early jurists, arguing that the Qur'ānic injunctions repudiated disagreement in the matters of religion.[26] Probably the first Muslim publicist

[25] Ghazzālī, *op. cit.*, Vol. I, pp. 121 ff; 'Alī 'Abd al-Rāziq, *al-Ijmā' fī al-Sharī 'a al-Islāmiyya* (Cairo, 1947), pp. 73-90.

[26] Q. III, 101; XCVIII, 4. For details on the early jurists' criticism of

who saw the futility of disagreement in the development of law was Ibn al-Muqaffa', who, while in the service of the Caliph al-Manṣūr (A.D. 754–75), addressed to the Caliph a treatise in which he suggested putting an end to the then existing anarchy of the law by its formal codification into a coherent system.[27]

The later jurists, however, favored disagreement rather than uniformity, a tendency reflecting the force of local particularism and precedents. Traditions ascribed to Muḥammad in support of disagreement were cited, the most important of which runs as follows: "the disagreement of my people is a mercy from Allah."[28]

This freedom in legal speculation set on foot the movement to develop a variety of schools, each led by a distinguished mujtahid, around whom a number of disciples gathered and discussed questions of law. Although these leading jurists often attacked each other, as in the case of Abū Ḥanīfa and his critics, there was on the whole a tolerant attitude on the part of the Muslim community towards their leading jurists, believing that in spite of their differences on matters of detail (furū') they all sought the truth, each according to his light. Al-Sha'rānī has compared the four orthodox schools of law to several roads, all leading to the truth.[29] But lack of direction in the ijtihād and disagreement tended to multiply the schools and to accentuate the rivalry among their followers. During the second

disagreement, see J. Schacht, *op. cit.*, p. 95; and I. Goldziher, *Die Zahiriten,* (Leipzig, 1884), p. 98.

27 Ibn al-Muqaffa', *op. cit.*, pp. 117-134.

28 A traditional story is related by several reporters that Mālik ibn Anas was requested by Caliph al-Manṣūr (some say by Caliph al-Mahdī) to permit the adoption of *al-Muwaṭṭa'* as the official law-book for the state. Mālik is reported to have politely refused favoring the enforcement of a variety of law-books rather than the enforcement of a single standard text. See Ibn 'Abd al-Barr, *al-Intiqā'* (Cairo, A.H. 1350), pp. 40-1.

29 Sha'rānī, *Kitāb al-Mīzān* (Cairo, 1932), Vol. I, pp. 2, 6-7.

and third centuries of the Islamic era (the eighth and ninth of the Christian era) the Islamic world was abounding with a great number of schools of law, major and minor. But at this stage no sharp distinction was yet recognized between them. These schools varied from the relatively liberal Ḥanafite and Mu'tazilite jurists—permitting large measures of independent reasoning (ijtihād)—to the conservative Zahirite and Ḥanbalite jurists, who not only restricted ijtihād, but also insisted on a literal interpretation of the Qur'ān and ḥadīth. Each school consisted at the outset of a group of disciples who followed their master in giving certain answers to specific questions, practical or speculative; it was not until the third century of the Islamic era, probably as a result of Shāfi'ī's systematizing effort in the study of the law, that the technical term madhhab (school of law) was applied to the followers of the founders of the recognized schools of law. Before that it was fashionable to call the followers of each jurist his aṣḥāb (singular, ṣāhib). Probably both Mālik and Abū Ḥanīfa died without realizing that they were the future founders of schools called after their names. Their followers were usually referred to respectively as the "people of tradition" (ahl al-ḥadīth) and the "people of opinion" (ahl al-ra'y). In the case of the latter school the reference was made to a number of Iraqi jurists, not to the Ḥanafīs only, and in this frame of reference the followers of Ibn abī Layla (great rival of Abū Ḥanīfa), Sufyān al-Thawrī and Ibn Shubruma were included.

In the fourth century of the Islamic era only four schools were recognized as orthodox, namely, the Ḥanafī, Mālikī, Shāfi'ī and Ḥanbalī schools. Their law-books became the standard text-books and any attempt to depart from them was denounced as innovation (bid'a). As a result ijtihād was gradually abandoned in favor of taqlīd (literally, "imitation") or submission to the canons of the four schools, and the door of ijtihād was shut. At first taqlīd reflected a tendency to reduce the differences among jurists and limit the number of schools, but the growing intolerence of the Muslims to legal reasoning rendered taqlīd an obstacle to legal development. The triumph of the followers of Ibn Ḥanbal coincided with this growing spirit of intolerence and was best expressed in their repudiation of ijtihād and their rejection of all forms of qiyās, seeking to find all the answers to their problems in the ḥadīth. Even the ijmā', which had been established as an infallible principle, ranked in their eyes inferior to a weak ḥadīth.[30]

The rigidity of the Ḥanbalī school and the austere life it required were opposed by many persons in authority who supported the Ḥanafī and Shāfi'ī schools. The Ḥanbalis would accept neither positions in the State nor gifts from supporters—two important factors which were fully exploited by their opponents and which weakened the Ḥanbalī followers.[31] Thus the Ḥanbalī teachings were abandoned in favor of other schools, in spite of occasional revivals of Ḥanbalism by a number of influential jurist-theologians, as in the eighteenth century of the Christian era when the teachings of Ibn Taymiyya (A.D. 1260-1327), a great Ḥanbalī jurist who revived interest in Ḥanbalism,[32] were adopted by the Wahhabi movement of Arabia as the official creed of the movement.

Outside Arabia the Ḥanafī and Shāfi'ī canons became dominant in Iraq, Syria, Egypt, and Turkey; and the Mālikī school, shrinking in the Ḥijāz, spread all over North Africa and Spain before the latter was restored to Christian rule. But there was,

30 For a detailed study of Ḥanbalī law, see Ibn Qudāma, *al-Mughnī*, ed. M. Rashīd Riḍa (Cairo, A.H. 1367), 9 vols; and Henri Laoust, *Le precis de droit d'ibn Qudama* (Beyrouth, 1950).

31 See Ibn Rajab al-Baghdādī, *Histoire des Hanbalites*, Arabic text (Damas, 1951), Vol. I, pp. 10-1, 189.

32 For a translation of Ibn Taymiyya's treatise on public law, see Henri Laoust, *Le traite de droit public d'Ibn Taimiya* (Beyrouth, 1948).

and still is, no restriction of the Muslim from changing his allegiance and religious practice from one school to another during his lifetime. A number of distinguished jurists as well as men in authority have, with facility and without incurring social criticism or prejudice, changed their allegiance from one school to another. It was possible to find in the same family one member belonging to one school and the other to another school; and in a certain family of four children, each purposely belonged to a different school.[33]

The Shī'ī Doctrine

The Sunnī sectarian division in Islam includes the four schools of law previously considered. The Shī'a comprises a heterodox group the historical importance of which requires separate treatment. The underlying difference between the Shī'ī and Sunnī legal theory is the doctrine of the imāmate (the Shī'ī term for the caliphate) which narrows the qualifications of the candidate for this position not merely to the tribe of Quraysh but still further to ahl al-bayt, the descendants of 'Alī and Fāṭima.[34] The Shī'a accepts the legitimist right of 'Alī to the imāmate as an article of faith; for, it is held, 'Alī was designated by Muḥammad and after him his descendants in direct line. This designation, made on a special occasion, entrusted 'Alī with divine authority; at the same time it confided to him a secret knowledge (ta'wīl), empowering him to interpret the Qur'ān as well as to make—some say even to abrogate—the law. This esoteric knowledge 'Alī passed on to his male descendants from generation to generation.[35]

[33] Sha'rānī, *op. cit.*, Vol. I, pp. 36-40; and Goldziher, *Les Dogme et le lois de l'Islam*, trans. Felix Arin (Paris, 1920), pp. 42-3.

[34] 'Alī was the cousin and son-in-law of Muḥammad; Fāṭima, the daughter of Muḥammad and wife of 'Alī.

[35] Ḥillī, *Al-Bābu'l-Ḥādi 'Ashar*, trans. W. M. Miller (London, 1928), pp. 62-81.

This doctrine, regarding 'Alī and his descendants as the repository of the Islamic truth, was further elaborated by 'Alī's devoted followers so as to ascribe superhuman qualities to him, raising him and his descendants to a level higher than fallible human beings. To many a Shi'a, Muḥammad is slightly eclipsed by 'Alī, and to certain extremists God's revelations, miscarried by the Angel Gabriel to Muḥammad, were originally intended for 'Alī.[36] To the majority of the Shī'a, however, 'Alī was to rule by divine right, armed with such authoritative knowledge bequeathed to him by Muḥammad—a knowledge which placed him beyond the reproach of human beings. He and his descendants formed, in contrast to the Sunnī caliphs, a caste of not only infallible, but also impeccable imāms.

Differences of opinions on the nature of the imāmate, itself the cause of division in Islam, gave rise to sub-divisions within the Shī'ī sect. Apart from the Zaydīs, who permit the election of the imām from among 'Alī's descendants, the principal subdivisions are two, the so-called Twelvers and Seveners. This dissension took place after the death of the sixth imām, Ja'far al-Ṣādiq (died A.D. 765); the Twelvers acknowledged his younger son Mūsa al-Kāzim and the Seveners supported the claim of the elder brother Ismā'īl. The minority, however, followed Ismā'īl, whose descendants established the Fāṭimid Caliphate in Egypt (A.D. 969-1171), and who are now to be found only in India, Central Asia, Syria, Persian Gulf, and East Africa. These are often called the Ismā'īlīs.[37]

The majority of the Shī'a were, and still are, the supporters of the imāmate of Mūsa al-Kāzim and his descendants until

[36] Ras'anī, *Mukhtaṣar al-Farq Bayn al-Firaq,* by 'Abd al-Qāhir al-Baghdādī, ed. P. K. Hitti (Cairo, 1924), p. 157.

[37] For an exposition of Ismā'īlī legal doctrine, see Qāḍī al-Nu'mān ibn Muḥammad, *Da'ā'im al-Islām,* ed. Āṣif ibn 'Ali Aṣghar Fayḍī (Fyzee) (Cairo 1951).

the disappearance of the twelfth Imām Muḥammad ibn al-Ḥasan al-'Askarī (A.H. 260, or A.D. 874).[38] These are called the Twelvers. No other imām had been selected since the disappearance of Muḥammad, because his absence (ghayba) did not mean that he had perished; his spirit, it is held, is still with his fold. The doctrine of the ghayba (absence of the imām) and his final return as the mahdī (messiah), to dispense justice and righteousness in a world now full of sin, forms the basis of the Twelvers' creed. During the imām's absence, the creed and the law have been interpreted by the mujtahids (scholars) who have acted as agents of the imām. Owing to continual persecution under succeeding Sunnī caliphs and sultans (mainly because the Shī'a were opposed to the Sunnī caliphate), the Shī'a developed the doctrine of kitmān or taqiyya (dissimulation) which permitted the members of this sect to hide their belief in order to secure protection. This principle is based on a vague Qur'ānic injunction,[39] but the mujtahids have regarded it as an integral part of their creed.

The Shī'ī conception of law, it will be noted, is more authoritarian and far more detached from social reality than the Sunnī conception, not only because the final authoritative interpretation of the law had been placed in the imām, but also because of his infallibility and his possession of an esoteric knowledge of the true meaning of the law. Not even the absence of the imām had transformed this character of the law, for the mujtahids acted only as agents of the imām, not as free representatives who followed their independent judgments. Thus ijtihād in Shī'ī law has a different meaning from that of

[38] Muḥammad is said to have disappeared in mysterious circumstances when he entered a cavern in search of his father who died at Sāmarrā', then capital of the caliph. From that cavern the child never returned, but the Shī'a believe that he is still alive and will return as the Mahdī-Imām.

[39] Q. III, 27.

the Sunnī conception, at least before the closure of the door of itjihād.[40]

In the Shī'ī, as in the Sunnī, legal theory the Qur'ān is accepted as an unquestionable source of law;[41] but the ḥadīth is not accepted unless related by an imām recognized by the Shī'a. The ijmā' is rejected unless the imām takes part in it because neither the community nor the scholars have the final legal authority to interpret the law. Analogical reasoning play a less significant part in legislation, at least in contrast to the liberal Sunnī schools, because the mujtahid's opinion must be supported by a tradition or the precedent of an imām.

The differences between the Shī'ī and Sunnī law in matters of detail (furū') are hardly more marked than those between one orthodox school of law and another. Apart from the doctrine of the imāmate, and the consequent emphasis on the authoritarian character of the law, the Shī'ī system, as it has been proposed, might have constituted a fifth madhhab, or school of law. However, the revolutionary character of Shī'ī opposition tended to accentuate the Sunnī-Shī'ī schism and rendered the recognition of their doctrine as Orthodox exceedingly difficult.[42]

[40] Cf. A. A. A. Fyzee, *Outline of Muhammadan Law* (Oxford, 1949), p. 35.

[41] Some Shī'ī extremists accused the Caliph 'Uthmān of deliberate suppression of certain Qur'ānic verses favorable to Shī'ism, but the majority accepted the same Qur'ān as the Sunnī, although they admit that it does not represent the original version.

[42] H. Lammens, *Islam: Beliefs and Institutions,* trans. Sir Denison Ross (London, 1929), p. 151-152; and H. A. R. Gibb, *Modern Trends in Islam,* (Chicago, 1947), p. 12.

"Toutes les nations ont un droit des gens; et les Iroquois mêmes, qui mangent leurs prisonniers, en ont un."

Montesquieu.

CHAPTER III

THE MUSLIM LAW OF NATIONS

It has been observed in the recorded history of mankind that the population of each civilization, in the absence of a vital external threat, has tended to develop within itself a community of political entities, that is, a "family of nations," whose interrelationships were regulated by a set of customary rules and practices, rather than a single nation governed by one authority and one system of law. This observation is to be substantiated by the fact that there existed, or coexisted, several families of nations in such regional areas as the ancient Near East, Greece and Rome, China, Islamdom, and Western Christendom: in each one of them at least one distinct civilization had flourished. Within each civilization a body of rules and practices developed for the purpose of regulating the conduct of each entity with the others in peace and war. "The mere fact of neighborly cohabitation," says Baron Korff, "creates moral and legal obligations, which in the course of time crystallize into a system of international law."[1] It has been observed that even among primitive people such rules seem to have existed as part of the mores before they developed into a coherent system among civilized nations. As Montesquieu stated, all nations, not excepting the Iroquois, who devoured their prisoners, have a law of nations. For even if conflict and anarchy had reigned among them, they inevitably found it to their common interest to agree on such rules as the exchange of prisoners and to refrain from certain practices from fear of retaliation. When a minimum of rules is deemed necessary for the cohabitation of territorial groups, a society of nations is bound to develop. *Ubi jus ibi societas est.*

Former systems of the law of nations, in contrast to the modern law of nations, were not world-wide or universal in character, since each system was primarily concerned with regulating the relations of entities and nations within a limited area and within one (though often more than one) civilization. Further, each past system of the law of nations, in contrast to the modern law of nations, was entirely exclusive, since it did not recognize the principle of legal equality among nations which is the basis of the modern law of nations. It is for this very reason that it was not possible for those systems to be integrated, although each borrowed freely from others without acknowledgement, as each system claimed an exclusive superiority over the other. Consequently, each system disappeared with the disappearance of the civilization (or civilizations) under which it flourished. Although the term "international law," since it was coined by Bentham, has gained more currency than the "law of nations," the latter term seems

[1] Baron S. A. Korff, "An Introduction to the History of International Law," *American Journal of International Law*, Vol. XVIII (1924), p. 248. See also Quincy Wright, *A Study of War* (Chicago, 1942), Vol. II, Chap. 26.

to be broad enough to cover the various historic patterns,[2] and therefore more convenient to use in this work.

The rise of Islam, with its mission to all people, inevitably raised for the Islamic state the problem as to how it would conduct its relations with the non-Muslim countries as well as with the tolerated religious communities within its territory. The ultimate aim of Islam was, of course, to win the whole world, but its failure to convert all people left outside its frontiers non-Muslim communities with which Islam had to deal throughout its history. Thus in its origin the Muslim law of nations, in contrast to almost all other systems, was designed to be a temporary institution—until all people, except perhaps those of the tolerated religions, would become Muslims. It follows, accordingly, that if the ideal of Islam were ever achieved, the *raison d'être* of a Muslim law of nations, at least with regard to Islam's relations with non-Muslim countries, would be non-existent.[3] The wave of Islamic expansion, however, could not continue indefinitely, so some law to govern the relations of Muslims with non-Muslims will remain so long as Muslims live in the world with non-Muslims.

The modern law of nations presupposes the existence of a family of nations composed of a community of states enjoying full sovereign rights and equality of status. The Muslim law

[2] See Arthur Nussbaum, *A Concise History of the Law of Nations* (New York, 1947), pp. 1-2.

[3] It is interesting to note that the Soviet Union, thirteen centuries after the rise of the Muslim state, has developed a similar idea of a world state, though of course different in nature, and recognized modern international law only temporarily until it could eventually achieve the ideal of world communism. See T. A. Taracouzio, *The Soviet Union and International Law* (New York, 1935) p. 10; John N. Hazard "Cleansing Soviet International Law of Anti-Marxist Theories," *American Journal of International Law*, Vol. XXXII (1938), pp. 244-52; Q. Wright, *Proceedings of the American Society of International Law*, 1953, pp. 79-80.

of nations recognizes no other nation than its own, since the ultimate goal of Islam was the subordination of the whole world to one system of law and religion, to be enforced by the supreme authority of the imām. Similar to the law of ancient Rome and the law of Medieval Christendom, the Muslim law of nations was based on the theory of a universal state. Both Christendom and Islamdom, as divine universal nomocracies, assumed that mankind constituted one community, bound by one law and governed ultimately by one ruler. Their aim was the proselytization of the whole of mankind. Their rules for foreign relations, accordingly, were the rules of an imperial state which would recognize no equal status for the other party (or parties) with whom they happened to fight or negotiate.[4] It follows therefore that the binding force of such a law of nations was not based on mutual consent or reciprocity, but on their own interpretation of their political, moral and religious interest, as they regarded their principles of morality and religion superior to others.

Furthermore, the Muslim law of nations was ordinarily binding upon individuals rather than territorial groups. For Islamic law, like all ancient law, had a personal rather than a territorial character and was obligatory upon the Muslims, as individuals or as a group, regardless of the territory they resided in.[5] It has only been in modern times, especially under the pressure of modern material civilization and culture, that the observance of law has been attached to people in relation to the territory they live in rather than in relation to the group they belong to.[6] We may argue, from a philosophical view-

[4] For a comparison with the *jus fetiale* of ancient Rome, see p. 57, below.

[5] See Ṭabarī, *Kitāb al-Jihād,* ed J. Schacht (Leiden, 1937), pp. 60-64. Only the Ḥanafī school permits relaxation of certain forbidden practices outside Islamic territory, *ibid.,* p. 62.

[6] See Q. Wright, *Mandates Under the League of Nations* (Chicago, 1930), pp. 267 ff.

point, that Islam, as a universal religion, laid emphasis on individual allegiance to a faith which recognized no boundaries for its kingdom: for under a system which claims to be universal territory ceases to be a deciding factor in the intercourse among people. Piety and obedience to God were the criteria of a good citizen under the Islamic ideology, rather than race, class, or attachment to a certain home or country. Failing to achieve this ideal, the Muslim jurists did not give up the concept of the personality of the law, that is, its binding character on individuals, not on territorial groups.

Finally, the Muslim law of nations is not a separate body of Muslim law; it is merely an extension of the law designed to govern the relations of the Muslims with non-Muslims, whether inside or outside the world of Islam.[7] Strictly speaking, there is no Muslim law of nations in the sense of the distinction between modern municipal (national) law and international law based on different sources and maintained by different sanctions. It is, perhaps, nearest to the ancient Jewish system, based on the Mosaic law, enforced upon Jews and Gentiles when they came into contact with each other.[8] The early Muslim jurists either dealt with the conduct of foreign relations in the general law corpora under such headings as "jihād," the

[7] Hugo Krabbe's conception of the modern law of nations is similar to that of the Muslim law of nations; it is an extension of constitutional law. He argues that the modern law of nations is different from municipal law only in "the extent of the community to which its commands apply" (Hugo Krabbe, *Modern Idea of the State,* tr. G. H. Sabine and W. J. Shepard [New York, 1922], p. 236). Kelsen argues that national and international law have the same norms, but that the norms of the latter are primitive and incomplete (Hans Kelsen, *General Theory of Law and State,* tr. Anders Wedberg [Cambridge, Mass., 1946], pp. 343, 363).

[8] Cf. T. A. Walker, *A History of the Law of Nations* (Cambridge, 1899), Vol. I, pp. 31-32. See J. M. Powis Smith, *The Origin and History of Hebrew Law* (Chicago, 1931).

"spoils of war," and the "amān,"[9] or in certain special studies such as al-kharāj.[10] Later on, the broad subject of foreign relations assumed a special significance and was discussed under the technical term al-siyar,[11] a branch of the law devoted to the conduct of foreign relations, although several publicists continued to use the term jihād.[12]

The Muslim law of nations (al-siyar), as part of the sharī'a, was in theory based on the same sources and maintained by the same sanctions as the sharī'a. In practice, however, if the term "law of nations" is taken to mean the sum total of the rules and practices of Islam's intercourse with other peoples, one should look further for evidences of the Muslim law of nations than to the conventional roots (uṣūl) or sources of the sharī'a. Some of the rules are to be found in the treaties which the Muslims concluded with non-Muslims,[13] others in public utterances and official instructions of the caliphs to commanders in the field,[14] which the jurists later incorporated in their canons; still others, the opinions and interpretations of the Muslim jurists on matters of foreign relations.[15] Analyzed in terms of the modern law of nations, the sources of the Muslim law of nations conform to the same categories defined by

[9] See e.g., Mālik ibn Anas, *Al-Muwaṭṭa'* with Suyūṭī's Commentary (Cairo, 1939), Vol. I, pp. 294-313.

[10] See e.g., Abū Yūsuf, *Kitāb al-Kharāj* (Cairo A.H. 1352); and Yaḥya ibn Ādam, *Kitāb al-Kharāj* (Cairo, 1931).

[11] See e.g., Shaybānī, *Kitāb al-Siyar al-Kabīr* with Sarakhsī's Commentary (Hyderabad, A.H. 1335), 4 Vols. Shaybānī may be regarded as the father of Muslim law of nations. (See Hans Kruse, "Die Begründung der islamischen Volkerrechtslehre," *Saeculum,* V, Heft 2, pp. 221-39.)

[12] See Ṭabarī, *Kitāb al-Jihād,* ed. by J. Schacht (Leiden, 1933).

[13] See chap. 18, below.

[14] See e.g., Abū Bakr's instructions to the Syrian Army, p. 102, below.

[15] See Ḥamīdullah, *The Muslim Conduct of State* (Revised ed. Lahore, 1945) Chap. 15.

modern jurists and the Statute of the International Court of Justice, namely, agreement, custom, reason, and authority.[16] The Qu'rān and the true Muḥammadan ḥadīths represent authority; the sunna, embodying the Arabian *jus gentium,* is equivalent to custom; rules expressed in treaties with non-Muslims fall into the category of agreement; and the fatwas and juristic commentaries of text-writers as well as the utterances and opinions of the caliphs in the interpretation and the application of the law, based on analogy and logical deductions from authoritative sources, may be said to form reason. Such utterances, opinions and decisions are to be found in the jurists' commentaries in early law textbooks and in the compilations of fatwas. These law books and digests had a great influence on the development of law generally and on the law of nations, in particular as commented and glossed upon more elaborately by later jurists.

[16] Cf. Abdur Rahim, *The Principles of Muhammadan Jurisprudence* (Madras, 1911) p. 68; and Edmund Rabbath, "Pour une theorie du droit international Musulman," *Revue Egyptienne de Droit International,* Vol. VI (1950), pp. 1-23.

BOOK II

THE LAW OF WAR:

THE JIHĀD

"The jihād is the peak of religion." a ḥadīth.

"War! War! War! War!
It has blazed up and scorched us sore.
The highlands are filled with its roar.
Well done, the morning when your heads ye shore!"

A Pre-Islamic Poet.

"Had thy Lord pleased, He would have made mankind one nation; but those only to whom thy Lord hath granted his mercy will cease to differ. . . ." Qu'rān XI, 120.

CHAPTER IV

INTRODUCTION

The state which is regarded as the instrument for universalizing a certain religion must perforce be an ever expanding state. The Islamic state, whose principal function was to put God's law into practice, sought to establish Islam as the dominant reigning ideology over the entire world. It refused to recognize the coexistence of non-Muslim communities, except perhaps as subordinate entities, because by its very nature a universal state tolerates the existence of no other state than itself. Although it was not a consciously formulated policy, Muḥammad's early successors, after Islam became supreme in Arabia, were determined to embark on a ceaseless war of conquest in the name of Islam. The jihād was therefore employed as an instrument for both the universalization of religion and the establishment of an imperial world state.[1] The mission of

[1]See chap. 5, below.

Islam was rapidly and successfully carried out during the first century of the Islamic era—although the peaceful penetration of Islam continued—and the empire extended over a large portion of the Old World and became as large as the Roman Empire.

But the expanding Muslim state, not unlike other universal states, could not extend *ad infinitum*. The hitherto victorious Muslim warriors were defeated in the West at Tours (A.D. 732) and in the East found they could not proceed further than the Indian borders.[2] Thus the wave of Muslim expansion, strong as it was, could not complete the Sun's circle; it imperceptibly subsided where it reached its utmost limits at the Pyrenees and the Indus.[3] The Muslim (world) state consequently did not correspond to the then known world. Outside it there remained communities which the Muslim authorities had to deal with, though in theory only temporarily, throughout all the subsequent history of Islam.

The world accordingly was sharply divided in Muslim law into the dār al-Islām (abode or territory of Islam) and the dār al-ḥarb (abode or territory of war). These terms may be rendered in less poetic words as the "world of Islam" and the "world of War." The first corresponded to the territory under Muslim rule. Its inhabitants were Muslims, by birth or conversion, and the communities of the tolerated religions (the dhimmīs) who preferred to hold fast to their own cult, at the price of paying the jizya (poll tax). The Muslims enjoyed full

[2] The Muslims suffered another defeat before the battle of Tours at Constantinople (A.D. 717-18).

[3] Edward Gibbon maintains that had the Muslims been successful at Tours the Qur'ān would have been taught at Oxford and Cambridge instead of the Bible (Gibbon, *History of the Decline and Fall of the Roman Empire*, ed. Bury [London, 1898], Vol. VI, p. 15); but in fact the Muslim Empire, due to internal forces, reached its utmost limits.

rights of citizenship; the subjects of the tolerated religions enjoyed only partial rights, and submitted to Muslim rule in accordance with special charters regulating their relations with the Muslims.[4] The dār al-ḥarb consisted of all the states and communities outside the world of Islam. Its inhabitants were often called infidels, or, better, unbelievers.[5]

On the assumption that the ultimate aim of Islam was world-wide, the dār al-Islām was always, in theory, at war with the dār al-ḥarb. The Muslims were required to preach Islam by persuasion, and the caliph or his commanders in the field to offer Islam as an alternative to paying the poll tax or fighting; but the Islamic state was under legal obligation to enforce Islamic law and to recognize no authority other than its own, superseding other authorities even when non-Muslim communities had willingly accepted the faith of Islam without fighting. Failure by non-Muslims to accept Islam or pay the poll tax made it incumbent on the Muslim State to declare a jihād (commonly called "holy war") upon the recalcitrant individuals and communities. Thus the jihād, reflecting the normal war relations existing between Muslims and non-Muslims, was the state's instrument for transforming the dār al-ḥarb into the dār al-Islām. It was the product of a warlike people who had embarked on a large-scale movement of expansion. Islam could not abolish the warlike character of the Arabs who were constantly at war with each other;[6] it indeed reaffirmed the war basis of intergroup relationship by institu-

[4] See chap. 17, below.

[5] For more precise definitions of dār al-Islam and dār al-ḥarb, see pp. 155-7, 170-1, below.

[6] "The primitive nomad of the desert and steppes," says Quincy Wright, "has a hard environment to conquer. . . . His terrain, adapted to distant raids and without natural defenses, leads him to institutionalize war for aggression and defense" (Q. Wright, *A Study of War* [Chicago, 1942], Vol. I, p. 64).

tionalizing war as part of the Muslim legal system and made use of it by transforming war into a holy war designed to be ceaselessly declared against those who failed to become Muslims. The short intervals which are not war—and these in theory should not exceed ten years—are periods of peace.[7] But the jihād was not the only legal means of dealing with non-Muslims since peaceful methods (negotiations, arbitration, and treaty making) were applied in regulating the relations of the believers with unbelievers when actual fighting ceased.

The Muslim law of nations was, accordingly, the product of the intercourse of an ever-expanding state with its neighbors which inevitably led to the development of a body of rules and practices followed by Muslims in war and peace. The practices followed by the Arabs before Islam in their intertribal warfare were regarded as too ungodly and brutal, because they were motivated by narrow tribal interests. Islam abolished all war except the jihād and the jurist-theologians consciously formulated its law subordinating all personal considerations to *raison d'état,* based on religious sanction.

[7] The idea that intergroup relationships were normally unpeaceful goes back to Antiquity (Plato, *The Laws,* Bk. I, 2) and it recurred in the writings of Medieval and modern thinkers. See Ibn Khaldūn, *al-Muqaddima,* ed. Quatremère (Paris, 1858), Vol. II, pp. 65-79; Hobbes, *Leviathan,* Chap. 13; *Elements of Law,* Pt. I, chap. 14, 2. See also Q. Wright, *op. cit.,* Vol. I, chaps. 6 and 7.

"Every nation has its monasticism, and the monasticism of this [Muslim] nation is the jihād." a ḥadīth.

CHAPTER V

THE DOCTRINE OF JIHĀD

The Meaning of Jihād

The term jihād is derived from the verb jāhada (abstract noun, juhd) which means "exerted";[1] its juridical-theological meaning is exertion of one's power in Allah's path, that is, the spread of the belief in Allah and in making His word supreme over this world. The individual's recompense would be the achievement of salvation, since the jihād is Allah's direct way to paradise. This definition is based on a Qur'ānic injunction which runs as follows:

O ye who believe! Shall I guide you to a gainful trade which will save you from painful punishment? Believe in Allah and His Apostle and carry on warfare (jihād) in the path of Allah with your possessions and your

[1] For the literal meaning of jihād, see Fayrūzabādī, *Qāmūs al-Muḥīṭ* (Cairo, 1933), Vol. I, p. 286. For the Quar'ānic use of jihād in the sense of exertion see Q. VI, 108; XXII, 77.

persons. That is better for you. If ye have knowledge, He will forgive your sins, and will place you in the Gardens beneath which the streams flow, and in fine houses in the Gardens of Eden: that is the great gain.[2]

The jihād, in the broad sense of exertion, does not necessarily mean war or fighting, since exertion in Allah's path may be achieved by peaceful as well as violent means. The jihād may be regarded as a form of religious propaganda that can be carried on by persuasion or by the sword. In the early Makkan revelations, the emphasis was in the main on persuasion. Muḥammad, in the discharge of his prophetic functions, seemed to have been satisfied by warning his people against idolatry and inviting them to worship Allah. This is evidenced by such a verse as the following: "He who exerts himself (jāhada), exerts only for his own soul,"[3] which expresses the jihād in terms of the salvation of the soul rather than a struggle for proselytization.[4] In the Madīnan revelations, the jihād is often expressed in terms of strife, and there is no doubt that in certain verses the conception of jihād is synonymous with the words war and fighting.[5]

The jurists, however, have distinguished four different ways in which the believer may fulfill his jihād obligation: by his heart; his tongue; his hands; and by the sword.[6] The first is

[2] Q. LXI, 10-13. See also Jurjānī, *Kitāb al-Ta'rīfāt*, ed. Gustavus Flügel (Leipzig, 1845), p. 84.

[3] Q. XXIX, 5.

[4] See Shāfi'ī, *Kitāb al-Umm* (Cairo, A.H. 1321), Vol. IV, pp. 84-85; 'Abd al-Qāhir al-Baghdādī, *Kitāb Uṣūl al-Dīn* (Istanbul, 1928) Vol. I, p. 193; Shaybānī, *al-Siyar al-Kabīr*, with Sarakhsī's Commentary (Hyderabad, A.H. 1335), Vol. I, p. 126.

[5] See Q. II, 215; IX, 41; XLIX, 15; LXI, 11; LXVI, 9.

[6] See Ibn Ḥazm, *Kitāb al-Faṣl fī al-Milal wa'l-Ahwā' wa'l-Niḥal* (Cairo, A.H. 1321), Vol. IV, p. 135; Ibn Rushd, *Kitāb al-Muqaddimāt al-Mumahhidāt* (Cairo, A.H. 1325), Vol. I, p. 259; Buhūtī, *Kashshāf al-Qinā' 'An Matn al-Iqnā'* (Cairo, A.H. 1366), Vol. III, p. 28.

concerned with combatting the devil and in the attempt to escape his persuasion to evil. This type of jihād, so significant in the eyes of the Prophet Muḥammad, was regarded as the greater jihād.[7] The second and third are mainly fulfilled in supporting the right and correcting the wrong. The fourth is precisely equivalent to the meaning of war, and is concerned with fighting the unbelievers and the enemies of the faith.[8] The believers are under the obligation of sacrificing their "wealth and lives" (Q. LXI, 11) in the prosecution of war.[9]

The Jihād as Bellum Justum

War is considered as just whether commenced and prosecuted in accordance with the necessary formalities required under a certain system of law, or waged for justifiable reasons in accordance with the tenets of the religion or the mores of a certain society. In Islam, as in ancient Rome, both of these concepts were included in their doctrine of the *bellum justum* since a justifiable reason as well as the formalities for prosecuting the war were necessary. In both Islam and ancient Rome, not only was war to be *justum,* but also to be *pium,* that is, in accordance with the sanction of religion and the implied commands of gods.[10]

[7] Ibn al-Humām, *Sharḥ Fatḥ al-Qadīr* (Cairo, A.H. 1316), Vol IV, p. 277.

[8] Ibn Ḥazm distinguishes between the jihād by the tongue and the jihād by ra'y and tadbīr (i.e., reason) and he maintains that the Prophet Muḥammad showed preference for reason over the sword. Ibn Ḥazm, Vol. IV, p. 135.

[9] Bukhārī, *Kitāb al-Jāmi' al-Ṣaḥīḥ,* ed. Krehl (Leiden, 1864), Vol. II, p. 199; Abū Dā'ūd *Sunan* (Cairo, 1935), Vol. III, p. 5; Dārimī, *Sunan* (Damascus, A.H. 1349), Vol. II, p. 213.

[10] See J. Von Elbe, "The Evolution of the Concept of the Just War in International Law," *American Journal of International Law,* Vol. XXXIII (1939), pp. 665-88; and Coleman Phillipson, *The International Law and Custom of Ancient Greece and Rome* (London, 1911), Vol. II, p. 180.

The idea that wars, when institutionalized as part of the mores of society, are just may be traced back to antiquity. It was implied in the concept of vendetta as an act of retaliation by one group against another. In the *Politics,* Aristotle refers to certain wars as just by nature.[11] The Romans instituted the *jus fetiale,* administered by a *collegium fetialium* (consisting of twenty members, presided over by *magister fetialium*), embodying the proper rules of waging war in order to be just.[12] In medieval Christendom, both St. Augustine and Isodore de Seville were influenced in their theory of just war by Cicero. St. Thomas Aquinas, who was acquainted with Muslim writings, formulated his theory of just war along lines similar to the Islamic doctrine of the jihād.[13] St. Thomas and other Medieval writers influenced in their turn the natural law theories of the sixteenth, seventeenth, and eighteenth centuries. Grotius, the father of the modern law of nations, developed his system under the impact of the natural law theory of just war, and his ideas remained predominant until the end of the eighteenth century.[14] Although the doctrine of war during the nineteenth century was by far less influenced by natural law than in previous centuries, the concept of just war reappeared after the First World War in the form of a doctrine of outlawing war, save that against an aggressor.

[11] *Politics,* Bk. I, chap. VIII.

[12] In the *Offices,* Cicero, who may be regarded as the representative legal philosopher of ancient Rome, has discussed the rules and formalities which constitute the *bellum justum.* See Cicero, *Offices, Essays and Letters* (Everyman's edition), Bk. I, § 11-12.

[13] See A. P. D'Entreves, *Aquinas: Selected Political Writings* (Oxford, 1948) pp. 59-61; John Epstein, *The Catholic Tradition of the Law of Nations* (London, 1935); William Ballis, *The Legal Position of War: Changes in its Practice and Theory* (The Hague, 1937), pp. 32-60.

[14] Hugo Grotius, *De Jure Belli ac Pacis,* first published in 1625 (Oxford, 1925).

Recurring as a pattern in the development of the concept of war from antiquity, it assumed in Islam a special position in its jural order because law and religion formed a unity; the law prescribed the way to achieve religious (or divine) purposes, and religion provided a sanction for the law.

In Muslim legal theory, Islam and shirk (associating other gods with Allah) cannot exist together in this world; it is the duty of the imām as well as every believer not only to see that God's word shall be supreme, but also that no infidel shall deny God or be ungrateful for His favors (ni'am).[15] This world would ultimately be reserved for believers;[16] as to unbelievers, "their abode is hell, and evil is the destination."[17] The jihād, in other words, is a sanction against polytheism and must be suffered by all non-Muslims who reject Islam, or, in the case of the dhimmīs (Scripturaries), refuse to pay the poll tax. The jihād, therefore, may be defined as the litigation between Islam and polytheism; it is also a form of punishment to be inflicted upon Islam's enemies and the renegades from the faith.[18] Thus in Islam, as in Western Christendom, the jihād is the *bellum justum*.

In Islam, however, the jihād is no less employed for punishing polytheists than for *raison d'état*. For inherent in the state's

[15] The Prophet Muḥammad is reported to have said: "I am ordered to fight polytheists until they say: 'there is no god but Allah.'" The validity of the rule of fighting polytheists is also based on a Qur'ānic injunction, in which Allah said to His Apostle, as follows: "slay the polytheists wherever you may find them" (Q. IX, 5). See also Tāj al-Dīn al-Subkī, *Kitāb Mu'īd al-Ni'am wa Mubīd al-Niqam*, ed. David W. Myhrman (London, 1908), p. 27.

[16] The idea that Islam would ultimately replace other religions (except perhaps the tolerated religions) is not stated in the Qur'ān, but it is implied in the objective of the jihād and expressed in the ḥadīth. See note 15, above.

[17] Q. IX, 74.

[18] For the forms or types of jihād, see Chap. 6, below.

action in waging a jihād is the establishment of Muslim sovereignty, since the supremacy of God's word carries necessarily with it God's political authority. This seems to be the reason why the jihād, important as it is, is not included—except in the Khārijī legal theory—among the five pillars of Islam. The reason is that the five pillars are not necessarily to be enforced by the state; they must be observed by the individuals regardless of the sanction of authority. The jihād, in order to achieve *raison d'état,* must, however, be enforced by the state. In the technical language the five pillars—the basic articles of the faith—are regarded as individual duties (farḍ 'ayn), like prayer or fasting, which each believer must individually perform and each is held liable to punishment if he failed to perform the duty. The jihād, on the other hand—unless the Muslim community is subjected to a sudden attack and therefore all believers, including women and children, are under the obligation to fight—is regarded by all jurists, with almost no exception, as a collective obligation of the whole Muslim community.[19] It is regarded as farḍ al-kifāya, binding on the Muslims as a collective group, not individually. If the duty is fulfilled by a part of the community it ceases to be obligatory on others; the whole community, however, falls into error if the duty is not performed at all.[20]

The imposition of the jihād duty on the community rather than on the individual is very significant and involved at least

[19] Sa'īd ibn al-Musayyib said that the jihād duty is farḍ 'ayn. Awzā'ī and Thawrī, however, advocated a defensive jihād (Shaybānī, *op. cit.,* Vol. I, p. 125) and an extremely pacifist sect, known as the Māziyāriyya, dropped both the jihād against polytheists and fasting from the articles of faith. See 'Abd al-Qāhir al-Baghdādī, *Mukhtaṣar Kitāb al-Farq Bayn al-Firaq,* summarized by al-Ras'anī and edited by Hitti (Cairo, 1924), p. 163.

[20] For a definition of this term, see Suyūṭī, *al-Ashbāh wa'l-Naẓā'ir* (Cairo, 1938), pp. 496-503; Ibn Qudāma, *al-Mughnī,* ed. Rashīd Riḍa *(Cairo,* A.H. 1367), Vol. VIII, pp. 345-6; Ibn al-Humām, *op. cit.,* p. 278.

two important implications. In the first place, it meant that the duty need not necessarily be fulfilled by all the believers. For the recruitment of all the believers as warriors was neither possible nor advisable.[21] Some of the believers were needed to prepare food and weapons, while the crippled, blind, and sick would not qualify as fighters.[22] Women and children were as a rule excused from actual fighting, although many a woman contributed indirectly to the war effort.

In the second place, the imposition of the obligation on the community rather than on the individual made possible the employment of the jihād as a community and, consequently, a state instrument; its control accordingly, is a state, not an individual, responsibility. Thus the head of the state can in a more effective way serve the common interest of the community than if the matter is left entirely to the discretion of the individual believer. Compensation for the fulfillment of such an important public duty has been amply emphasized in both the authoritative sources of the creed[23] and in formal utterances of public men.[24] All of them give lavish promises of martyrdom and eternal life in paradise immediately and without trial on resurrection and judgment day for those who die

[21] Q. IX, 123: "The believers must not march forth all to war."

[22] Q. XXIV, 60: "There is no blame on the blind man, nor on the lame, nor on the sick. . . ."

[23] Q. III, 163: "Count not those who are killed in the path of Allah as dead; they are alive with their Lord." A woman complained to Muḥammad about the death of her son in the battle of Badr, and then she asked whether her son went to hell or paradise, Muḥammad replied: "Your son is in the higher Paradise!" (Bukhārī, Vol. II, p. 202.) Another ḥadīth runs as follows: "There are one hundred stages in Paradise that are provided by Allah for those who fight in His path" (Bukhārī, II, p. 200). See also Ibn Hudhayl, *Tuḥfat al-Anfus wa Shi'ār Sukkān al-Andalus*, ed. Louis Mercier (Paris, 1936), chaps. 10 and 20.

[24] See a speech given by Caliph Abū Bakr to Syrian expedition in Ṭabarī, *Ta'rīkh*, ed. de Goeje (Leiden, 1890), Series I, Vol. IV, p. 1850.

in Allah's path. Such martyrs are not washed but are buried where they fall on the battlefield, not in the usual type of grave, after washing in a mosque. It is true that a promise of paradise is given to every believer who performs the five basic duties, but none of them would enable him to gain paradise as surely as participation in the jihād.[25]

The Jihād as Permanent War

War, however, was not introduced into Arabia by Islam. It was already in existence among the Arabs; but it was essentially a tribal war. Its nature was peculiar to the existing social order and its rules and procedure were thoroughly integrated as part of the sunna. Since the tribe (in certain instances the clan) was the basic political unit, wars took the form of raids; mainly for robbery or vendetta (tha'r). This state of affairs had, as observed by Ibn Khaldūn, developed among the Arabs a spirit of self-reliance, courage, and co-operation among the members of the single tribe.[26] But these very traits intensified the character of warfare and rivalry among the tribes and created a state of instability and unrest.

The importance of the jihād in Islam lay in shifting the focus of attention of the tribes from their intertribal warfare to the outside world; Islam outlawed all forms of war except the jihād, that is, the war in Allah's path. It would, indeed, have been very difficult for the Islamic state to survive had it not been for the doctrine of the jihād, replacing tribal raids, and directing that enormous energy of the tribes from an inevitable internal conflict to unite and fight against the outside world in the name of the new faith.

[25] Shaybānī, *op. cit.,* Vol. I, p. 20; and Herman Theodorus Obbink, *De Heilige Oorlog Volgen den Koran* (Leiden, 1901), pp. 110-1.

[26] Ibn Khaldūn, *al-Muqaddima,* ed. Quatremère (Paris, 1858), Vol. II, pp. 220-1.

The jihād as such was not a casual phenomenon of violence; it was rather a product of complex factors while Islam worked out its jural-doctrinal character. Some writers have emphasized the economic changes within Arabia which produced dissatisfaction and unrest and inevitably led the Arabs to seek more fertile lands outside Arabia.[27] Yet this theory—plausible as it is in explaining the outburst of the Arabs from within their peninsula—is not enough to interpret the character of a war permanently declared against the unbelievers even after the Muslims had established themselves outside Arabia. There were other factors which created in the minds of the Muslims a politico-religious mission and conditioned their attitude as a conquering nation.

To begin with, there is the universal element in Islam which made it the duty of every able-bodied Muslim to contribute to its spread. In this Islam combined elements from Judaism and Christianity to create something which was not in either: a divine nomocratic state on an imperialistic basis. Judaism was not a missionary religion, for the Jews were God's chosen people; a holy war was, accordingly, for the defense of their religion, not for its spread. Christianity on the other hand was a redemptive and, at the outset, a non-state religion. Even when it was associated with politics, the Church and state remained apart. Islam was radically different from both. It combined the dualism of a universal religion and a universal state. It resorted to peaceful as well as violent means for achieving that ultimate objective. The universality of Islam provided a unifying element for all believers, within the world of Islam,

[27] The economic factors are discussed by Carl H. Becker in *The Cambridge Medieval History* (Cambridge, 1913), Vol. II, pp. 329 ff; Henri Lammens, *Le Berceau de l'Islam* (Rome, 1914), Vol. I, pp. 114 ff; the Semitic migratory theory is discussed in Prince Caetani, *Annali dell'Islam* (Milan, 1907) Vol. II, 831-61.

and its defensive-offensive character produced a state of warfare permanently declared against the outside world, the world of war.

Thus the jihād may be regarded as Islam's instrument for carrying out its ultimate objective by turning all people into believers, if not in the prophethood of Muḥammad (as in the case of the dhimmis), at least in the belief in God. The Prophet Muḥammad is reported to have declared "some of my people will continue to fight victoriously for the sake of the *truth* until the last one of them will combat the anti-Christ."[28] Until that moment is reached the jihād, in one form or another, will remain as a permanent obligation upon the entire Muslim community. It follows that the existence of a dār al-ḥarb is ultimately outlawed under the Islamic jural order; that the dār al-Islām is permanently under jihād obligation until the dār al-ḥarb is reduced to nonexistence; and that any community which prefers to remain non-Islamic—in the status of a tolerated religious community accepting certain disabilities—must submit to Islamic rule and reside in the dār al-Islām or be bound as clients to the Muslim community. The universalism of Islam, in its all-embracing creed, is imposed on the believers as a continuous process of warfare, psychological and political if not strictly military.

Although the jihād was regarded as the permanent basis of Islam's relations with its neighbors, it did not at all mean continuous fighting. Not only could the obligation be performed by nonviolent means, but relations with the enemy did not necessarily mean an endless or constant violent conflict with him. The jihād, accordingly, may be stated as a doctrine of a permanent state of war, not a continuous fighting. Thus some of the jurists argued that the mere preparation for the jihād

[28] Abū Dā'ūd, *Sunan* (Cairo, 1935), Vol. III, p. 4.

is a fulfillment of its obligation.[29] The state, however, must be prepared militarily not only to repel a sudden attack on Islam, but also to use its forces for offensive purposes when the caliph deems it necessary to do so.

In practice, however, the jihād underwent certain changes in its meaning to suit the changing circumstances of life. Islam often made peace with the enemy, not always on its own terms. Thus the jurists began to reinterpret the law with a view to justifying suspension of the jihād, even though temporarily. They seem to have agreed about the necessity of peace and the length of its duration.[30] When Muslim power began to decline, Muslim publicists seem to have tacitly admitted that in principle the jihād as a permanent war had become obsolete; it was no longer compatible with Muslim interests. The concept of the jihād as a state of war underwent certain changes. This change, as a matter of fact, did not imply abandonment of the jihād duty; it only meant the entry of the obligation into a period of suspension—it assumed a dormant status, from which the imām may revive it at any time he deems necessary. In practice, however, the Muslims came to think of this as more of a normal condition of life than an active jihād.

The shift in the conception of the jihād from active to dormant war reflects a reaction on the part of the Muslims from further expansion. This coincided with the intellectual and philosophical revival of Islam at the turn of the fourth century of the Muslim era (tenth century A.D.), when the Muslims were probably more stirred by the controversy between orthodoxy and rationalism than by fighting Byzantine encroachments on the frontiers. To certain Muslim thinkers, like Ibn Khaldūn (d. 1406),[31] the relaxation of the jihād marked the

29 Ibn Hudhayl, *op. cit.*, p. 15.

30 See chap. 13, below.

31 Ibn Khaldūn, *op. cit.*, Vol. I, pp. 309 ff.

change in the character of the nation from the warlike to the civilized stage. Thus the change in the concept of the jihād was not merely an apologia for weakness and failure to live up to a doctrine, but a process of evolution dictated by Islam's interests and social conditions.

The Shī'ī and Khārijī Doctrines of the Jihād

Generally speaking, the Shī'ī law of the jihād is not different from the Sunnī; but in linking the special duty of prosecuting the jihād with the doctrine of walāya (allegiance to the imām), the concept of jihād assumed in Shī'ism a special doctrinal significance.[32] In Shī'ī legal theory, not only would the failure of a non-Muslim to believe in Allah justify waging a jihād, but also the failure of a Muslim to obey the imām would make him liable for punishment by a jihād.[33] While to a Sunnī the jihād is the sure way to Heaven, a jihād without an allegiance to the imām would not constitute an imān (a necessary requirement for salvation) in the Shī'ī creed.

The jihād is regarded as one of the chief functions of the imāmate, the performance of which would fulfill one of the requirements for the best (afḍal) qualified person for this position. If the imām fails to fulfill the jihād obligation, he disqualifies his claim as the best candidate, according to the Zaydī creed.[34] The imām, as an infallible ruler, is the only one who can judge when the jihād should be declared and under what circumstances it would be advisable not to go to war

[32] For an exposition of the Shī'ī law of the jihād, see Ṭūsī, *Kitāb Masā'il al-Khilāf* (Tehrān, A.H. 1370), Vol. II, pp. 196-9; and Qāḍī Nu'mān, *Da'ā'im al-Islām*, ed. Āṣif ibn 'Alī Fayḍī (Fyzee) (Cairo, 1951), Vol. I, pp. 399-466. For a translation of the Shī'ī law of the jihād, see A. Querry, *Recueil de lois concernant les Musulmans Schyites* (Paris, 1881), Vol. I, pp. 321-53.

[33] 'Abd-Allah ibn Muftāḥ, *Sharḥ al-Azhār* (Cairo, A.H. 1358), Vol. V, p. 525.

[34] See R. Strothmann, *Das Staatrecht de Zaiditen* (Strassburg, 1912), p. 61.

with the enemy. If the imām finds it necessary to come to terms with the enemy, he may do so; he may even deem it necessary to seek the support of non-Muslims (including polytheists) in order to avoid risking defeat by the enemy.[35] Under no circumstances, however, should the imām risk a jihād if he considers the enemy too powerful for him to win a victory, namely, if the enemy is at least twice as powerful as the Muslims.[36]

The disappearance of the imām, however, has left the duty of declaring the jihād unfulfilled.[37] Opinion differed as to the capacity of the mujtahids to act in the name of the imām in fulfilling the jihād obligation; but since the duty of calling the believers to battle is a matter in which an infallible judgment is necessary—since the interest of the entire community would be at stake—only an imām is capable of fulfilling such a duty. Further, it is deemed impossible to combat evil during the absence of the imām; the jihād, accordingly, is regarded unconsequential. Thus in the Shī'ī legal theory, the jihād has entered into a dormant stage—it is in a state of suspension. In contrast to the Sunnī doctrine which requires the revival of the dormant jihād when Muslim power is regained, the resumption of the jihād in the Shī'ī doctrine would be dependent on the return of the imām from his ghayba (absence), in the capacity of a Mahdī, who will triumphantly combat evil and re-establish justice and righteousness.[38]

In contrast to the Shī'ī doctrine of the jihād, the Khārijīs maintain that the jihād is a fundamental article of the faith which could not possibly be abandoned or relaxed. To them

35 *Ibid.*, p. 105.

36 Qāḍī Nu'mān, Vol. I, p. 434; Ḥillī, *Tabṣirat al-Muta'allimīn fī Aḥkām al-Dīn* (Damascus, A.H. 1342), p. 103; Strothmann, p. 91.

37 This situation has not arisen among the Zaydis, since technically they elect their imāms.

38 For an exposition of the Shī'ī doctrine of Mahdism, see Dwight M. Donaldson, *The Shiite Religion* (London, 1933), Chap. 21.

the jihād is a sixth pillar of the faith, binding individually on every believer and on the community as a whole.[39] They also go as far as to enforce imān on all who do not accept their version of Islam, Muslims as well as non-Muslims, by the jihād; for, they argue, that since the Prophet Muḥammad had spent almost all his life in war, all true believers must also do so. Their strict belief in their religion and their fanaticism made them uncompromising in the fulfillment of their jihād duty. Thus their conception of the state was that of a garrison state; an ever-ready community, led by its imām, to wage war on the enemies of the faith. Even if the imām does not lead in war, the jihād is incumbent on each believer to fulfill by himself, for he falls in error if he fails to do so.

The Khārijī conception of the jihād, in contrast to the Sunnī doctrine is that of violence rather than strife or religious propaganda.[40] To them true belief is a matter of conviction which should be imposed on reluctant individuals, not a subject of debate and argumentation; for, if evil is to be exterminated and justice re-established, obstinate heretics must be either forced to believe or be killed by the sword. This is based on a ḥadīth in which the Prophet Muḥammad is reported to have said: "My fate is under the shadow of my spear."[41]

Strict and fanatical, the Khārijīs were as fierce and brutal in war as their desert life was austere and puritanical. The humane and moral aspect of religion made little impact on their tribal character. In war they killed women and children and condemned to death prisoners of war. Although these rules were not always followed, the extremist Khārijīs, such as the

[39] The Khārijīs do not actually add a sixth pillar to the already recognized five pillars of the Sunnīs, because they substitute jihād for imān (which to them is synonymous with Islam) and thus the number of the pillars is not increased.

[40] See p. 12, note 19, above.

[41] Bukhārī, Vol. II, p. 227.

followers of Nāfi' ibn al-Azraq (A.H. 686), insisted that they should always be enforced.[42]

The Jihād and Secular War

Islam, it will be recalled, abolished all kinds of warfare except the jihād. Only a war which has an ultimate religious purpose, that is, to enforce God's law or to check transgression against it, is a just war. No other form of fighting is permitted within or without the Muslim brotherhood.

Throughout the history of Islam, however, fighting between Muslim rulers and contending parties was as continuous as between Islam and its external enemies. The *casus foederis* of a jihād was frequently invoked on the grounds of suppressing innovations and punishing the leaders of secession from the faith. Not infrequently the naked ambition of opposition leaders who resorted to war for the sake of a throne or high political offices was too apparent to be ignored. When the caliph's prestige and power declined, lack of respect for and opposition to the central authority became fashionable among local rulers. This state of affairs accentuated the struggle for power and created instability and anarchy in the world of Islam. Ignoring existing realities, the jurists continued to argue—following the example of al-Māwardī—that ultimate authority belonged to the caliph and that no one else had the right to renounce it even if the caliph proved to be unjust and oppressive, since tyranny, it was then contended, was preferrable to anarchy[43]—a sad comment on existing conditions.

A few publicists, in their reflections on the state of affairs as they then existed, have said that wars, in forms other than the

[42] Shahrastānī, *Kitāb al-Milal wa'l-Niḥal*, ed. Cureton (London, 1840), pp. 90, 93; and Ras'anī's *Mukhtaṣar*, pp. 73, 80, 97.

[43] Badr al-Dīn Ibn Jamā'a, *Taḥrīr al-Aḥkām fī Tadbīr Ahl al-Islām*, ed. H. Koefler in *Islamica*, Vol. VI (1934), p. 365.

jihād, had often recurred in the Islamic society. Paying lip service to the jihād as a religious duty, they looked upon wars as dangers which Muslim rulers should avoid. Al-Ṭarṭūshī (died A.H. 520) described "war crises" as social anomalies[44] and al-Ḥasan ibn 'Abd-Allah compared them to diseases of society.[45] Both of these writers, who expatiated on the ways and means of conducting fighting, advised their rulers that the best way to win wars, if they found it impossible to avert them, was to be adequately prepared militarily. Thus Muslim publicists, like their Roman predecessors, seemed to have been convinced that *si vis pacem, para bellum.*

It was, perhaps, Ibn Khaldūn (A.D. 1332-1406) who for the first time recognized that wars were not, as his Muslim predecessors thought, casual social calamities. He maintained that war has existed in society ever since "Creation." Its real cause, which accounts for its persistence in society, is man's will-to-revenge. Man, in other words, is by nature warlike. He is forever moved to fight either for his own selfish interests or by such emotional motives as jealousy, anger, or a feeling of divine guilt. Thus the members of one group or nation, in order to attain their objectives, combined against others and the inevitable result was war.

Wars, according to Ibn Khaldūn, are of four kinds. First is

[44] Ṭarṭūshī, *Sirāj al-Mulūk*, pp. 150-153.

[45] Ibn 'Abd-Allah, who wrote his book in A.H. 708, gives seven reasons for the recurrence of war in society: First, for the establishment of a new state (dawla) or dynasty; second, for the consolidation of an already established state or dynasty; third, the wars of a just state (dawla 'ādila) against rebels and dissenters; fourth, wars between two nations or tribes in the form of raids; fifth, the annexation of one state by another, regardless of whether the latter was just or unjust; sixth, wars for the purpose of mere robbery, not for any political purpose; seventh, intertribal warfare as those existed in pre-Islamic Arabia. Al-Ḥasan ibn 'Abd-Allah, *Āthār al-Uwal fī Tartīb al-Duwal* (Cairo, A.H. 1295), pp. 167-8.

the tribal warfare, such as that which existed among the Arabian tribes; second, feuds and raids which are characteristic of primitive people; third, the wars prescribed by the sharī'a, i.e., the jihād; fourth, wars against rebels and dissenters. Ibn Khaldūn contends that the first two are unjustified, because they are wars of disobedience; the other two are just wars ('adl).

Ibn Khaldūn was not of the opinion, as Ṭarṭūshī contended, that victory could be attained by sheer military preparedness. He believed that there are always deeper causes for victory—more important than arms and armaments—which he called al-asbāb al-khafiyya, that is, the hidden causes. He does not mean, however, by khafiyya the morale of the army (although he regards this as absolutely necessary); but rather the application of certain skills and tactics which enable an army to attain victory, such as making use of certain highlands which helps to start an offensive, and deceiving tactics which tend to mislead the enemy.[46]

It is to be noted that Muslim thinkers, from the rise of Islam to the time of Ibn Khaldūn, regarded secular wars as an evil to be avoided since they were inconsistent with God's law which prohibited all forms of war except those waged for religious purposes. A close examination of society taught Muslim thinkers that secular wars were not easily avoided by fallible human beings; peace within the Muslim brotherhood needed the inspiring influence of a Prophet or the prestige and power of an 'Umar I. When the caliphs departed from the sunna of the Prophet, holy wars were no longer the only kind of warfare waged; nor were they always devoid of secular purposes. A war, called ḥarb, in distinction from a holy war (jihād), was looked upon as an unnatural phenomenon which befell society only because of man's carelessness and sins. Ibn 'Abd-Allah, it will

[46] Ibn Khaldūn, *op. cit.*, Vol. II, pp. 65-79.

be remembered, described wars as diseases; but Ibn Khaldūn thought that their frequency in society, arising from the very nature of man, makes their recurrence as permanent as social life itself. Ibn Khaldūn based his conclusions not only on his own personal observations on the state of constant warfare that existed among the petty Muslim states in North Africa, but also on the experiences of various nations with whose history he was acquainted. Ibn Khaldūn's observation, which shows keen insight in understanding human society, is corroborated by modern research, which has demonstrated that early societies tended to be more warlike and that peace was by no means the normal state of affairs.[47] As Sir Henry Maine stated, "it is not peace which was natural and primitive and old, but rather war. War appears to be as old as mankind, but peace is a modern invention."[48] Islam, unlike Christianity, sought to establish the Kingdom of Heaven on earth; but, like

[47] Ibn Khaldūn is not the first thinker who said that warfare is the normal state in society, but he was the first Muslim thinker to say so. Plato (*The Laws,* Bk. I, 2) before him as well as others after in Medieval and modern times have expressed similar ideas. Hobbes, in an often quoted statement, said: "Hereby it is manifest, that during the time men live without a common power to keep them all in awe, they are in that condition which is called war; and such a war, as is of every man, against every man. For war, consisteth not in battle only, or the act of fighting; but in a tract of time, wherein the will to contend by battle is sufficiently known: and therefore the notion of time, is to be considered in the nature of war; as it is in the nature of weather. For as the nature of foul weather, lieth not in a shower or two of rain; but in an inclination thereto of many days together: so the nature of war consisteth not in actual fighting; but in the known disposition thereto, during all the time there is no assurance to the contrary. All other time is peace." (Hobbes, *Leviathan,* Chap. 13). See also Leo Strauss, *The Political Philosophy of Hobbes* (Oxford, 1936), pp. 160-3.

[48] Sir Henry Maine, *International Law* (London, 1888), p. 8. See also Quincy Wright, *A Study of War* (Chicago, 1942), Vol. I, Chapters 6, 7, appendices, 6, 8, 9, and 10.

Christianity, could not produce that world brotherhood and God-fearing society which would live permanently in peace. War was as problematic to our forefathers as to ourselves; they sought earnestly to abolish it by the faiths they honored no less than we do by our own faith in the scientific approach.

"Allah gave the Prophet Muḥammad four swords [for fighting the unbelievers]: the first against polytheists, which Muḥammad himself fought with; the second against apostates, which Caliph Abū Bakr fought with; the third against the People of the Book, which Caliph 'Umar fought with; and the fourth against dissenters, which Caliph 'Alī fought with."
Shaybānī, *Kitāb al-Siyar al-Kabīr,* I, 14-5.

CHAPTER VI

TYPES OF JIHĀD

Muslim jurists distinguished between the jihād against nonbelievers and the jihād against believers who either renegaded from the faith or, professing dissenting views, renounced the authority of the imām or his lieutenants. While the jurists agreed that war was just when waged against such people, they disagreed on its conduct and termination. Al-Māwardī subdivided the jihād against believers into three categories: first, the jihād against apostasy, (al-ridda); second, the jihād against dissension (al-baghī); and third, the jihād against secession (al-muḥārībūn).[1] Other jurists added a category known as al-ribāṭ, or the safeguarding of frontiers. There may be added still another type, the jihād against the People of the Book or the Scripturaries.

[1] Māwardī, *Kitāb al-Aḥkām al-Sulṭāniyya,* ed. Enger (Bonn, 1853), p. 89.

The Jihād Against Polytheists

No compromise is permitted with those who fail to believe in God, they have either to accept Islam or fight. In several Qur'ānic injunctions, the Muslims are under the obligation to "fight the polytheists wherever ye may find them;"[2] to "fight those who are near to you of the polytheists, and let them find in you sternness";[3] and "when you meet those who misbelieve, strike off their heads until you have massacred them. . . ."[4] In the ḥadīth the Prophet Muḥammad is reported to have declared: "I am ordered to fight polytheists until they say: 'there is no god but Allah.' "[5] All the jurists, perhaps without exception, assert that polytheism and Islam cannot exist together; the polytheists, who enjoin other gods with Allah, must choose between war or Islam. The definition of a polytheist, however, has not been precisely given by any jurist. They exclude not only Scripturaries (who believe in Allah though not in His Apostle) but also the Magians (Zoroastrains) whose belief in Allah is obscure, but they had some sort of a book. Polytheism seems to have been confined narrowly to paganism, with no implied concept of a supreme deity.

In the Ḥijāz the principle was carried out to the letter, but in certain parts of Arabia, like al-Yaman, Jews were permitted to reside. No one was permitted to reside within Arabia, save those who either adopted Islam or remained Scripturaries. After Muḥammad's death, however, the Christians of Najrān, who were given a pledge of security, were required by the Caliph 'Umar to leave for settlement in the Fertile Crescent.[6]

[2] Q. IX, 5.

[3] Q. IX, 124.

[4] Q. XLVII, 4.

[5] Bukhāri, *Kitāb al-Jāmi' al-Ṣaḥīḥ,* ed. Krehl (Leiden, 1864), Vol. II, p. 236; and Abū Da'ūd, *Sunan* (Cairo, 1935), Vol. III, p. 44.

[6] See Chap. 17, below.

Later, the rule was relaxed and at the present Scripturaries are forbidden from residing only in Makka.[7] Outside the Arabian peninsula polytheists were rarely to be found, except perhaps Zoroastrians in Persia and pagan elements in the distant provinces of the borders of Islam in Asia and Africa.

The Jihād Against Apostasy

Apostasy may take place in one of two forms: (a) either the believer reverted from (irtadda, literally turned his back against) Islam with no intention of joining the dar al-ḥarb, (b) or a group of believers, having renounced Islam, joined the dar al-ḥarb or separated themselves in a territory constituting their own dār. The latter situation is relevant to our discussion on the jihād; the former, which relates to the law of peace, will be discussed later under jurisdiction.[8]

If the apostates were numerous and powerful enough to defy authority, the imām was under obligation to invoke the jihād against them. The jurists, however, advise negotiation before fighting begins, since this may succeed in persuading them to return to Islam. Neither peace nor tribute nor poll tax is acceptable, since the law tolerates no secession from Islam. The apostates must either return to Islam or accept the challenge of jihād. As in the case of unbelievers, they should be notified (in the course of negotiations) that fighting will follow. This satisfies the rule of a declaration of war.

Should the apostates refuse and fighting begin, the rules governing the conduct of war would be the same as those gov-

[7] The Ḥanbalī jurist Ibn Qudāma permits Scripturaries to pass through the Ḥijāz, including Makka, provided they do not intend to reside (Ibn Qudāma, *al-Mughnī,* ed. Rashīd Riḍa [Cairo, A.H. 1367], Vol. VIII, p. 530-31). Present practice forbids Scripturaries from entering Makka alone, allowing non-Muslims to travel elsewhere and even to reside in Jidda.

[8] See Chap. 14.

erning a war with the people of dār al-ḥarb.[9] Neither their property nor themselves become subject to the general rule of submission of unbelievers, namely, they and their wives are not liable to be condemned into slavery, nor their property confiscated or divided as spoil. The property of those killed in battle is taken over by the state as fay'. Some jurists, such as the Ḥanafīs, maintain that the apostate wife should become a sabī, that is, condemned to be a slave-woman and taken as a spoil or sold. So are the children born after apostasy, but the majority of jurists do not think that is necessary.

The outstanding case of apostasy was the secession of the tribes of Arabia after the death of Muḥammad. Abū Bakr, the first caliph, warned them first to return to Islam, and those who did not return were severely fought, especially by Khālid ibn al-Walīd, who burned a great number of them in spite of objections raised regarding the penalty of burning. The leaders of the apostate tribes were severely punished and most of them were slain. An eminent chronicler, al-Balādhurī, reports that nobody escaped death save those who returned to Islam.[10]

The Jihād Against Baghī

Baghī is an attempt at dissension. If the dissenters did not renounce the authority of the imām, they were not fought and were allowed to reside peacefully in the dār al-Islām. The imām, however, should persuade them to abandon their dissenting ideas and to conform to orthodoxy; if they refused and failed to conform to the law, then they were fought against. If dissension were the result of certain grievances which did not touch the creed, such as against their own governor, an attempt should be made to reconcile them. If there were very few so that they

[9] See Chap. 9.

[10] Balādhurī, *Futūḥ al-Buldān,* ed. de Goeje (Leiden, 1866), pp. 105-6; Hitti's translation, pp. 159-61.

could be controlled without difficulty, there was no need for a jihād. The Khārijīs were a case in point. When they disagreed with the Caliph 'Alī, they were offered three propositions; they were permitted to say their prayers in the mosques, they were not attacked by the caliph, and were allowed to live in the dār al-Islām.[11] But once they opposed the caliph, 'Alī marched against them and crushed their power in the battle of al-Nahruwān (A.D. 658).

While, in early Islam, Muslim public opinion was not inclined to support an imām who himself seemed to have departed from the law, the jurist-theologians seem to have gradually tended to support the authority of the imām against any element revolting against him. They upheld the theory that the imām, even if he committed an error, must be obeyed. The Ash'arīs and almost all the later Sunni jurists supported authority against dissension and argued that rebellion is worse than tyranny.[12] To them once the bay'a (homage or fealty) was given to the new imām there was no legal way of taking it back. For, according to a Qur'ānic injunction, the believers must "obey Allah and the Apostle and those in authority among you"; if the Muslims differ from the imām on an issue, "bring it before Allah and the Apostle, if you believe in Allah and in the last day." [13] But when Allah's Apostle has died then the imām takes his place. Thus in practice the imām has the ultimate authority in the state, and he can invoke the jihād to enforce his commands. It follows that baghī, in the sense of dissension, would constitute the negation of the imām's au-

[11] Saḥnūn, *al-Mudawwana al-Kubra* (Cairo, A.H. 1323), Vol. III, pp. 47-50; and Māwardī, p. 97.

[12] Ash'arī, *Kitāb al-Ibāna* (Hyderabad, 2nd. ed., A.H. 1367), p. 9; and Ibn Jamā'a, "Taḥīr al Aḥkām fī Tadbīr Ahl al-Islām," ed. Kofler in *Islamica*, Vol. VI (1934), pp. 354 ff.

[13] Q. IV, 62.

thority; hence both the imām and his subject must oppose the dissenters in order to re-establish the unity of the imāmate.

The rules governing the conduct of war against dissenters are somewhat different from those of fighting the unbelievers; the main differences being that the dissenter prisoners are not liable for killing nor their property for confiscation as spoils. Their arms and armaments should be returned to them after their submission to the imām. Such destructive measures as burning the cattle or an attack by the mangonels and fire should not be resorted to unless deemed absolutely necessary.[14]

The Jihād Against Deserters and Highway Robbers

Acts committed by deserters from the community of believers and highway robbers are called the great theft. The law concerning their treatment is provided in the Qur'ān as follows:

> The punishment of those who combat Allah and His Apostle, and go about to commit disorders on the earth, they should be slain or crucified or have their hands and their feet cut off or be banished from the land; this shall be as a disgrace for them in this world, and in the next they shall have a great torment.[15]

The jurists agree, on the basis of the foregoing Qur'ānic verse, that deserters and highway robbers should be punished by the imām; but they disagreed on the degree of punishment. Some ordered slaying and crucification; others cutting off their hands and feet; still others were satisfied with banishment. The punishment depended on the character of the criminal as well as the seriousness of his act.[16] There was also a difference of

[14] Shāfi'ī, *Kitāb al-Umm* (Cairo, A.H. 1321), Vol. IV, pp. 133 ff; Māwardī, pp. 96-101; Ibn Qāsim al-Ghazzī, *Fatḥ al-Qarīb*, ed. Van den Berg (Leiden, 1894), pp. 592-6; Ibn Qudāma, *al-Mughnī*, ed. Rashīd Riḍa (Cairo, A.H. 1367), Vol. VIII, pp. 104-22; Marghinānī, *al-Hidāya* (Cairo, 1936), Vol. II, pp. 126-8.

[15] Q. V, 37.

[16] Māwardī, pp. 102-3.

opinion regarding banishment. Mālik contended that the criminal should be banished to the dār al-ḥarb; other jurists insisted that he should be kept in the dār al-Islām, but banished from his own town (according to the Caliph 'Umar ibn 'Abd al-'Azīz) or thrown into prison (according to Abū Ḥanīfa).

In fighting such groups, the imām has the choice of treating them on the same footing as the bughāt (singular, baghī) or being more lenient to them, depending on the degree of the seriousness of their conduct.[17]

The Jihād Against Scripturaries

The People of the Book or Scripturaries (Ahl al-Kitāb) are the Jews, Sabians, and Christians who believed in Allah but, according to the Muslim creed, who distorted their Scriptures and fell into Allah's disfavor. When Allah sent the last of His Prophets to call them to the truth, they accepted belief in Allah but not in His Prophet or the Qur'ān. Hence, the Scripturaries, like the polytheists must be punished; but since they believe in Allah, they are only partially liable to punishment. The jihād, accordingly, is invoked but not in the same degree of effectiveness as against polytheists.

The polytheists have the limited choice between Islam or the jihād; the Scripturaries can choose one of three propositions: Islam, the poll tax, or the jihād. If they accept Islam, they are entitled under the law to full citizenship as other believers; if they prefer to remain Scripturaries at the sacrifice of paying the poll tax, they suffer certain disabilities which reduce them to second-class citizens; if they fight they are to be treated in war on the same footing as polytheists.

[17] Māwardī, p. 105-6; and M. Ḥamīdullah, *Muslim Conduct of State* (Lahore, 1945), pp. 177-9.

The Ribāṭ

The ribāṭ is the safeguarding of the frontiers of the dār al-Islām by stationing forces in the harbors and frontier-towns (thughūr) for defense purposes. This type of jihād, although based on a Qur'ānic injunction, developed at a time when the Islamic state was on the defensive. The Qur'ānic rule, making no distinction between defensive or offensive purposes, states: "Prepare ye against them what force and companies of horse ye can, to make the enemies of God, and your enemies, and others beside them, in dread thereof." [18] But the jurists, especially the Mālikī jurists of Spain and North Africa (whose frontiers had become constantly the targets of attack from European forces), emphasized the defensive purpose of the ribāṭ. In the ḥadīth, the defensive character of the ribāṭ is emphasized, probably because these ḥadīths were circulated at the time the ribāṭ was fulfilling defensive purposes. Thus one ḥadīth runs as follows: " 'Abd-Allah ibn 'Umar stated that the jihād is for combatting the unbelievers, and the ribāṭ for safeguarding the believers." In Spain the ribāṭ assumed in the eyes of the Muslims more significance than the jihād since their frontiers were constantly under attack by Christian forces. It was for this reason that Ibn Hudhayl, writing his treatise on the jihād in the twelfth century of the Christian era (when Islamic rule in Spain had been reduced to the southern part), devoted the second chapter to ribāṭ and stressed the defense of Spain against the unbelievers, from land and sea, as the most essential obligation upon the believers. Ḥadīths, ascribed to the Prophet Muḥammad, with references to Andalus as the Western frontier of Islam, are cited to stress the significance of ribāṭ for the protection of Spain from European attack.[19] The

[18] Q. VIII, 62.

[19] Ibn Hudhayl, *Tuḥfat al-Anfus wa Shi'ār Sukkān al-Andalus*, ed. Louis Mercier (Paris, 1936), pp. 8-10.

Prophet Muḥammad is also reported to have said that the ribāṭ is given preference over the jihād, and that spending one night in a ribāṭ is worth more than a thousand in prayer.[20]

[20] Bukhārī, *Kitāb al-Jāmi' al-Ṣaḥīḥ,* ed. Krehl (Leiden, 1864), Vol. II, p. 222; Shaybānī, *al-Siyar al-Kabīr,* with Sarakhsī's Commentary (Hyderabad, A.H. 1335), Vol. I, pp. 6, 7, 9, 31.

In reply to the Emperor Heraclius who inquired about the Muslims, a Byzantine who had been among them said: "They are horse-riders during the day and monks during the night!"

Ṭabarī's *Ta'rīkh,* I, 2395.

CHAPTER VII

MILITARY METHODS

The Jihādists

In the early career of the Prophet Muḥammad, all of his followers including even women, agreed to fight for the cause of Islam.[1] In practice, however, that was impossible; the whole Muslim community, small and embryonic as it was, could not be mobilized in the field, for economic as well as for physical reasons.[2] From the military point of view, therefore, the Mus-

[1] In the second oath taken at 'Aqaba (A.D. 621), all of Muḥammad's followers agreed to fight, in the words of Ibn Hishām, "the red and black war" for the cause of Islam. This incident marked the passing in the way of preaching Islam from persuasion to propagation by the jihād. See Ibn Hishām, *Kitāb al-Sīra,* ed. Wüstenfeld (Göttingen, 1858), Vol. I, pp. 293-300.

[2] It is certain that Muḥammad often left behind him a number of his followers when he took the field (Wāqidī, *Kitāb al-Maghāzī,* ed. von Kremer (Calcutta, 1856), pp. 12-3.) This practice has been sanctioned by a Qur'ānic injunction to the effect that "the believers must not march forth all together to war. . . ." Q. IX, 23.

lims were divided, in the words of Shāfi'ī, into those "under jihād obligation" and those "under no jihād obligation."[3] These terms may be simplified however into jihādists and non-jihādists. The jihādists must possess certain qualifications, in order to be allowed to go to battle and fight in Allah's path, which may be stated as follows:

In the first place, the jihādist must be a believer. Mālik and Shāfi'ī support this position and argue that the Prophet Muḥammad refused to admit nonbelievers into his army.[4] Other jurists, especially the Ḥanafīs, saw no reason why nonbelievers could not be employed, arguing that the Prophet Muḥammad himself sought the support of nonbelievers.[5] They cited a ḥadīth to the effect that Islam might be supported even by sinners.[6] While the practice of excluding nonbelievers was generally accepted, it was not always followed. It is certain that at the battle of al-Qādisiyya the Muslims were supported by polytheists who accepted Islam only after they had won the battle.[7]

In the second place, the jihādist must be a mature and sound-minded person. Children and the insane were excused until the latter were cured and the former became mature.[8]

[3] Shāfi'ī, *Kitāb al-Umm* (Cairo, A.H. 1321), Vol. IV, p. 85.

[4] *Ibid.*, p. 89; Saḥnūn, *al-Mudawwana al-Kubra* (Cairo, A.H. 1323) Vol. III, pp. 40-1. For the case of Khubayb ibn Isāf, who was refused by Muḥammad permission to fight before he professed Islam, see Wāqidī, pp. 40-1.

[5] Shaybānī, *al-Siyar al-Kabīr*, (Hyderabad, A.H. 1335), Vol. III, pp. 186-8.

[6] Bukhārī, *Kitāb al-Jāmi' al-Ṣaḥīḥ*, ed. Krehl (Leiden, 1864), Vol. II, pp. 263-4. Muhammad's practice, however, seems to have varied between refusal and acceptance of nonbelievers (See Wāqidī, pp. 215, 222.)

[7] Ṭabarī, *Ta'rīkh*, ed. de Goeje (Leiden, 1893), Series I, Vol. V, p. 2261.

[8] Ibn 'Umar is reported to have said that Muḥammad refused his offer to participate in the battle of Uḥud, when he was fourteen years old, and allowed him to do so a year later, in the battle of the Trench (Shāfi'ī, Vol. IV, p. 85).

In the third place, the jihādist must be a male; women are, in principle, non-jihādist.[9] The reason is that the Qur'ānic verses of the jihād refer only to the mu'minīn (believers, which is masculine in Arabic) and the word mu'mināt (which is feminine) is not added to it. Only in case of a sudden attack on Islam, might women participate in fighting. The jurists permit women to help indirectly in war, especially in taking care of wounded Muslims or in encouraging them in the prosecution of the war.[10]

In the third place, the jihādist must be an able-bodied person. The Qur'ān is explicit in excluding the weak, crippled, and sick, "so long as they are sincere to Allah and His Apostle."[11] In another verse the rule is stated as follows: "Allah will not burden any soul beyond its power."[12] Muslims who are well-to-do but unable to fight may fulfill their jihād obligation by contribution in money or weapons.[13]

In the fourth place, the jihādist must be independent economically. He must be under no debt obligation, unless he is excused by his debtor, and must possess wealth enough to support himself and his family.[14] A slave accordingly, who is dependent on his master, was under no jihād obligation.[15] If

[9] The Prophet Muḥammad said: "The jihād of women is a pilgrimage" (Bukhārī, Vol. II, p. 218).

[10] Shāfi'ī, Vol. IV, p. 88; Wāqidī, p. 206; Shaybānī, Vol. I, p. 125; Vol. III, p. 206. Yet some women took part in actual fighting during the life of Muḥammad and later in the conquest of Iraq and Syria. See Ṭabarī, *Ta'rīkh,* Series I, Vol. IV, p. 2100. It had been the practice in pre-Islamic Arabia that occasionally women took part in fighting.

[11] Q. IX, 92; XLVIII, 17.

[12] Q. II, 286.

[13] Shaybānī, Vol. I, pp. 95-6.

[14] Shāfi'ī, Vol. IV, p. 86; and Shaybānī, Vol. III, pp. 201-5.

[15] Shāfi'ī, Vol. IV, p. 85; Ibn Rushd, *al-Muqaddimāt al-Mumahhidāt* (Cairo, A.H. 1325), Vol. I, p. 267.

the slave were set free, he was of course allowed to fight. In case of attack, slaves, like women, are under obligation to help in repelling the aggressor.

In the fifth place, the jihādist must get his parents' permission before he goes to battle. In case of sudden attack, the believers must rise to defend themselves without prior authorization of their parents or the imām.[16]

In the sixth place, the jihādist must proceed to action with good intentions. This is the principle of *bona fide* which is embodied in Muḥammad's saying that "deeds are to be judged by intentions."[17] In Muslim legal theory the jihādist's main purpose is to uphold and further the cause of religion, not to take his share of the spoils; the latter comes as a matter of course, since victory is assured by Allah.

Finally, the jihādist must fulfill certain duties while he is on active service. One of them is obedience and loyalty to the commander of the army in accordance with the Qur'ānic rule: "Obey Allah, and the Apostle and those in authority among you."[18] He is likewise expected to accept the commander's decisions in matters of military affairs as well as in the division of the spoil.[19] Nor should the jihādist ever entertain the idea of desertion from service, unless the enemy is very powerful—at least twice the number of Muslims—and no retreat is permitted unless he is overpowered by the enemy and threatened with extermination.[20] Furthermore, the jihādist must be honest

[16] Shāfi'ī, Vol. IV, p. 86; Shaybānī, Vol. I, pp. 123, 128, 133. A believer once joined Muḥammad without his parents' approval and was sent back to get their authorization.

[17] See p. 27, above.

[18] Q. IV, 62. See also Shaybānī, Vol. I, pp. 114.

[19] Māwardī, *al-Aḥkām al-Sulṭāniyya,* ed. Enger (Bonn, 1853), pp. 79-80; and Ibn Hudhayl, *Tuḥfat al-Anfus wa Shi'ār Sukkān al-Andalus,* ed. Louis Mercier (Paris, 1936), pp. 15-6.

[20] See chap. 12, below.

and straightforward and avoid treacherous acts. For instance, if he gave an amān,[21] he must abide by it; and if he has killed, he must not mutilate.[22]

Command of the Jihādists

The caliph, enthroned to enforce the law, is the chief of both civil and military authority. He appoints civil as well as military governors; but these act only as his deputies, since the caliph is the chief responsible (in theory to God only) for public duties as prescribed by the law. The Prophet Muḥammad as well as many of his successors often took the field as commanders of the army, but at other times they appointed commanders who acted as their deputies in the prosecution of the jihād.[23] The Jurists conceived of military power as an instrument in the hand of the caliph for fulfilling his public duties, but when the authority of the caliph waned and his deputy commanders became in fact more powerful than he was, the jurists often justified the assumption of authority by force. To many jurists, military force was regarded as a basic qualification for authority, a view which reflects the increasing tendency

[21] See chap. 15, below.

[22] Māwardī, pp. 75-6; and Ibn Rushd, p. 268.

[23] Out of the fifty-five expeditions dispatched during his lifetime, the Prophet Muḥammad commanded twenty-six or twenty-seven of them (Ibn Hishām, *op. cit.*, Vol. II; and Ṭabarī, *op. cit.*, Series I, Vol. IV, p. 1756.) Those expeditions which the Prophet himself commanded were called ghazwas; those whose command was entrusted to companions were called sariyyas.

Abū Bakr was anxious to command the expeditions sent to Syria, but was persuaded by 'Umar to remain in Madīna for a better strategic control of public affairs. 'Ali was at the head of his army in the battle of Ṣiffīn. Not infrequently succeeding caliphs during the Umayyad and 'Abbāsid periods themselves commanded the army. Hārūn al-Rashīd acquired the reputation of leading his army in one year and pilgrimage in the other.

to subordinate institutions to those who have command of the army.

The military command was of two kinds: special and general. The first is concerned only with the military policy of the army, and the other with diplomatic as well as with military matters. The duties of the special command are included in the general and may be summarized as follows:

(1) The leading of the army, including taking care of individual warriors, the inspection of horses and equipment.

(2) The conducting of fighting and the encouragement of the army in fighting.

(3) Application of military skills and techniques, in accordance with the Prophet's saying that "war is a trickery," so as to protect the army from sudden attack and to win victory.[24] The commander has also to choose the best possible strategic position for attack.

(4) Observation of military duties such as patience and perseverance in fighting the enemy,[25] and to see that no jihādist deserts the army.[26] The jihādists, on the other hand, are under obligation to obey the commander's orders and to accept his decisions in cases of personal conflict.

The general command includes the foregoing duties together with a mandate to negotiate and sign peace treaties and direct division of the spoils of war.[27]

Composition of the Army

Muḥammad's early followers had been completely converted into a militia, but when the Muslim community grew in number only those who could fulfill the jihād obligation were

[24] Bukhārī, Vol. II, p. 254.

[25] Q. III, 200.

[26] A faithful jihādist is permitted to take leave, if necessary for rest. Shāfi'ī, Vol. IV, p. 92.

[27] Māwardī, pp. 57 ff.; and Ibn Hudhayl, pp. 17 ff.

recruited. The jihādists formed the muqātila (fighters) and those who stayed at home were known as the qa'āda. The muqātila were also called the muhājira, or *émigrés,* for those who took active part in the occupation of the newly conquered territories took their wives and children and settled there, forming the forces as well as the ruling class that held those territories under Muslim rule. The number of the muqātila was increased enormously by the occupation of southern Iraq and Syria where the resident Arab tribes, some of whom were Christian Arabs, joined the Muslim forces against their Persian and Byzantine masters.[28]

From the rise of Islam to its reorganization under Caliph Marwān II (A.D. 744-50) the army was divided into five units (al-khamīs): the center (qalb), the two wings (maymana and maysara), the vanguard (muqaddama), and the rear-guard (saqa).[29] The tribal unit was preserved in each division of the army and each tribe had its own standard. Horsemen or the calvary played an important role in fighting and were usually in the wings, as they were quicker and more decisive in action. Their weapon was the rumḥ (lance). The infantry used the bow and arrow and, later, the shield and sword. The number of the army in the early days of expansion was not very considerable; it comprised from four to twelve thousand men. Ṭabarī reports that the Muslim force at the battle of al-Qādisiyya (A.D. 637) was made up of 12,000 men against 120,000 Persians.[30]

[28] Balādhurī, *Futūḥ al-Buldān,* ed. de Goeje (Leiden, 1866), pp. 136, 182; Hitti's translation, p. 284.

[29] This organization of the army existed in Arabia before Islam, although the term was borrowed from the Hebrew, and it meant an army of five divisions. See Harold W. Glidden, "A Note on Early Arabian Military Organization," *Journal of the American Oriental Society,* Vol. 56 (1936), pp. 88-91.

[30] Ṭabarī, Series I, Vol. V, pp. 2250-1, 2261.

The jihādists were divided into ajnād (singular, jund or regiment), each of which resided in a camp such as Jābiya, Ṭabariyya, and Ḥoms, in Syria; Baṣra and Kūfa, in 'Iraq, Fusṭāṭ and Alexandria, in Egypt. These fighting men had to do nothing but fight. They were the privileged citizens of the state, to be compensated in this world by the spoils of war, and in the next by paradise. The caliph was advised to prevent them from being engaged in agriculture—a policy instituted by Caliph 'Umar—on the ground that their eventual settlement would make it increasingly difficult to mobilize them on the battlefield. Yet the inevitable settlement took place and the army camps continued to grow until the camps became important cities in the empire.

Gradually the army took on more of a professional character, especially under the Umayyads who constantly needed an efficient army to suppress revolts and civil wars. The division of the army according to the khamīs system was abandoned and the army became one compact body called kurdūs. This reorganization was made under Marwān II when the system of recruiting the army became conscription.[31] Owing to Byzantine influence the jihādist was hard to distinguish in appearance from the Greek and his weapons were largely the same. While Ibn Khaldūn regrets the decline of its morale, the army gained both in efficiency and experience under Umayyad rule.[32]

The 'Abbāsid caliphs distinguished between the regular army, always on active service (called the murtaziqa, regularly paid), and the volunteers (mutaṭawwi'a) who were recruited for temporary service and received grants while on duty. The caliphial bodyguard was made up of a select regiment of the regular army which not infrequently constituted the only

[31] Ṭabarī, Series I, Vol. II, p. 1944.

[32] Ibn Khaldūn, *al-Muqaddima,* ed. Quatremère (Paris, 1858), Vol. II, pp. 70-1.

standing army. In order to assert their own authority, the caliphs recruited foreign elements as their bodyguard and paid them heavily. This mercenary army, at a time when the prestige and authority of the caliphate declined, became more powerful than its masters. The Turkish guard of the caliph played the same role as that of the Praetorian guard, deposing one ruler after another at its pleasure, replacing them by its own nominees.

Conduct of Fighting

Fighting starts by an order of the commander of the army. The order was usually followed by the takbīr or du'ā' (Allah is the greatest) as good omen before the actual fighting should begin.[33] Ṭabarī reports that Sa'd, the commander-in-chief at al-Qādisiyya, ordered his army not to fight until after the noon prayer, and soon after that gave his signal of the takbīr, repeated four times.[34] Some of the caliphs and army chiefs, as in the ceremonies of the *jus fetiale,* were advised to abstain from starting war on certain days or incidents, and to choose more auspicious occasions.[35]

It was also the custom before fighting started to strengthen the morale of the army by reading Qur'ānic verses on the jihād, the reciting of chivalrous poetry by writers who actually took part in fighting, and by an appeal to certain emotional traits of the Arabs such as courage, honor, or religious zeal.[36] Verses

[33] Bukhārī, Vol. II, p. 245; and Shaybānī, Vol. I, p. 56.

[34] Ṭabarī, Series I, Vol. V, pp. 2294-5.

[35] The Caliph 'Alī advised against fighting during an eclipse, and Muḥammad preferred to travel or take the field on Thursdays. See Ibn Qutayba, *Kitāb 'Uyūn al-Akhbār* (Cairo, 1925), Vol. I, p. 122.

[36] In the decisive battle of Yarmūk (A.D. 636) the commander addressed the army, for encouragement by saying: "*Allah! Allah!* your believers are the defenders of the Arabs and guardians of Islam; they (the Byzantines) are the defenders of Rūm (Byzantines) and guardians of polytheism!"

from the Qur'ān and chivalrous poetry were recited even during fighting. Poetry was composed by fighting poets while they were taking part in battles. These poems were by no means of low standard; in fact some of the most excellent poetry was the product of great battles, when the poets were at their highest level of excitement and passion.

Actual fighting was not as well organized at first as in the later periods. In the early wars of expansion the nature of fighting was no different from the pre-Islamic tribal warfare. Fighting started by courageous individual warriors who proceeded towards the enemy and issued challenges. Duels between individuals of both sides may have taken a few hours in certain battles (and it may have decided the issue of the war) or may have taken place for several days. Then the rest of the warriors, more or less in groups, followed into battle. The Muslims made use of a technique of fighting, fashionable in pre-Islamic Arabia, that of following the so-called rule of karr and farr, namely, with a sudden attack by the full strength of the army on the enemy followed by a quick retreat. This was repeated during the battle and it often inflicted damage and confusion in the enemy ranks while the Muslim forces remained intact.[37] In these operations the calvary usually played a more important role, for they were quicker and more effective.[38]

As the Muslim army gained more experience and acquired

Ṭabarī, Series I, Vol. IV, p. 2095. See also Sir William Muir, *The Caliphate: Its Rise and Decline,* ed. Weir (Edinburgh, 1924), pp. 82, 87.

[37] "The strength of the Moslem Arabian army lay neither in the superiority of its arms nor in the excellence of its organization, but in its higher morale, to which religion undoubtedly contributed its share; in its power of endurance, which the desert breeding fostered; and in its remarkable mobility, due mainly to camel transport" (Philip K. Hitti, *History of the Arabs* [London, 1952], p. 174).

[38] See, e.g., the story of the poet-horsemen Abū Miḥjan al-Thaqafī and his exploits in attack in Ṭabarī, Series I, Vol. V, pp. 2312-6.

efficiency, it not only followed more regular methods of attack but also used its organization and equipment more effectively. Military techniques of other nations were soon adopted and used against the enemy. While these military techniques were not regulated by the sharī'a, they were practices which were permitted by the law, since they were in conformity with such broad principles as "war is trickery" and certain traditions which advised alertness, patience, and perseverence in war.[39]

[39] Ibn Qutayba, Vol. I, p. 110 ff; Ṭarṭūshī, *Sirāj al-Mulūk* (Cairo, A.H. 1319), pp. 150-7; Ibn Hudhayl, pp. 63-73; Ibn Khaldūn, Vol. II, pp. 65-79. For a comparison with Byzantine military organization, under whose influence the Muslim army developed, see Charles Oman, *A History of the Art of War: The Middle Ages* (London, 1905), Bk. 4, pp. 169 ff.

"We have never punished until we had first sent an Apostle. . . ." Qur'ān XVII, 16.

CHAPTER VIII

THE INITIATION OF WAR

The Call for Fighting

The jihād, it will be recalled, is a collective as well as an individual duty; the latter is to be fulfilled without a call or an authorization of the imām. If Islam is threatened by a sudden attack it becomes the duty of every believer, including women and children, to rise up in arms for the defense of Islam. As a collective duty, the jihād is a state instrument; the imām, accordingly, as head or deputy head of the state, is charged with the duty of declaring it.

Together with declaring the jihād goes the duty of calling the believers to battle. The declaration of the jihād creates a legal state of hostilities.[1] The call to the believers is the execu-

[1] If we take the position that the jihād was the normal legal condition in Islam (the doctrine of permanent war), the duty of the caliph would be merely reduced to reviving a dormant jihād, for in practice the jihād did not mean continuous fighting.

tion of the jihād. The imām must appeal to the inner conscience of the believers and to remind them of the religious duty of the jihād, "to fight in Allah's path." The believers are under the obligation of responding to the imām's call, as the Prophet Muḥammad had said: "when you are convoked, bestir yourself and respond." The call might be implemented after a public speech, a prayer or by messages sent by the imām to the provinces.[2] During the wars of expansion, the early caliphs had to write to the tribes near their capital and, in the words of Balādhurī, "all the Arabs of Najd and Ḥijāz," in order to call them to battle and have them consent to take the field.[3] This rule was followed by the caliphs and sultans during the subsequent history of Islam.

The giving of the call for fighting may be delegated from the caliph to his governors, especially those in the provinces bordering the enemy. The caliph had to send out orders and the governors, in the name of the amīr al-mu'minīn (commander of the believers), to call to battle the believers who were in their turn under obligation of fealty.[4] The commanders of the frontier forces (ribāṭ) were under permanent orders to call for fighting when they were attacked; indeed, if the enemy overruns the frontiers, the jihād at once becomes an individual obligation, and all the believers have to rise up in arms without a call to expel the enemy from the land.

[2] The Caliph Abū Bakr, in his inaugural speech, asked his people to "obey him as they obeyed Allah and His Apostle," and reminded them of the jihād obligation and said: "those who would abandon it would be humiliated by Allah" (Ṭabarī, *Ta'rīkh,* ed. de Goeje (Leiden, 1890), Series I, Vol. IV, p. 1829).

[3] Balādhurī, *Kitāb Futūḥ al-Buldān,* ed. de Goeje (Leiden, 1866), p. 107; Hitti's translation, p. 165.

[4] Māwardī, *Kitāb al-Aḥkām al-Sulṭāniyya,* ed. Enger (Bonn, 1853), pp. 58, 79.

Necessity of "Invitation"

Like the *jus fetiale* which required the Romans to observe regular ceremonies with regard to the declaration of war,[5] the jihād must be preceded by an "invitation to Islam," and only failure to accept the new faith, or pay the poll tax in the case of Scripturaries, would precipitate fighting with the enemy.[6] In the Qur'ān, Allah said: "We never punished until we had first sent an Apostle";[7] and in the ḥadīth, the Prophet Muḥammad is reported to have said: "I have been ordered to fight polytheists until they say there is no god but Allah; if they say it, they are secured in their blood and property."[8] These two citations signify that an invitation should be extended first to the unbelievers, to find out whether they are ready to accept Islam or fight.[9]

The Prophet Muḥammad had followed the rule which he

[5] See Coleman Phillipson, *International Law and Custom of Ancient Greece and Rome* (London, 1911), Vol. I, pp. 96-7.

[6] Cf. Deut. XX, 10-12: "When thou comest nigh unto a city to fight against it, then proclaim peace unto it. And it shall be, if it make thee answer of peace, and open unto thee, then it shall be, that all the people that are found therein shall become tributaries unto thee, and they shall serve thee. And if it will make no peace with thee, but will make war against thee, then thou shalt besiege it. . . ."

[7] Q. XVII, 18.

[8] Bukhārī, *Kitāb al-Jāmiʿ al-Ṣaḥīḥ*, ed. Krehl (Leiden, 1864), Vol. II, p. 236.

[9] Some commentators maintain that the rule of "invitation" was based on the precedent of Solomon and the Queen of Sheba as reported in a communication between Solomon and the Queen in the Qur'ān. Solomon, according to this communication, had extended an invitation to the Queen to worship Allah and abandon the cult of the Sun. The story goes on to say that the Queen, after deliberation, accepted finally the worship of Allah and submitted to the authority of Solomon (Q. XXVII, 23-44). See Ibn Rushd, *Kitāb al-Muqaddimmāt al-Mumahhidāt* (Cairo, A.H. 1325), Vol. I, p. 267.

had himself laid down, and his early successors seem to have followed their master's rule faithfully.[10] In the campaigns against the Byzantines and Persians, the Arab commanders addressed invitations officially to their enemies, inviting them first to accept Islam or pay the tribute, before they launched their offensives. The official invitation was, in its most complete form, presented by a commission of a few prominent warriors who carried the invitation either verbally or in written form, to the enemy commander, which contained, essentially, an invitation to adopt the new faith. The following is a traditional report of an official letter sent by Khālid ibn al-Walīd, before the capture of Madā'in (A.D. 634):

> From Khālid ibn al-Walīd to the Persian authorities. Peace be on those who follow the path of the truth. Thanks be to Allah who humiliated you and caused the collapse of your kingdom . . . those who pray our prayer . . . and eat our meals are Muslims and will have the same rights as ours. After you receive my letter send me guarantees and you will have peace; otherwise, in the name of Allah, I shall send you men who like death as much as you like life.[11]

While the jurist-theologians agreed on the general principle that an invitation should be sent to the enemy before fighting begins, they disagreed on matters of detail. The Ḥanafī and Mālikī jurists, following the precedents of the early caliphs, maintained that an invitation should be sent before fighting begins.[12] Even if the enemy had already received an invitation, says al-Qudūrī (A.D. 973-1037) a Ḥanafī jurist, it is preferrable that it should be renewed.[13] The Shāfi'ī jurists held that

[10] For Muḥammad's instructions to this effect, see Ṭabarī, Series I, Vol. IV, pp. 1724-1725.

[11] Ṭabarī, Series I, Vol. IV, p. 2020. For similar cases, see Balādhurī, *op. cit.*, p. 97; and Sir William Muir, *The Caliphate: Its Rise, Decline and Fall*, ed. T. H. Weir (Edinburgh, 1924), pp. 101-103.

[12] Abū Yūsuf, *Kitāb al-Kharāj* (Cairo, A. H. 1352), pp. 23, 191.

[13] Qudūrī, *al-Mukhtaṣar* (Istanbul, A.H. 1309), p. 132.

in the case of those who had already received an invitation, the imām has the choice of fighting them without notification—if he deems this to be in the interests of Islam—and of extending another invitation, if he thought there was a possibility of their submission to Islam without war. The Ḥanbalī jurists insist that those who had received an invitation, such as the Scripturaries, should never be reinvited or notified; only those pagan nations that had not yet received the invitation or ever heard of Islam should be notified.[14] Later jurist-theologians, who thought of the jihād as a defensive measure, have either regarded the rule of invitation as obsolete—since Islam had become known to the world at large—or remained silent about it.[15]

Negotiation

In the early Muslim conquests, the commander often waited for three days after the invitation had been sent before actual fighting took place.[16] During this interim period the Muslims were ready to negotiate when the enemy demanded it. This often led to a peaceful settlement, in such cases as the surrender of a number of towns in Iraq and Syria, but not infrequently such negotiations reflecting divergent points of views, were cut short and fighting started immediately afterwards. An outstanding case of negotiations, which illustrates the character of formal negotiations between the Muslims and their enemies, is that which took place before the battle of al-Qādisiyya (A.D.

[14] Ibn Qudāma, *al-Mughnī*, ed Rashīd Riḍa (Cairo, A.H. 1367), Vol. VIII, pp. 361-2.

[15] Ibn Rushd, *op. cit.*, p. 266.

[16] In his instructions to army commanders, the Prophet Muḥammad had set the rule for the Muslims to wait for three days after the invitation was sent to the enemy, before they were permitted to start fighting. See his instructions to Khālid ibn al-Walīd in the campaign against the tribe of Banū Ḥarith (Ṭabarī, Series I, Vol. IV, pp. 1724).

637) between Sa'd ibn Abi Waqqāṣ, the Arab Commander-in-Chief, and Rustum, the Persian commander. Sa'd sent out for this purpose a commission of prominent warriors, headed by al-Mughīra ibn Shu'ba, who negotiated directly with Rustum.

The *procès-verbal* of this case is preserved in part in Ṭabarī and in Balādhurī. But although both of these eminent historians agree on the essentials, they differ on some minor points of detail. Thus Balādhurī reports that the commission proceeded to the Persian side and ibn Shu'ba entered the camp of Rustum and tried to sit beside Rustum on his dignified seat. Rustum's aides, however, hurried up and prevented him. Ibn Shu'ba is reported to have remarked that, to him, this sort of behavior was the cause of the decline of Persia.[17] The other members of the commission also entered Rustum's camp and took part in the negotiation.

Rustum opened the negotiation by putting this question: "Why did you come here?"

Rab'ī, one of the commissioners, replied: "Allah has sent us to ask you people to abstain from the worship of man and to worship Allah . . . and [also] under the pressure of necessity. . . ."[18]

Rustum then demanded a postponement of fighting for an indefinite period of time. Rab'ī replied that the Prophet Muḥammad ordered the Muslims not to delay fighting after the invitation for more than three days. Then negotiation was postponed for the next day.

Rustum resumed negotiation, on the following day, in which he said: "I understand that the motive of your coming here is the poverty of your country, and under such circumstances I shall be willing to order a suit of clothing, a mule and one

17 Balādhurī, p. 256; Hitti's translation, p. 410.

18 Ṭabarī, Series I, Vol. V, p. 2271.

thousand dinārs[19] for your commander, and a Waqr[20] of dates for each warrior with cloths . . . as I have no desire to kill you or to imprison you."[21]

Ibn Shu'ba replied: ". . . what you have said concerning our poverty is clear to us and we do not ignore that. . . . But the conclusion you reached as to the motive of our coming here is not correct . . . for Allah has sent to us a Prophet and we are united and honored by him. . . ."[22]

Further discussion took place and the Muslim commission insisted that Rustum had to accept one of three positions: to join Islam, pay the poll tax, or fight. Rustum seems to have become completely disgusted and is reported to have said in despair that there could be no peace between him and the Muslims. Balādhurī reports that one of the commissioners replied, "Our Prophet has promised us victory over your country."[23]

Ṭabarī reports other negotiations with the Persians and Byzantines which were not essentially different from the foregoing. Similar negotiations took place between the Muslims and the Egyptians during the course of the Muslim conquest of Egypt. Ibn 'Abd al-Ḥakam reports that the Patriarch of Egypt sent a mission to 'Amr ibn al-'Āṣ, commander of the Muslim army, inviting him to negotiate a treaty of peace. 'Amr responded and although negotiations did not lead at first to successful results, it did eventually bring the Copts to terms

[19] Greek *denarius,* the unit of currency.

[20] A measure of dates.

[21] Ṭabarī, Series I, Vol. V, p. 2276.

[22] *Ibid.,* pp. 2276-7.

[23] Balādhurī, p. 257; Hitti's translation, p. 411-12. There was an almost unanimous belief on the part of the Muslims, based on a divine revelation to Muḥammad, that they would successfully conquer Persian and Byzantine dominions. See Wāqidī, *Kitāb al-Maghāzī,* ed., von Kremer (Calcutta, 1856), p. 363; and Ṭabarī, *op. cit.,* Series I, Vol. III, p. 1469.

with the Muslims.[24] Unfortunately the existing authorities hardly report more than the text of the treaties and neglect the *procès-verbaux* of the negotiations which preceded their conclusion.

Negotiations leading to the signing of treaties or the exchange of prisoners became more frequent after the establishment of Muslim rule outside Arabia, especially with the Byzantines.[25] During the Crusades, attempts at negotiation made before and during fighting, were often crowned with success. Such negotiations had usually limited purposes, such as the release of prisoners, the signing of truces and, not infrequently, leading to combinations and alliances of provincial rulers against the Franks or Muslim with Frankish governors.[26] Sometimes negotiations led to the surrender of a city after prolonged siege or the signing of a peace treaty which terminated some military phase of the war.[27]

[24] Ibn 'Abd al-Ḥakam, *Kitāb Futūḥ Miṣr,* ed. C. C. Torrey (New Haven, 1922), pp. 63-65; Ibn Taghrī Bardī, *al-Nujūm al-Zāhira* (Cairo, 1929), Vol. I, pp. 10-17; A. J. Butler, *The Arab Conquest of Egypt* (Oxford, 1902).

[25] See chap. 18.

[26] See Ibn al-Qalānisī, *The Damascus Chronicle of the Crusades,* trans. H. A. R. Gibb, (London, 1932), pp. 48, 68, 90.

[27] *Ibid.,* pp. 269-72; and Stevenson, *The Crusades in the East* (Cambridge, 1907), pp. 220-24, 269-72, 277-84.

"In a celebrated address to the first Syrian expedition Abū Bakr, the first Caliph, said: Stop, O people, that I may give you ten rules to keep by heart! Do not commit treachery, nor depart from the right path. You must not mutilate, neither kill a child or aged man or woman. Do not destroy a palm-tree, nor burn it with fire and do not cut any fruitful tree. You must not slay any of the flock or the herds or the camels, save for your subsistence. You are likely to pass by people who have devoted their lives to monastic services; leave them to that to which they have devoted their lives. You are likely, likewise, to find people who will present to you meals of many kinds. You may eat; but do not forget to mention the name of Allah." Ṭabarī, *Ta'rīkh,* I, 1850.

CHAPTER IX

LAND WARFARE

In Muslim legal theory, the objective of war is neither the achievement of victory nor the acquisition of the enemy's property; it is rather the fulfillment of a duty—the jihād in Allah's path—by universalizing the Islamic faith.[1] The jihādists, accordingly, were advised to refrain from the shedding of blood or the destruction of property unnecessary for the achievement of their objective. This general rule is based on Abū Bakr's address to the first expedition sent to the Syrian borders as well as to other similar utterances by succeeding caliphs.

Prohibited Acts

Although the jurists accepted in principle the doctrine of unnecessary destruction, based on Abū Bakr's instructions,

[1] Ibn Rushd, *Kitāb al-Muqaddimāt al-Mumahhidāt* (Cairo, A.H. 1325), Vol. I, p. 266.

they disagreed on certain matters of detail. Only al-Awzā'ī (A.D. 774) and al-Thawrī (A.D. 778), as far as existing records show, accepted the doctrine of unnecessary destruction without qualifications. Other jurists, including the founders of the four schools, have greatly restricted this doctrine on the basis of certain Qur'ānic injunctions and the sunna. Al-Awzā'ī argued, however, that the Qur'ān and the *sunna* must be interpreted in the light of the practice established by Abū Bakr and the companions, who "knew the interpretation of the Qur'ān better than Abū Ḥanīfa," and therefore their interpretations must be accepted.[2]

Mālik in his treatment of the law of war in the *Muwaṭṭa'*, prohibited only the slaying of the flock and the destruction of beehives.[3] Abū Ḥanīfa laid down the rule that everything that the jihādists cannot bring under their control must be destroyed, including the houses, churches, trees, flocks and herds. Shāfi'ī contended that everything which is lifeless must be destroyed, including trees; but animals can be slain only if the jihādists believed they would strengthen their enemies.[4]

The jurists agreed that noncombatants who did not take

[2] Ṭabarī, *Kitāb al-Jihād*, ed. J. Schacht (Leiden, 1933), p. 103-4; and Abū Yūsuf, *al-Radd 'Ala Siyar al-Awzā'ī*, ed. Abū al-Wafa al-Afghānī (Cairo, A.H. 1357), pp. 83-7. See also Schacht, *Origins of Muhammadan Jurisprudence* (Oxford, 1950), p. 34.

[3] Ibn Ḥazm prohibits the slaying of animals except pigs. See Ibn Ḥazm, *al-Mahallī* (Cairo, A.H. 1349), Vol. VII, p. 294.

[4] Ṭabarī, p. 106-7. The rules concerning the flocks and trees are old going back to ancient Israelite practice. See Deut. XX, 19, 20: "When thou shalt besiege a city a long time, in making war against it to take it, thou shalt not destroy the trees thereof by forcing an axe against them: for thou mayest eat of them, and thou shalt not cut them down (for the tree of the field is man's life) to employ them in the siege: only the trees which thou knowest that they be not trees for meat, thou shalt destroy and cut them down; and thou shalt build bulwarks against the city that maketh war with thee, until it be subdued."

part in fighting, such as women, children, monks and hermits, the aged, blind, and insane, were excluded from molestation.[5] If the aged and monks indirectly helped their people, they were subject to molestation.[6] Ibn Hisham reports that in the battle of Ḥunayn the Muslims killed, in the presence of Muḥammad, Durayd ibn al-Ṣimma, a man more than one hundred years old, because he gave useful advice to his people during the battle.[7] Some Ḥanafī and Shāfi'ī jurists would also exclude from molestation peasants and merchants who do not take part in fighting.[8]

The jurists advise abstention from carrying the heads of killed enemies on the points of lances—a practice known to the Arabs before Islam.[9] They also advise the jihādist to abstain from slaying his polytheist father, if he happens to be seen fighting against the Muslims. The Mālikī jurist Khalīl advises against the use of poisoned arrows and Ḥillī goes so far as to prohibit their use in any form against the enemy.[10]

[5] On women and children see Bukhārī, *Kitāb al-Jāmi' al-Ṣaḥīḥ*, ed. Krehl (Leiden, 1864), Vol. II, p. 251; The slaying of women and children is only permitted by the followers of Nāfi' ibn al-Azraq, of the Khārijī sect, who argued that women and children are as guilty of polytheism as adults and therefore should not be spared their lives. See 'Abd al-Qāhir al-Baghdādī, *Mukhtaṣar Kitāb al-Farq Bayn al-Firaq*, ed. Philip Hitti (Cairo, 1924), pp. 73, 97. The rule regarding monks and hermits is based on the ḥadith: "Do not kill people of the monasteries." On the blind and insane, see Sarakhsī, *Kitāb al-Mabsūt* (Cairo, A.H. 1324), Vol. X, p. 69.

[6] See Shaybānī, *al-Siyar al-Kabīr*, with Sarakhsī's Commentary (Hyderabad, A.H. 1335), Vol. I, p. 33.

[7] Ibn Hishām, *Kitāb al-Sira*, ed. Wüstenfeld (Göttingen, 1860), Vol. II, pp. 841-2, 852.

[8] Shaybānī, Vol. IV, p. 79; Yaḥya ibn Ādam, *Kitāb al-Kharāj* (Cairo, A.H. 1347), p. 34; Ibn Rushd (al-Ḥafīd), *Bidāyat al-Mujtahid* (Istanbul, A.H. 1333), Vol. I, p. 311. Cf. Deut. XX, 17-19; I Sam. XV, 3, 33; XVIII, 27.

[9] Shaybānī, Vol. I, p. 78.

[10] See Muḥammad al-Amīr, *Kitāb al-Iklīl Sharḥ Muktaṣar Khalīl* (Cairo,

The Muslims, following a pre-Islamic customary rule, were not allowed to go to war during the sacred months (al-ashhur al-ḥarām); these constituted the grace of God when all people should abstain from fighting.[11] This rule is based on a Qur'ānic injunction which runs as follows:

> And when the sacred months are passed, kill those who associate other gods with Allah wherever ye shall find them. . . .[12]

This Qur'ānic rule, however, was later abrogated by another (indeed the pre-Islamic rule of the grace of God was already on the decline as it was violated during the War of the Fijār, circa A.D. 585) which runs as follows:

> They will ask thee concerning war in the sacred month. Say: To war therein is bad, but to turn aside from the cause of Allah, and to have no faith in Him, and in the sacred Temple, and to drive out its people, is worse in the sight of Allah.[13]

All the jurists are agreed, except 'Aṭā', that the principle of the grace of God is no longer valid in Muslim law, although it may be said that abstention is recommended.[14]

Treatment of Enemy Persons

Once the unbelievers in the dār al-ḥarb had been invited to adopt Islam and refused to accept one of the alternatives (i.e. Islam or the poll tax), the jihādists were allowed in principle to kill any one of them, combatants or noncombatants, provided

---

A.H. 1224), p. 160; and Ḥillī, *Tabṣirat al-Muta'allimīn* (Damascus, A.H. 1342), p. 103.

11 The sacred months are: Shawwāl, Dhu'l-Qi'da, Dhu'l-Hijja, and Muḥarram.

12 Q. IX, 5.

13 Q. II, 214. For the war of the Fijār, see Ibn Hishām, *op. cit.*, Vol. I, pp. 117-9.

14 Shaybānī, Vol. I, p. 68; Sarakhsī, *Kitāb al-Mabsūt*, Vol. X, p. 26.

they were not killed treacherously and with mutilation.[15] The ḥarbis, in other words, had to submit to battle as the deciding test between Islam and their faith.

The jihādists are permitted to besiege enemy cities, to use siege artillery (hurling machines)[16] for the destruction of city walls and houses, and to burn or flood enemy territory. They are also permitted to cut water canals and destroy water supplies to prevent the ḥarbis from using them. Poison, blood, or any material that may spoil the drinking water may be thrown into the water supplies or canals in order to force the enemy to capitulate.[17] Poisoned arrows, and arrows carrying bundles of fire, are ordinarily permitted to be used.[18]

If, however, the ḥarbis had captured Muslims (including women and children) and were all besieged with the unbelievers by the jihādist, the jurists are agreed that the jihādists should use limited means of violence in fighting the enemy.[19] They disagreed, however, on the limitations of violent means. Al-Awzā'ī goes so far as to advise abstention from direct attack, unless individual ḥarbis show themselves whom the jihādist can shoot, depending on the following Qur'ānic verse (revealed on the occasion of the capture of Makka):

> . . . had it not been for believing men and believing women whom ye knew not, whom ye might have trampled on, and so crime might have occurred to you on their account without your knowledge.[20]

[15] The Prophet Muḥammad was against the practice of treacherous killing and mutilation, but when the Makkans did not respect this rule he ordered his followers to retaliate. See Wāqidī, *Kitāb al-Maghāzī,* ed. von Kremer (Calcutta, 1856), p. 284; and Ṭabarī, *Ta'rīkh,* ed. de Geoje (Leiden, 1882-5), Series i, Vol. III, p. 160. See also Shaybānī, Vol. III, p. 249.

[16] Manjanīq (mangonels). Muḥammad made use of them in the capture of Ṭā'if.

[17] Shaybānī, Vol. III, pp. 212-3.

[18] *Ibid.,* p. 217.

[19] Ṭabarī, *Kitāb al-Jihād,* pp. 3-4.

[20] Q. XLVIII, 25.

Sufyān al-Thawrī and Abū Ḥanīfa permitted attack even if shooting by arrows or hurling machines would kill the believers, provided that the jihādists intend to shoot the unbelievers; the killing of believers (including women and children) would be regarded as killing by mistake.[21] Shāfi'ī advises attack on the fortified places and castles, but not on the houses; if, however, fighting was at close range, they ought not abstain from shooting, even if it results in killing believers.[22] Ghazzālī, a Shāfi'ī jurist-theologian, justifies the shooting of believers in attacking the ḥarbis on the ground of istiṣlāḥ, or public interest; that is, the killing of a few believers is justified on the ground that it would serve the greater interests of the Muslim community.[23]

Spies

While Muslim commanders saw the value of spying and made use of this time-honored practice, they, like other nations, punished severely foreign spies. If the ḥarbī entered the dār al-Islam by amān (safe-conduct) and proved later to be a spy, he was killed and, if the imām decided, was crucified to discourage others from this practice.[25] If the ḥarbī under an amān were a woman or a child, the woman should be killed (but not subject to crucifixion); the child becomes fay' but is not subject to killing.[26]

In the case of a Muslim spy, who transmits intelligence to the enemy, the law does not require killing, although Shafi'i and Mālik leave the matter to the imām to punish him.[27]

21 Ṭabarī, pp. 6-7; and Abū Yūsuf, *Kitāb al-Radd 'ala Siyar al-Awzā'ī*, pp. 65-6.

22 *Ibid.*, pp. 5-6.

23 Ghazzālī, *al-Mustaṣfa fī Uṣūl al-Fiqh* (Cairo, 1937), Vol. I, p. 141.

25 Shaybānī, Vol. IV, pp. 226-7.

26 *Ibid.*, p. 227.

27 Ṭabarī, *Kitāb al-Jihād*, pp. 172-3.

Awzā'ī advises exile or tortuous punishment, and Abū Ḥanīfa orders him to be imprisoned until he repents. The same rule applies to a Scripturary spy.[28]

Treatment of the Dead

Once the ḥarbī is killed, his dead body should never be mutilated or his head cut off and raised at the point of a lance. Abū Ya'la advises burial of the dead, though they need not be placed in coffins. His opinion is based on Muḥammad's practice after the battle of Badr.[29]

[28] *Ibid.*, p. 173; and Shaybānī, Vol. IV, p. 226.

[29] Abū Ya'la, *Kitāb al-Aḥkām al-Sulṭāniyya*, ed. al-Fiqqi (Cairo, 1938), p. 34; and M. Ḥamīdullah, *Muslim Conduct of State* (Lahore, 1945), p. 246.

"He it is who has subjected the sea, that from it ye might eat fresh meat, and from it ye might seek ornaments to wear and in it see ships cleaving, and that ye might seek of its abundance and that ye might be grateful." Qur'ān XVI, 14.

CHAPTER X

MARITIME WARFARE

Islam and Sea Power

Few subjects has the juristic literature of Islam treated so inadequately as salt-water warfare. This indifference reflects not only early Muslim mistrust of the sea, but also, perhaps more important, the fact that Muslim power was essentially a land—not sea—power.[1] Islamic sovereignty emerged in an inland area and expanded into the interior of the Byzantine and Persian dominions from their desert approaches. The collapse of the Persian Empire was rapid and complete because Persia

[1] Neither in the Arabian Peninsula nor in the Fertile Crescent was it possible to develop a system of river navigation, owing to the limited number of navigable rivers in the latter and the lack of them in the former. For a discussion of the inadequate system of river navigation in the Islamic world, see Adam Mez, *Die Renaissance des Islam* (Heidelberg, 1922), Chap. 27.

was a land power which Islam could beat; but when the Muslims reached the sea at Alexandria and the Syrian seaboard, where Byzantine sea power was intact, they faced stiff resistance. For a long while the Muslims continued to control their conquered territories from the interior—from their newly established headquarters at Jābiya, Kūfa, and Fusṭāṭ, where they could trust themselves to the desert. The sea remained a constant threat to Islam until a fleet was built up to protect the coast of the Empire from foreign attack. It was indeed the dictate of geography no less than the wise statesmanship of Mu'āwiya that opened the eyes of the Muslims to sea power: for so long as the Mediterranean belonged to Byzantium the position of Islam in both Egypt and Syria was far from being secure.

My'āwiya's occupation of Cyprus in A.D. 648 marked the beginning of Muslim sea power; it also helped to make his hold over Syria more secure than ever. The Muslim raids on Rhodes and Sicily added to their experience in preparation for the first major naval battle they won in A.D. 655. The battle of Dhāt al-Ṣawārī, won by some new naval tactics,[2] gave evidence that the Muslims had at last trusted themselves to the sea. Although Byzantine sea power remained unchallenged, the Mediterranean no longer belonged to Christian powers alone. Naval supremacy changed hands between Christianity and Islam, because each time one of them had perfected her tactics or discovered a new weapon (as in the case of Greek fire which broke the Muslim siege of Constantinople in A.D. 673-97),[3] the other was either quick to use the same weapons or to counterattack

[2] Ṭabarī, *Tar'īkh*, ed. de Goeje (Leiden, 1893), Series I, Vol. V, pp. 2865-70; Balādhurī, *Futūḥ al-Buldān*, ed. de Geoje (Leiden, 1866), pp. 117-8; George F. Hourani, *Arab Seafaring* (Princeton, 1951), pp. 57-9.

[3] Archibald R. Lewis, *Naval Power and Trade in the Mediterranean, 500-1100* (Princeton, 1951), pp. 60-1.

with new tactics. This explains, at least in part, why the Byzantine Empire was able to hold out against continued Muslim assault (including another attack on Constantinople in A.D. 717) under both the Umayyad and 'Abbāsid dynasties.

In the western Mediterranean Sea, Islam's naval power grew steadily in strength. By the tenth century of the Christian era Islam had established its complete supremacy owing to its effective control over the whole North African seaboard and Spain, and its occupation of Sicily, Sardinia and southern Italy. The significance of Islam's mastery of this sea was far-reaching. Not only did it result in reviving international commerce between the eastern and western Mediterranean, but also in providing maritime commerce with certain financial facilities,[4] new naval tactics as well as rules and practices governing navigation. When Muslim sea power began to decline, the Christian powers began to take the initiative in encroaching upon Muslim territory in the western Mediterranean. The establishment of Christian naval supremacy, as Ibn Khaldūn keenly observed, was the chief factor in losses of Muslim territory in the Mediterranean and Spain.[5] Islam's sea power was reestablished at the turn of the fifteenth century when the Ottoman Turks controlled a large area of the eastern Mediterranean and the African coasts and continued to do so for over three centuries.

Muslim Law and the Sea

Most of the Muslim jurists are silent about the sea and those few who treated the subject scarcely provide us with adequate materials to reconstruct a legal theory of the sea as a vehicle

[4] Such as the use of the gold dīnār and banking techniques. See p. 229-30, below.

[5] Ibn Khaldūn, *al-Muqaddima,* ed. Quatermère (Paris, 1858), Vol. II, pp. 38-40.

between nations in war and peace. The Qur'ān makes several references to the sea, not all of them are favorable. "Satan takes its way into the sea," said Allah in one of them.[6] In another we are warned that Allah punished Pharaoh's people by drowning them in the sea.[7] In still another, a distinction is made between two kinds of seas: the one fresh and pleasant, and the other salt and bitter; from both, says Allah, the believer may eat meat and take ornaments and go in quest of bounties.[8] More favorable Qur'ānic injunctions to navigation are those in which Allah has "subjected the sea" in order that the "ships may move in it."[9] Further, He has "ordained the stars for you that you may be guided thereby in the darkness of the land and of the sea."[10]

The ḥadīth provides us with little more than the Qur'ān. Neither Muḥammad nor his early successors, perhaps owing to lack of experience with salt water, had given instructions regarding the sea. Indeed, we are informed that the Caliph 'Umar I had advised the believers to abstain from travel by sea, and to him are ascribed the instructions to his commanders to rely on the desert in their military calculations. Mu'āwiya's suggestion to occupy Cyprus, it will be recalled, was opposed by 'Umar and only reluctantly authorized by 'Uthmān.

In the circumstances, the jurists had little guidance in the authoritative sources of Islam to formulate rules governing peaceful navigation or naval warfare. They had to depend, accordingly, either on the analogy of rules governing land warfare or on the practices and usages of other nations which were adopted through a recognized source. Owing to the aversion of

[6] Q. XVIII, 62.
[7] Q. II, 47.
[8] Q. XXXV, 13.
[9] Q. XLV, 11.
[10] Q. VI, 97.

the Prophet Muḥammad to the sea, it is not likely that the ḥadīths relating to sea warfare were of early origin but rather circulated at a time when Islam had reconciled itself to the sea and was not opposed to adopting usages of other nations into the body of Muslim law.

Rules and Practices of Naval Warfare

Traditions are cited to the effect that the Prophet Muḥammad once said that those who perish while fighting on the sea will receive double the compensation for fighting on land.[11] This emphasis on the double reward reflects the legacy of traditional fear of the sea and the necessity for encouraging recruitment for a sea jihād.[12] Shaybānī adds that any Muslim who takes part in a sea expedition would be doubly compensated and that once the jihādist puts his foot on the ship all his sins are forgiven as if he were born anew.[13]

As a general rule the jurists agreed to apply, by analogy, the rules governing a castle in land warfare to a vessel in sea warfare. In the same way as the jihādists were permitted to besiege and attack a castle by hurling machines and to cut or destroy any outside forthcoming support, so were the sea jihādists permitted to attack and destroy enemy vessels by fire or by sinking until their crews were brought to their knees and capitulated. By

[11] Bukhārī, *Kitāb al-Jāmi' al-Ṣaḥīḥ*, ed. Krehl (Leiden, 1864), Vol. II, pp. 199-200, 202, 218, 222. Abū Dā'ūd, *Sunan* (Cairo, 1935), Vol. I, pp. 6-7; Ibn Qudāma, *al-Mughnī*, ed. Rashīd Riḍa (Cairo, 1367), Vol. VIII, pp. 349-50; Hajjāwī, *al-Iqnā'*, (Cairo, n.d.), Vol. II, p. 5.

[12] Ibn Qudāma, Vol. VIII, pp. 349-50. Fear of sea travel continued even after the Islamic Empire had established commercial relations with neighboring countries. The stories of the exploits of Sindbad in the Indian Ocean reflect the exaggerated fear and danger from sea travel. It was the practice that after terminating their trips, sea travelers would congratulate each other on their safe return.

[13] Shaybānī, *al-Siyar al-Kabīr*, with Sarakhsī's Commentary (Hyderabad, 1335), Vol. I, pp. 25-6; Hajjāwī, p. 5.

virtue of the same rule, the sea jihādists often resorted to measures which were intended to lower the morale of the enemy as well as to create panic and help a direct assault on their vessels. Thus the Muslims often hurled on enemy vessels not only stones and fire bundles, but also snakes and scorpions and harmful powders in order to injure as well as to scare the enemy and create confusion and panic among all on board their vessels.[14]

If the enemy resorted to protecting their vessels by shielding them with Muslims, the same rule in the case of a besieged castle in land warfare would be applicable, namely, the enemy vessel would not be regarded as immune from Muslim attack even if the enemy were shielded with Muslim women and children.[15] Awzā'ī, it will be recalled,[16] who dissented from other jurists in advising against an attack on an enemy castle if shielded by Muslims, was opposed to the sinking of enemy vessels or destroying them by fire or otherwise if they were shielded by Muslims.[17]

If, in the course of a naval battle, the Muslim vessels were wrecked, the jihādist might choose either to remain in the vessel and sink with it, or he may throw himself into the sea and face death by drowning.[18] In the latter case the chance of being picked up by the enemy was not very great and even then he might be killed by the enemy.[19]

[14] Ḥasan ibn 'Abd-Allah, *Athār al-Uwal fī Tartīb al-Duwal* (Cairo, A.H. 1295), pp. 195-8.

[15] Shaybānī, Vol. III, p. 265.

[16] See p. 106, above.

[17] Ṭabarī, *Kitāb al-Jihād*, ed. Joseph Schacht (Leiden, 1933), pp. 4-5.

[18] Shaybānī, Vol. III, pp. 327-8.

[19] Mālik is of the opinion that the sea jihādist should not throw himself into the sea if he saw the possibility of being picked up by the enemy. If, however, the vessel was on fire, he advises leaving it. See Saḥnūn, *al-Mudawwana al-Kubra* (Cairo, 1323), Vol. III, pp. 25-6.

It was likely that after a naval battle Muslim vessels might take spoils of war in persons and property. The jurists are agreed that the law governing the division of the spoil on land is applicable to the spoils of sea warfare.[20] If the Muslim sea jihādists found that their spoils were too heavy and that their vessels were likely to sink, they were permitted not only to throw into the sea property, but also their prisoners of war, including women and children.[21] But if the jihādists had on board Muslim women and children, they were not permitted to throw them into the sea if they were in great danger, since throwing them into the sea would amount to killing them which was prohibited by the law.[22] The fact that such a contingency may happen led some jurists, like al-Suyūṭī, to advise against taking women and children on board war vessels.[23] The same rule applied if the Muslims had on board dhimmis or even non-Muslims under an amān (safe conduct), since the Muslims were under an obligation to abide by their promises.[24]

If an enemy vessel were not seaworthy and its crew were seen on the coast of dār al-Islam without an amān, they were not liable to molestation.[25] Awzā'ī is of the opinion that if the enemy persons asked for an amān, they were entitled to it; if they did not want an amān, they were liable to molestation.[26] If the enemy vessel were adrift along the coast and the mer-

[20] Ṭabarī, *Kitāb al-Jihād,* p. 86. See chap. 11.

[21] Shaybānī, Vol. III, p. 269; and Ardabīlī, *al-Anwār lī-'Amāl al-Abrār* (Cairo, n.d.), Vol. II, p. 289.

[22] Ibid., pp. 269-70. Even if the Muslim vessel fell into the hands of the enemy, the jihādists were not permitted to throw their women and children into the sea on the ground that this amounts to deliberate killing. See *Ibid.,* p. 272.

[23] Suyūṭī, *al-Ashbāh wa'l-Nazā'ir,* ed. al-Fiqqy (Cairo, 1938), p. 509.

[24] For amān, see chap. 15 below; Shaybānī, Vol. III, p. 270.

[25] Ṭabarī, *Kitāb al-Jihād,* p. 31.

[26] *Ibid.,* p. 32.

chants on board were without an amān, they were liable to be taken as fay'; if, however, they claimed they were on a diplomatic mission, they were entitled to diplomatic immunity and permitted to proceed to the imām. If the imām found that they lacked the letters of credence necessary, they were liable to be taken prisoners, turned into slaves or killed, and their property confiscated.[27]

Naval Organization

As the Muslim navy acquired more and more experience, its efficiency and organization greatly improved. By the tenth century of the Christian era, when Muslim sea power became supreme, Muslim war and mercantile vessels attained the highest quality then known. There is a good deal of information on Muslim naval organization in the western Mediterranean, which probably could be applied to other Muslim areas as well. The Mediterranean vessels were by far larger and higher in quality than the Red Sea and Indian Ocean vessels. The Muslims imported the best quality of wood for the building of their vessels and provided them with instruments for efficiency and speed. While traveling on the high seas, cracks, fractures, and openings in the vessels were closed without much difficulty. A number of the crew were specially trained to swim round the vessel while cruising, filling up the openings with wax or other available materials.[28]

The admiral (amīr al-baḥr) of the fleet, like the governor of a province, was delegated with full powers. In many respects, he shared authority with the caliph: the one reigned on land, and the other on the sea. Each ship had a captain (qā'id), at the head of the sea jihādists and armaments, and a sailing master (ra'īs) who directed the sails and oars. A subordinate

[27] Abū Yūsuf, *Kitāb al-Kharāj* (Cairo, A.H. 1352), p. 189.

[28] Adam Mez, *op. cit.*, chap. 29.

amīr may take charge of a naval expedition, unless the amīr al-baḥr (admiral) himself took charge. After having suffered from Greek fire, the Muslims themselves learned to arm their war vessels with Greek fire. These were called the ḥarrāqas, fire-ships which threw a combustible substance at enemy vessels.[29]

The Muslims used the compass, but its adoption seems to have been late, since early Muslim publicists do not mention it. There are thirty-two points in the compass card, following the European pattern, but here the similarity ends. Except for the four cardinal points, the Muslims do not subdivide the points, but name them after certain constellations and stars. The cardinal points are called al-jihāt al-arba'a (four directions); these are given the names of ya' (for north), which is one of the names of the Pole Star, the Maṭla' (for east), maghrib (for west), both of these terms are derived from the rising and the setting sun. Quṭb stands for south, which also means pole. The points of the compass are then named westward from north to south, each name is derived from the appropriate star which sets in that direction. The same names are applied in the corresponding points eastward, with addition of the word maṭla'.[30]

[29] Ibn Khaldūn, *op. cit.*, Vol. II, pp. 38 ff; Vasiliev, *Byzance et les Arabes*, tr. Grégoire et Canard (Brussels, 1935), Vol. I, p. 132; Lewis, *op. cit.* pp. 155-6.

[30] The writer acknowledges the help of Colonel Lionel Dimmock on the description of the compass.

"Allah promised ye much booty which ye may take and He hastened this for you. . . ." Qur'ān XLVIII, 20.

CHAPTER XI

SPOILS OF WAR

Meaning and Nature of the Spoils

Ownership of property under the general principles of Muslim law is acquired either by iḥrāz, that is, taking possession of things in the state of nature, which may be called original acquisition; by naql, or the transfer of property from one person to another through one of the recognized contractual arrangements; or by inheritance.[1] The taking of property from non-Muslims in war, whether by force or without force confers upon Muslim warriors collectively (until division is undertaken) the right of original acquisition. For although such property belongs to non-Muslims, ownership is alienated as a punishment for persistence in disbelief by all those who refused

[1] See Abdur Rahim, *Principles of Muhammadan Jurisprudence*, (Madras, 1911), p. 280.

to adopt Islam (or submit to Islamic rule) and resorted to fighting with the Muslims.

The term spoil (ghanīma) is applied specifically to property acquired by force from non-Muslims. It includes, however, not only property (movable and immovable) but also persons, whether in the capacity of asra (prisoners of war) or sabī (women and children).[2] The element of force ('anwatan) and the imām's permission are essential prerequisites, since property taken without force would be regarded as fay', and if the imām's permission were lacking the possessed property, whether taken by one or a group of jihādists, would be regarded as theft, not spoil.[3] The imām's permission formalizes fighting as the fulfillment of the jihād duty and invokes the law governing the conduct of fighting as well as the acquisition and the division of the spoil among those who have a right to it.

The spoil belongs to those believers who take part in the battle; those who may appear after the battle is over have no right to it, unless they arrive before actual acquisition takes place. This rule is based on the Caliph 'Umar's report that the Prophet Muḥammad said: "The spoil belongs to those who witnessed the battle."[4] The jurists agree on this general rule,

[2] Yaḥya ibn Ādam, *Kitāb al-Kharāj* (Cairo, A.H. 1347), pp. 17, 19; and Māwardī, *Kitāb al-Aḥkām al-Sulṭāniyya,* ed. Enger (Bonn, 1853), p. 226. Cf. Aghnides, *Mohammedan Theories of Finance* (New York, 1916), p. 409.

[3] Although the jurists agree that the jihādists must first obtain the imām's permission before they go to war, they disagree as to the spoil whether it is theft or legally acquired if the imām's permission were lacking. Shāfi'ī regards spoil without the imām's permission as *makrūh* (objectionable), and Awzā'ī leaves it to the imām to punish the jihādists or divide the spoil among them. Abū Ḥanīfa, however, permits the jihādists to acquire the spoil without even giving the state a share in it. See Ṭabarī, *Kitāb al-Jihād,* ed. Schacht (Leiden, 1933), pp. 78-80.

[4] See Sarakhsī, *Kitāb al-Mabsūṭ* (Cairo, A.H. 1324), Vol. X, p. 22. See also Shaybānī, *al-Siyar al-Kabīr,* with Sarakhsī's Commentary (Hyderabad, A.H. 1335), Vol. II, p. 250; Marghinānī, *al-Hidāya* (Cairo, 1936), Vol. II, p. 106.

although some are inclined to recommend share in the spoil if reinforcements were on their way before the battle was won or if some of the jihādists were prevented from actual participation by sickness or by *force majeur*.[5] If one of the participating jihādists died before the battle is over, his share must be given to his heirs.[6]

Division of the Spoil

The spoil should be divided after, not before, the winning of the battle. The reason being that the acquisition of the spoil is determined by victory, which alienates the enemy's rights of ownership and enables the Muslims to claim or divide the enemy's property. Even if the battle is won and the war continues, division of the spoil must be postponed until the Muslims attain victory. For if victory is not achieved, the division and even the discussion of the spoil might turn the attention of the jihādists from the fighting to the spoil.[7]

The spoil may either be divided in the dār al-ḥarb or carried to dār al-Islam and there divided. The Ḥanafī school prohibits division in the dār al-ḥarb, unless the imām deems it necessary to do so under compelling circumstances.[8] Awzā'ī orders the division of the spoil in the dār al-ḥarb in accordance with the

[5] For differences among the various schools, see Ṭabarī, pp. 69-71.

[6] Shāfi'ī and Thawrī recommend giving the share of the dead to his heir only if death took place after the winning of the battle and before division of the spoil. Mālik and Awzā'ī advise giving the dead's share to his heirs regardless of the time of his death. See Ṭabarī, pp. 76-7; and Saḥnūn, *al Mudawwana al-Kubra* (Cairo, A.H. 1323), pp. 34-5.

[7] Māwardī, p. 240. It is alleged that one of the reasons which contributed to defeat at the battle of Tours (A.D. 732) was discussion of the spoil before winning the battle.

[8] Abū Yūsuf, *Kitāb al-Radd 'Ala Siyar al-Awzā'ī*, ed. Abū al-Wafā al-Afghānī (Cairo, A.H. 1357), pp. 1-4; Shaybānī, Vol. II, p. 254; Marghinānī, Vol. II, p. 106.

practice of the Prophet Muḥammad in the cases of Banū Muṣṭaliq, Hawāzin, Ḥunayn, and Khaybar. Abū Yūsuf contends that the Prophet did so because the territory in these cases had become part of dār al-Islam after victory, while in the case of the spoils of Badr he did not divide the spoils until after the Muslims returned to Madīna.[9] Mālik agrees with Awzā'ī, but the Shāfi'ī school leaves the matter to the imām to decide in accordance with the Muslims' interests: if he thought division was advisable in the dār al-ḥarb he might so order, but if he deemed it necessary to postpone division, the spoils should be carried to dār al-Islam.[10]

Before the battle of Badr (A.D. 624) the Prophet Muḥammad had free choice in the division of the spoil, guided only by Arab customary law. But this led to quarrels among his followers and consequently the matter was settled by divine legislation as follows:

". . . when ye have taken any booty, one-fifth belongs to Allah and to the Apostle, and to the near kin, and to orphans, and to the poor, and to the wayfarer. . . ."[11]

The one-fifth share may be regarded as the share of the state. But its expenditure led to serious differences of opinion. The leading jurists have stated their opinions as follows:

Ibn 'Abbās maintained that the one-fifth share should be divided into six parts: one for Allah (to be spent on al-Ka'ba), the second for the Prophet, the third to the near kin of the Prophet, the fourth for the orphans, the fifth for the poor, and the sixth for the wayfarer.[12] 'Atā' ibn Abi Rabāḥ and al-Ḥasan ibn Muḥammad contended that Allah and the Apostle have one part of the one-fifth, since the clause concerning Allah is

[9] Abū Yūsuf, pp. 8-9, 10.

[10] Saḥnūn, *op. cit.*, Vol. III, pp. 12-13; and Māwardī, p. 240.

[11] Q. VIII, 42.

[12] Māwardī, p. 240.

only a prelude for the other parts, and it should not be counted.[13] This view is also accepted by the Ḥanbalī jurists.[14]

The Ḥanafī jurists held that the one-fifth should be divided into three parts only: one for the Prophet (which goes to the caliph after his death), the other to the near kin, and the third to be divided among the orphans, the poor, and wayfarers.[15]

The Mālikī jurists argued that the division of the one-fifth should be similar to the fay',[16] namely, to be divided evenly among the poor and the rich of the Muslim community. But Mālik also held that the imām may, if he so desires, give part of the spoil to the Prophet's kin.[17]

The Shāfi'ī jurists maintained that the one-fifth should be divided into five parts in accordance with the Qur'ānic injunction, with Allah and the Apostle having one part.[18]

There was difference of opinion also as to the treatment of Allah and the Apostle after the death of Muḥammad. One point of view was to redistribute this share among the rest of the recipients; others argued that it should be given to the imām.[19] Still others believed that it should be spent on preparation for fighting.

There was difference also as to whom the phrase "near kin" refers. Some considered the near kin to be Banū Hāshim; others Banū Hāshim and Banū 'Abd al-Muṭṭalib.[20]

[13] See Ibn Sallām, *Kitāb al-Amwāl* (Cairo, A.H. 1303), p. 14.

[14] Abū Ya'la, *al-Aḥkām al-Sulṭāniyya* (Cairo, 1938), p. 121.

[15] Abū Yūsuf, *Kitāb al-Kharāj* (Cairo, A.H. 1352), p. 21.

[16] See p. 191, below.

[17] Saḥnūn, Vol. III, pp. 26-9; and Ibn Rushd (al-Ḥafīd), *Bidāyat al-Mujtahid* (Istanbul, A.H. 1333), Vol. I, p. 315.

[18] Shāfi'ī, *Kitāb al-Umm* (Cairo, A.H. 1325), Vol. IV, p. 64.

[19] This is based on a ḥadīth to the effect that "whenever Allah has rewarded His Apostle, the reward should go to his successors after his death." See Ibn Rushd (al-Ḥafīd), Vol. I, p. 230.

[20] Abū Yūsuf, *Kitāb al-Kharāj*, p. 11.

The four-fifths share was usually divided among the mature male jihādists who were in the field. Awzā'ī held that women and children should also be given part of the spoil,[21] but other jurists objected to this.[22] Ibn Ḥanbal would give them some compensation, but this should be less than that for men.[23]

The four-fifths share was divided differently according to the various schools. Mālik and Shāfi'ī give three parts to the horseman (two to the horse and one to its rider) and one to the foot soldier.[24] Ibn Ḥanbal agrees with Mālik and Shāfi'ī.[25] Abū Ḥanīfa gives only two parts to the horseman (one to the horse and one to the rider), arguing that he does not want to give to the animal a larger share than to a human being, and one to the footsoldier.[26] Abū Yūsuf, however, who was the foremost disciple of Abū Ḥanīfa, disagreed with his master on this point and gave the horseman three parts.[27] No further shares were given to the horseman if he brought to battle more than one horse, according to both Abū Ḥanīfa and Shaybānī.[28] Abū Yūsuf and Ibn Ḥanbal gave shares to two horses.[29] Most of the jurists agreed that riders bringing to battle animals other than horses received no further shares than footsoldiers.[30]

The imām has the authority to promise additional shares of

21 Abū Yūsuf, *Kitāb al-Radd 'ala al-Awzā'ī,* p. 42; Ibn Rushd (al-Ḥafid), Vol. I, p. 231.

22 Saḥnūn, Vol. III, pp. 33-4; Shāfi'ī, Vol. IV, p. 79.

23 Ibn Qudāma, *al-Mughnī,* ed. Rashīd Riḍa (Cairo, A.H. 1367), Vol. VIII, p. 410.

24 Shāfi'ī, Vol. IV, p. 69; Saḥnūn, Vol. III, p. 32.

25 Abū Ya'la, p. 135; and Ibn Qudāma, Vol. VIII, pp. 404-5.

26 Shaybānī, Vol. II, p. 175; and Marghinānī, Vol. II, p. 108.

27 Abū Yūsuf, *Kitāb al-Kharāj,* p. 18.

28 Shaybānī, Vol. II, p. 177.

29 Abū Yūsuf, p. 19; Ibn Qudāma, Vol. VIII, pp. 407-8.

30 Some jurists permitted additional compensation for a mule or other types of breeds. See Shaybānī, Vol. II, pp. 178-183; and Ibn Qudāma, Vol. VIII, pp. 405-6.

the booty to certain jihādists before the battle is won or even before the battle begins.[31] In technical terms, the imām had the power of tanfīl (supererogation), which permits him to use his judgment in increasing the jihādists' share if there is need for it.[32] The additional quantity to the share given by the imām to a jihādist is called nafal. All the jurists agreed on the power of tanfīl;[33] but they disagreed on the source and the quantity of the nafal to be given. The Mālikī and Ḥanafī jurists held that the nafal should be given from the state share (the one-fifth),[34] and Shāfi'ī said that the quantity should not exceed a fifth of the one-fifth share (i.e., the imām's share of the one-fifth).[35] Other jurists argued that the imām had the power to give the nafal from the spoil itself, up to a maximum of one-fourth or even one-third.

The imām may allow the jihādist to appropriate the property of unbelievers whom they happen to kill. There was, however, serious difference of opinion on the way this power was to be exercised. Mālik insisted that the killer should not be allowed to appropriate the property unless the imām, through the tanfīl power, had allowed him to do so.[36] Shāfi'ī permitted killers to appropriate the property provided that they did not take it from deserting unbelievers. Still others held that looted property could be divided according to the general rule for the division of the spoil.[37]

[31] Cf. Saḥnūn, Vol. III, pp. 29-31; and Ibn Rushd (al-Ḥafīd), Vol I, p. 233.

[32] Shāfi'ī, Vol. IV, p. 68; Ibn Sallām, p. 303; Shaybānī, Vol. II, pp. 2-3.

[33] This is based on a Qur'ānic injunction which runs as follows: "They will ask you about the anfāl (plural of nafal); Say, the anfāl are Allah's and the Apostle's; fear Allah and settle it among yourselves. . . ." (Q. VIII, 1).

[34] Shaybānī, Vol. II, pp. 11-12; Marghinānī, Vol. II, pp. 110-1; Saḥnūn, Vol. III, pp. 29 ff; Ibn Rushd (al-Ḥafīd), Vol. I, p. 233.

[35] Shāfi'ī, Vol. IV, p. 68.

[36] Saḥnūn, Vol. III, p. 31.

[37] Ibn Rushd (al-Ḥafīd), Vol. I, p. 234.

Finally, restored property of believers which had been appropriated by unbelievers was treated according to one of the following rules. First, according to a view ascribed to Caliph 'Alī (A.D. 661) it was to be treated as part of the spoil. Secondly, Shāfi'ī held that it should be restored to its original owner. Thirdly, if restored property was claimed after its division as part of the spoil, the owner lost his right; if he claimed it before the division, he could regain it. Fourthly, if the restored property had been seized by the unbelievers by force, the original owner could only regain it before the division of the spoil; if the restored property had been taken by the unbelievers without force, the original owner could regain it before or after the division of the spoils.[38]

Immovable Property

Immovable property, like movable property, forms part of the spoil when acquired by force. Unlike movable property, however, its disposition or ownership by the state presented a more complex problem which was solved differently in different areas by special rules of law. These rules vary according to the several schools of law.

While practice changed, during the life of the Prophet Muḥammad, from the distribution of land among the jihādists to ownership by the state, there seems to have been no definite rule established prior to 'Umar's land regulations. For military reasons 'Umar, after consultation with leading Muslims, decided to immobilize the land with its inhabitants, imposing on them for it the kharāj—as a land tax—and the jizya as a poll tax.[39] The proceeds of these taxes were to constitute a permanent source of expenditure for the maintenance of the be-

[38] *Ibid.*, Vol. I, p. 235.

[39] For a discussion on the origins and development of 'Umar's land regulations see chap. XVII, below.

lievers who were neither disposed nor permitted to engage in agriculture. This rule, originally adopted in connection with the Sawād (southern Mesopotamia or Iraq), became the basic rule for the regulation of lands acquired as part of the spoil. While in theory the transfer of land from the original tenant to another, either by conversion of the possessor or through sale to a Muslim, was not permitted, such transfer was not infrequently permitted by the imām.

Mass conversion and validation of transfer by the imām induced the jurists to reconsider the situation and the different schools of law give different rules. The Ḥanafī jurists held that the imām had free choice to divide the land among the jihādists, to regard it as state land, or let its inhabitants retain ownership of it, provided they paid the kharāj. Abū Ḥanīfa argued, on the precedent of Khaybar, that the Prophet divided part of its land and the rest became state land. Mālik ordered all immovable property to be regarded as public property owned by the state, and its produce as part of the revenue. No land was permitted to be divided according to the Mālikī jurists. The Shāfi'ī jurists, depending upon practice, classified land in the same category as other property and as such to be divided among the jihādists. If the jihādists, however, declined to take it, it became public land.[40]

Prisoners of War

The practice of taking prisoners of war as part of the spoil is very old and goes back to antiquity. The Persians treated their captives with relentless cruelty: they were blinded, tortured, and finally killed or crucified.[41] The Hebraic rule was

[40] See *ibid.;* and Frede Løkkegaard, *Islamic Taxation in the Classic Period* (Copenhagan, 1950), chaps. 3 and 6.

[41] Thomas A. Walker, *History of the Law of Nations* (Cambridge, 1899), Vol. I, p. 61.

no less severe than Persian practice.[42] The Muslims, regarding captives also as part of the spoil, often treated them no less cruelly than their predecessors. The law governing prisoners of war is based on two Qur'ānic injunctions which run as follows:

> It has not been for any prophet to have captives until he slaughters in the land.[43]
>
> So, when ye meet *in battle* those who disbelieve, then *let there* be the striking off of heads until, when ye have slaughtered them, then make the bond strong. Then *grant* either favor afterwards, or ransom, till war lays down its burdens.[44]

The treatment to which they were liable varied, however, with the different schools of law. The imām is advised by the jurists to follow one of four courses:

First, he may order the immediate execution of some or all of the captives. Both Abū Yūsuf and Shāfi'ī insist that this should not be done unless dictated by certain reasons, such as the need of weakening the enemy, or required by high Muslim interests.[45] Awzā'ī recommends, however, that before execution the prisoner should be given the opportunity of adopting Islam as an alternative to death.[46]

Second, he may release them on paying ransom (fidā') as provided in the Qur'ān, or set free without compensation. The Caliph Abū Bakr was against release by ransom.[47]

Third, he may exchange them for Muslim prisoners. The

[42] Deut. XX, 10-17: "When thou comest nigh unto a city to fight against it . . . thou shalt smite every male thereof with the edge of the sword: but the women, and the little ones, and the cattle, and all that is in the city, even all the spoil thereof, shalt thou take for a prey unto thyself. . . ."

[43] Q. VIII, 68.

[44] Q. XLVII, 4-5.

[45] Abū Yūsuf, *Kitāb al-Kharāj,* pp. 195-6; Shāfi'ī, Vol. IV, p. 316.

[46] Ṭabarī, *Kitāb al-Jihād,* pp. 141-42.

[47] *Ibid.,* p. 145. See also Ḥamīdullah, *Muslim Conduct of State* (Lahore, 1945), p. 211-13.

Caliph 'Umar insisted that earnest efforts should be made to release Muslim prisoners by payment from the spoil or by paying ransom from the treasury. If the prisoners were not condemned to slavery, Mālik restricts their treatment either to execution or exchange with Muslim prisoners.[48] During the 'Abbāsid period this practice became very common, and was regulated by treaties.[49]

Fourth, he may condemn them to be slaves. The treatment of slaves will be dealt with in the following section.

An outstanding case of an eminent prisoner of war was that of al-Hurmuzān, the famous Persian commander who fought the Muslims early in the conquest of Iraq. Al-Hurmuzān was captured (A.D. 640) and sent to Madīna. The Caliph 'Umar determined to order his execution and called his attention to the result of fighting the Muslims. Al-Hurmuzān (al-Mughīra ibn Shu'ba interpreting) replied: "In the pre-Islamic time Allah was on the neutral side, leaving both of us to fight, and thus we were victorious over you."

'Umar said: "No! It was because you were united and we were not . . . and now tell me why did you not respect your pledges of peace?"

Al-Hurmuzān said: "I am afraid you will kill me before I tell you," and gasping like one faint with thirst, he begged for a draught of water.

"Give it," said the Caliph, "and let him drink in peace."

"Nay," said the captive, trembling, "I fear to drink, lest someone slay me unawares."

"Your life is safe," said 'Umar, "until you have drunk the water up."

Al-Hurmuzān, believing that he had won his case, poured the water upon the ground. The Caliph ordered another cup

[48] Ṭabarī, pp. 144-45.

[49] See p. 217, below.

to be brought, but al-Hurmuzān said that he was no longer in need of water. "I wanted not the water," he said, "but safety (amān),[50] and now you have given it me."

"Liar!" cried 'Umar angrily and said: "I am going to kill you." The people around the Caliph interposed and said that an amān was given. 'Umar tried to find a legal justification for execution, but failing for once, had to yield and said: "The fellow has deceived me, and yet I cannot spare the life of one who had slain so many believers by reiterated treachery. I swear that you shall not gain by deceit, unless you embrace Islam." Al-Hurmuzān at once made profession of the faith upon the spot and, thenceforth, residing freely in Madīna, received a pension from the treasury.[51]

The jurists agree that the sabī, which includes women and children prisoners, were not liable to be killed, but enslaved and divided as property. While in practice a few women and children were killed, the Prophet Muḥammad always warned against the killing of women and children. The Prophet also set the precedent of securing the release of Muslim prisoners by exchange for sabī.[52]

Muslim prisoners, captured by the enemy, were under no obligation to submit or obey the orders of the enemy; if they were able to escape or destroy enemy property, they should do so. If however, the Muslim prisoner pledged himself not to escape, he must observe faithfully his parole.[53] Muslim prisoners were under obligation to refuse to give information

[50] See chap. 15, below.

[51] For a full account of the case see, Ṭabarī, *Ta'rīkh,* ed. de Goeje (Leiden, 1893), Series I, Vol. V, pp. 2557-9. See also Sir William Muir, *The Caliphate: Its Rise, Decline and Fall,* ed. T. H. Weir (Edinburgh, 1924), pp. 171-2. For a similar case, see Balādhurī, *Futūḥ al-Buldān,* ed. de Goeje (Leiden, 1866) pp. 41-2.

[52] Ṭabarī, *Kitāb al-Jihād,* pp. 145-6.

[53] Shaybānī, Vol. IV, pp. 223-5.

valuable to the enemy, to refuse to take part in war against Islam, and to refuse to abandon the faith unless forced to do so.[54] If a female Muslim prisoner should fall into the hands of the enemy, she must refuse to respond to their demands, even if she were severely beaten, unless she felt her life was in danger. The imām, in his turn, is under obligation to make every effort to release the Muslim captives by exchange in persons or property.

Slaves

Enslavement by war is an ancient custom which existed in the ancient East and was practiced in pre-Islamic Arabia. The majority of the slaves were of foreign origin, although there also existed Arab slaves who, in accordance with Arab customary law, were able to obtain freedom by ransom.

Islamic law, which has its roots in Arab customary law, recognized slavery, although, both legally and doctrinally, Islam endeavored to raise the moral standard of the slave and afforded him the possibility of emancipation. The pious Muslim is urged to free a slave as a recommended act to be amply rewarded in Heaven. However, slavery persisted as an integral part of Muslim society down to its abolition in almost all Muslim countries in the nineteenth century.

Slaves were acquired either by purchase or as spoils of war: the latter is the manner in which the Muslim law of war regulates, the former, outside the scope of our study, falls under the law of sale.[55]

As a consequence of attaining victory over the enemy, the

[54] Ṭabarī, *Kitāb al-Jihād*, pp. 194-6, 196-8.

[55] In almost every standard law book the subject of slavery is discussed under the relevent section governing the status of the slave. For a comprehensive treatment of the subject in both Muslim law and history, see R. Brunschwig, "'Abd," *Encyclopaedia of Islam*, new edition, Vol. I, pp. 24-40.

imām may condemn part of the whole of the population of the conquered territory, in case they did not accept Islam and the imām did not demand that they work and pay the kharāj, to be slaves and be divided among the jihādists as spoils of war. The recipient had the legal right to regard the slave as his property, but he was under a moral obligation to treat him gently and to show him real kindness. If the slave were a woman, the master was permitted to have sexual connection with her as a concubine. In the division of the spoil, however, women were not separated from their husbands, nor the children from their parents.

Arabs were ordinarily not enslaved, although certain cases of Arab enslavement occurred during the life of the Prophet Muḥammad and the Caliph Abū Bakr. The Prophet had enslaved the Arabs of Banū Muṣṭaliq; but when he married Juwayriyya, a beautiful woman of this tribe, he ordered set free one hundred slaves of her tribe.[56] He also enslaved several thousands of the tribe of Hawāzin; and, on account of kinship and in response to their demands for his favor, set six thousand of them free.[57] The Caliph Abū Bakr also enslaved the Banū Nājiba Arabs. The Caliph 'Umar, however, was against the enslavement of Arabs. He is reported to have declared: "No ownership of an Arab is permitted."[58] 'Umar was inspired by the spirit of Arabism and considered the Arabs to be, in his own words, "the essence of Islam."[59] He seems to have been

[56] 'Ā'isha, one of the Prophet's wives, is reported to have remarked: "I know of no woman who was more merciful to her people than Juwayriyya." See Sha'rānī, *Kitāb Kashf al-Ghimma* (Cairo, A.H. 1303), Vol. II, p. 167.

[57] See Ibn Hishām, *Kitāb al-Sīra,* ed. Wüstenfeld (Göttingen, 1859), Vol. II, p. 877.

[58] Sha'rānī, Vol. II, p. 167.

[59] Ṭabarī, *Ta'rīkh,* Series I, Vol. V, p. 2742; and Abū Yūsuf, *Kitāb al-Kharāj,* p. 8.

unfavorable even to non-Arab enslavement and was more interested in having the population of the occupied territories of Syria and Iraq work and pay kharāj than to be enslaved. From 'Umar's time, custom ran against the enslavement of Arabs, although certain jurists held to the possibility of enslavement.[60]

The Muslim system of slavery carried with it the possibility of emancipation. A slave might obtain his liberty from his master either by an act of favor or by ransom. Both in the Qur'ān and ḥadīth, Muslims were urged to free slaves whether for worldly or heavenly compensation.[61] Thus the slave in Muslim society was not condemned to live permanently in servitude; he had a chance of obtaining liberty in his life time in an age when the rule was more rigid outside the World of Islam.

[60] Sha'rānī criticizes the Caliph 'Umar for his ruling against Arab enslavement and insists that the precedents in the time of the Prophet and Abū Bakr were sufficient to justify Arab enslavement. (Sha'rānī, Vol. II, p. 167).

[61] Q. XXIV, 33.

"O ye who believe! When ye meet those who disbelieve in battle, turn not your backs to them; for he who turns his back to them on that day, unless manoeuvring for battle or intent to join a company, shall incur wrath from Allah: hell shall be his abode and wretched the journey thither." Qur'ān VIII, 15-16.

CHAPTER XII

TERMINATION OF FIGHTING

The cessation of hostilities by a people who had already been promised victory by God could only mean that Islam's enemies must capitulate at the end. For inherent in Islam is God's power: failure would certainly be on the side of its enemies since success could not be divorced from Islam. If the imām, or his commanders in the field, found victory difficult to attain, he was advised to have continuous patience for the continuation of fighting until victory is achieved however long it might take to reach that end. "O you who believe!," said Allah to His Apostle, "be patient, and vie in patience, and be firm, and fear Allah, that you may be successful."[1]

There are warnings in the Qur'ān against desertion,[2] and

[1] Q. III, 200; and Q. II, 149.

[2] Q. VIII, 15-16, 36.

the ḥadīth not only warns against it but goes so far as to regard it as a great sin.[3]

In his *Kitāb al-Aḥkām al-Sulṭāniyya,* Māwardī advises the imām never to give up his fight with the enemy until victory is achieved. "Constant patience for the [continuation] of the jihād," Māwardī goes on to say, "is indispensable until [the imām] attains one of four results. First [the enemy] will adopt Islam and will have the same rights and obligations as ours. . . . Second, [the imām] will have, by the grace of Allah, victory over [the enemies] who will remain polytheists and consequently their lives and property are liable to molestation. . . . Third, [the enemy] will pay tribute by virtue of a peace treaty. . . . Fourth, [the enemy] will have peace by an amān. . . ."[4] Māwardī, however, is silent about an unsuccessful war with the enemy, and to him, as well as to many other jurists, the possibility of a defeat is dismissed as if entirely nonexistent.

Some jurists, however, argued that if a catastrophe had befallen the Muslims (qualifying their remark by istaghfir Allah, God forbid) the imām might come to terms with the enemy for a period not exceeding the terms of the Hudaybiya treaty,[5] on the grounds of *force majeur,* provided that the Muslims should resume the jihād after the expiration of the treaty if the imām decided that he was able to do so. If the imām feels that the Muslims are not powerful enough to resume the fighting, he may renew the truce for a similar period—but not longer—for if he concluded a truce for a longer period, it would be null and void.[6]

[3] Abū Dā'ūd, *Sunan* (Cairo, 1935), Vol. III, pp. 42, 46; and Shaybānī, *al-Siyar al-Kabīr,* with Sarakhsī's Commentary (Hyberabad, A.H. 1335), Vol. I, pp. 86-7.

[4] Māwardī, *Kitāb al-Aḥkām al-Sulṭāniyya,* ed. Enger (Bonn, 1853), p. 81.

[5] See p. 210 ff., below.

[6] Shāfi'ī, *Kitāb al-Umm* (Cairo, A.H. 1322), Vol. IV, p. 110.

On the basis of a Qur'ānic injunction which stated that twenty believers can fight two hundred, later abrogated by another that one thousand believers can fight two thousand—for Allah "knows that there is a weakness amongst you"[7]—some jurists concluded that the Muslims were to be relieved of fighting if their numerical strength were less than half that of their enemy.[8] Other jurists maintained that the term "strength" should not be construed on strictly numerical grounds, but on the power of resistance and the equipment of the enemy. Thus if a Muslim were confronted with an enemy soldier more adequately armed than himself, he was permitted to retreat.[9] Abū Ḥanīfa, however, argued that retreat should be resorted to only after a trial in which the Muslim would be convinced of the impossibility of attaining victory.[10] The Mālikī jurists permit retreat if the believers were certain to face death; if, however, they felt that retreat would not save their life, they should fight until the finish.[11] Ibn Ḥanbal permits retreat if the enemy's power exceeded twice that of the believers.[12] Ibn Hudhayl adds that if the believers were under

[7] Q. VIII, 66-67: "O Prophet! urge on the believers to fight. If there be of you twenty patient men, they shall conquer two hundred; if there be of you a hundred, they shall conquer a thousand of those who misbelieve, because they are a people who did not discern. Now has Allah made light your burden; He knows that there is a weakness amongst you: but if there be amongst you but a patient hundred, they will conquer two hundred; and if there be of you a thousand, they will conquer two thousand, by the permission of Allah—for Allah is with the patient. . . .

[8] Shaybānī, Vol. I, p. 87; Shīrāzī, *Kitāb al-Muhadhdhab*, (Cairo, 1343), Vol. II, pp. 248-9.

[9] Ibn Rushd (al-Ḥafīd), *Bidāyat al-Mujtahid* (Istanbul, A.H. 1333), Vol. I, p. 313.

[10] Shaybānī, Vol. I, pp. 86-8; Vol. III, p. 238.

[11] Nawawī, *Minhāj al-Ṭālibīn*, ed. L. W. C. Van Den Berg (Batavia, 1884), Vol. III, p. 258-9.

[12] Ibn Qudāma, *al-Mughnī*, ed. Rashīd Riḍa (Cairo, A.H. 1367), Vol. VIII, pp. 483-6.

extreme hardships, such as constant thirst and hunger to the extent that they could no longer fight, retreat was permitted.[13]

Awzā'ī goes further in elaborating this rule and argues that, if the imām feels weakness in his forces, or if the Muslims are engaged in a civil war, he might come to terms with the enemy even at the sacrifice of paying an annual tribute.[14] In giving this opinion Awzā'ī, who lived under Umayyad rule, no doubt tried to validate a practice which several Umayyad caliphs were forced to adopt in their treaty relations with the Byzantines.[15]

It follows that in Muslim legal theory, defeat is an anomaly which could be tolerated only under *force majeur;* thus the imām is advised either to abstain from going to war if his forces are insufficient to attain victory, or, if he should suffer defeat, to withdraw and save the lives of surviving believers. Defeated Muslims always maintained that their battle with the enemy would be resumed, however long they had to wait for the second round.[16] When secular war became fashionable in Islam, victory or defeat depended less on the just causes for its declaration, as in the case of a jihād, than on the morale of the army and the maneuvres followed by commanders. Ṭarṭūshī emphasized the courage and morale of the army, while al-Ḥasan ibn 'Abd-Allah stressed the effectiveness of arms.[17]

[13] Ibn Hudhayl, *Tuḥfat al-Anfus wa Shi'ār Sukkān al-Andalus,* ed. Louis Mercier (Paris, 1936), pp. 42-7.

[14] See Ṭabarī, *Kitāb al-Jihād,* ed. Schacht (Leiden, 1933), pp. 17-8; cf. Abū Ḥanīfa's position in *Ibid.,* p. 19.

[15] Both Mu'āwiya I and 'Abd al-Malik, during civil wars, signed peace treaties in which they paid annual tribute to the Byzantines.

[16] This is based on a ḥadīth in which a few Muslims reported to the Prophet Muḥammad their defeat in battle; the Prophet replied that "they were not deserters, but 'akkarūn," i.e., that they will resume later their fight for victory. See Shaybānī, Vol. I, p. 87.

[17] Ṭarṭūshī, *Sirāj al-Mulūk* (Cairo, A.H. 1319), pp. 150-7; and Al-Ḥasan

Ibn Khaldūn, it will be recalled, held that certain hidden forces played a more decisive role in the attainment of victory than sheer numerical strength, such as the ability to make use of the physical nature of the terrain on which the army fought and certain tactical skills.[18] These publicists did not take it for granted, as their predecessors thought, that victory was a matter of divine intervention.[19] When the Muslim ruler fought a secular war—in which the religious purpose was not apparent—no sin was necessarily to be incurred if he suffered defeat by another ruler, be he a believer or an unbeliever.

---

ibn 'Abd-Allah, *Athār al-Uwal fī Tartīb al-Duwal* (Cairo, A.H. 1295), pp. 184-8.

18 Ibn Khaldūn, *al-Muqddima*, ed. Qatremère (Paris, 1858), Vol. II, pp. 65-79.

19 Ṭarṭūshī advises the commander of the army to be prepared, among other things, to know how to lead the army in retreat before the battle begins. See Ṭarṭūshī, *op. cit.*, p. 151.

BOOK III

THE LAW OF PEACE

"If they lean to peace, then lean thou also to it. . . ."

Qur'ān, VIII, 63.

"Now Allah has made light your burden, for he knows there is a weakness amongst you. . . ." Qur'ān VIII, 67.

CHAPTER XIII

INTRODUCTION

The jihād, it will be recalled, was regarded as Islam's instrument to transform the dār al-ḥarb into dār al-Islām. If that end had ever been achieved, the dār al-ḥarb would have been reduced to nonexistence and the *raison d'être* of the jihād, except perhaps for combatting Islam's internal enemies, would eventually have disappeared. We may argue, therefore, that in Islamic legal theory, the ultimate objective of Islam was not war *per se,* but the ultimate establishment of peace. This may be regarded as another reason why the jihād was not made, as it has been by the Khārijīs, the sixth pillar of the faith, since in theory it was merely a temporary instrument to establish ultimate peace, rather than a permanent article of the faith.

It is interesting to note that Islam presented in its jural-doctrinal theory another utopia to realize a peaceful world state. Like Christianity, it sought to achieve the salvation of mankind; but, unlike Christianity, it began to achieve it first on earth. The Muslim jurists and philosophers, even when Muslim power had declined, worked out elaborate theories of the state in which they sought, as in all utopias, to offer a corrective to existing conditions by providing the ideal representation of the *civitas dei* under which all men can live in perfect harmony as God-fearing Muslims. 'Abd al-Qāhir al-Baghdādī and al-Māwardī conceived of the Islamic world state as a jural superstructure embracing all believers, presided over by an imām whose authority, even though it was often challenged or usurped by local governors, was indivisible; and al-Fārābī and Ibn Sīnā (Avicenna) characterized the caliph, the head of the *civitas dei,* as a philosopher-imām. To al-Fārābī the perfect state was the truly universal state.

For various reasons the Islamic state, like other world states, carried out only partially its ideal. Islam dominated a vast area of western Asia, North Africa, and Spain; but its experiment, like other attempts at world unity, was frustrated by internal no less than by external resistance. Internally, there was a growing tendency within Islam to develop successive schismatic jural-doctrinal orders; the inevitable result was the division of Islam into different factions within the original organization. This tendency has indeed been inherent in all the world empires known in recorded history: for every new world empire was inclined to make possible the spread of its political concepts and institutions over as large as possible an area of the world. There was also a tendency toward a continuous cumulation of civilization: for the achievement of a world empire requires development and increase in communication, wealth, and population. As the spread of civilization becomes more and more uniform, the distribution of power tends toward equilibrium, and the empire changes into either a sort of federation of sub-groups or splits into independent political entities. The schismatic development of the Islamic state, with all the efforts to rationalize the Sunni system with a view to justifying its historical development, inevitably resulted in the rise of several caliphates—some of them coexisting as rival states—and other sub-entities.

The internal process of disintegration might often be checked by the existence of a vital external threat, or a supposed threat, which would make it possible to keep the internal elements of the state in harmony, i.e., combined against the external threat, rather than to be in conflict. At the height of Muslim power in the ninth century of the Christian era, the Byzantine threat to Islam was limited only to the eastern empire; thus North Africa and Spain failed to rally to the 'Abbāsid caliphs. On the contrary, the effects of Byzantine pressure on the 'Abbāsids in the East relieved the Umayyads of Spain from 'Abbāsid attack and afforded them an opportunity to repel local encroachments from Western Christendom. The division of Christianity into rival Western (Roman) and Eastern (Orthodox) kingdoms was thus matched by a similar division of Islam, creating a balance of power as the basis of international relations; otherwise Christendom and Islamdom would have been facing one another as the only two rival great powers, with the inevitability of continuous conflict for world domination. As a result, the process of decentralization and division in both the eastern and western Islamic empires developed in the tenth century of the Christian era. In the eastern Islamic empire this process was checked by the coming of the Crusaders, who, for two centuries, gave a fresh impetus to the petty states to unite and fight against the external enemy. But the internal disintegration went too far when later the Mongols attacked the 'Abbāsid Caliphate from the East. Its collapse made possible the rise of two Muslim dynasties in Egypt and Asia Minor: the Mamlūks and the Ottomans. A similar process was set on foot in Western Islamdom.

The impossibility of establishing a Muslim universal state or of universalizing Islam inevitably divided the world into the world of Islam and the world of war. In Muslim legal theory, it will be recalled, this division was only temporary; but in practice it persisted throughout Islamic history. The relations between these two worlds were in theory not peaceful; each world was at war with the other. But this state of war should not be construed as actual hostilities; it was rather equivalent to what is called in Western legal terminology non-recognition, that is, the incompetence of the world of war to possess a legal status under Muslim law so long as it lacked the essential doctrinal prerequisite of the true faith. This non-recognition did not imply, as in the case of the modern law of nations, the impossibility of initiating negotiations and concluding treaties, for such actions were neither considered to imply equality between the two contracting parties nor necessarily to possess a permanent character. The nearest equivalent, perhaps, to this situation in the modern law of nations is the recognition of insurgency which neither precludes an intention of later *de facto* or *de jure* recognition nor approval of the regime under insurgency; it merely means that an authority to enforce the law in a certain territory was needed under certain circumstances.[1] The Islamic state, in like manner, in entering into diplomatic negotiations with a non-Muslim state, does not intend to recognize (in the modern sense of the term), that is, to extend the area of validity of Muslim law to the non-Muslim state, but merely to admit that a certain authority or authorities were needed in the world of war so long as it remained beyond Muslim sovereignty.

Some of the jurists, however—especially the Shāfi'īs—devised a third temporary division of the world, called dār al-ṣulḥ (world of peace) or dār al-'ahd (world of covenant), giving

[1] H. Lauterpacht, *Recognition in International Law* (Cambridge, 1947), chap. 16.

qualified recognition to a non-Muslim state if it entered into treaty relations with Islam either before hostilities began or after offering stiff resistance, on condition that the non-Muslim state should either pay an annual tribute, a poll tax (jizya), or cede a portion of its territory.[2] Other jurists, especially the Ḥanafīs, never recognized the existence of a third division of the world; they argued that if the inhabitants of a territory concluded a peace treaty and paid a tribute or a poll tax, it became part of the dār al-Islām and its inhabitants were entitled to protection by the imām, since otherwise it would be a part of the dār al-ḥarb.

To sum up, the law of peace, like the jihād, was in theory only a temporary device to regulate the relations of Muslims with the outside world during non-hostile periods (i.e., when the jihād was in suspense), until the dār al-Islām should comprise the whole world. Nor did the peaceful relations between dār al-Islām and dār al-ḥarb, which were often conducted on the basis of mutual respect and interest, carry with it the implied idea of equality between the two dārs, since dār al-ḥarb could not possibly attain a normal or permanent status unless its inhabitants either adopted Islam or accepted the status of the tolerated religions. In practice, however, the more habituated the Muslims became to a dormant jihād the more reconciled they tended to be to the permanency of a law of peace.

[2] Shāfi'ī, *Kitāb al-Umm,* Vol. IV, pp. 103-4. Māwardī states the legal situation as follows: territories acquired by Muslims fall into three categories: (a) those taken by force ('anwatan); (b) those taken without fighting after the flight of their previous owners; and (c) those taken by treaty (ṣulḥ). The last may either put the inhabitants in the status of dhimmīs and their land is tilled by them, though owned by Islam, or the territory became in special tributary relations as dār al-ṣulḥ, with the land both owned and retained by its inhabitants. This last division constitutes a third division of the world which is neither dār al-Islām nor dār al-ḥarb. See Māwardī, *al-Aḥkām al-Sulṭāniyya,* ed. Enger (Bonn, 1853), pp. 237-8.

This tendency fitted well into the pattern of the modern trend of integrating the various regions of the world into the Family of Nations.[3]

[3] See chap. XXIII, below.

"Islam is binding on the Muslim wherever he may be . . . for [the duty] of worship is not waived if he is in the land of the infidels." Shāfi'ī.

CHAPTER XIV

JURISDICTION

Persons: Believers

Muslim law binds individuals, not territorial groups; the believer, accordingly, must ordinarily observe the law even if he happens to be in a non-Muslim territory. Conversely, a non-Muslim who resides in a Muslim territory is not bound to observe the law in the same manner as Muslims do, except perhaps in the case of certain obligations which he must fulfill as a condition of permission to reside in a Muslim territory. Thus the state's jurisdiction is essentially dependent on the individual's religion which entitles him both to membership in the Muslim brotherhood as well as to citizenship of the Muslim state. It is a commonplace that any one who believes in Allah and in His Apostle is regarded as a Muslim; but from a jural-doctrinal viewpoint the question may not be as easy as that. What then constitutes a Muslim?

Some Muslim jurists have maintained that everyone who affirms the prophecy of Muḥammad and the truth of all that he preached, no matter what he asserts after his declaration, is a Muslim.[1] Others held that anyone who observed the five pillars of faith or who merely acknowledged the necessity of turning in the direction of the Ka'ba in the worship is a Muslim. Abū Ḥanīfa went so far as to say that even if he were in doubt as to the Ka'ba location he would still be regarded as a Muslim. 'Abd al-Qāhir al-Baghdādī, however, regarded these definitions as too broad and inadequate; he maintained that all are Muslims who:

> profess the view that the world is created, the unity of its Maker, his pre-existence, his attributes, his equity, his wisdom, the denial of his anthropomorphic character, the prophetic character of Muḥammad, and his universal apostolate, the acknowledgment of the constant validity of his law, that all that he enjoined was truth, that the Koran is the source of all legal regulations, and the Ka'ba is the direction in which all prayers should be turned. Everyone who professes all this and does not follow a heresy that might lead him to unbelief, he is an orthodox Sunnite. . . .[2]

But if the Muslim were inclined to one of the heresies of the sects, Baghdādī contended, then his rights and duties under Islam would be qualified. "He would be entitled," said Baghdādī, "to be buried in the graveyard of the Muslims, and to have a share in the tribute and booty which is procured by the true believers in war with the idolaters provided he fights with the true believers. Nor should he be prevented from praying in the mosques. But he is not of the umma in other respects: namely, no prayer should be allowed over his dead body, nor behind him [it]; moreover, any animal slaughtered by him is not lawful food; nor may he marry an orthodox

[1] Shahrastānī, *Kitāb al-Milal wa'l-Niḥal,* ed. Cureton (London, 1846), pp. 25-6; Ash'arī, *Kitāb al-Ibāna* (Hyderabad, 1948), pp. 5 ff.

[2] Baghdādī, *Al-Farq Bayn al-Firaq,* trans. Kate C. Seelye (New York, 1920), pp. 29-30.

Muslim woman. It is also not lawful for an orthodox man to marry one of their women if she partake of their belief."

It should be noted that Islam requires the external submission of the person to the foregoing articles of the faith which qualify him for membership in the congregation. Thus Islam represents both a religion and a nationality for the citizen of its state. Some of the jurist-theologians have distinguished between Islam, emphasizing external submission, and the imān, the internal submission (i.e., faith[3]); although others, such as Nasafī, have regarded the two as synonymous.[4]

The Shī'a stress the distinction between Islam and imān, since the latter implies the additional belief in walāya (allegiance) to an infallible appointed imām. To the Shī'a, therefore, Islam is the religion of all believers; imān is the creed of the chosen few, the believers in the true faith.[5]

Persons: Kāfirs (unbelievers) and Murtadds (apostates)

The opposite of imān is kufr (unbelief); thus he who denies Allah or who merely commits a great sin is a kāfir.[6] A Muslim who reverts to polytheism or adopts another religion is murtadd (apostate). While the theologians disagree as to the punishment of a kāfir, ranging from full damnation and eternal fire in the next life to partial earthly punishment, both jurists and theologians agree that apostasy constitutes a viola-

[3] 'Abd al-Qāhir al-Baghdādī, *Kitāb Uṣūl al-Dīn* (Istanbul, 1928), Vol. I, pp. 247-51; Shahrastānī, *op. cit.*, p. 27; A. J. Wensinck, *The Muslim Creed* (Cambridge, 1932), pp. 23, 38-9.

[4] Taftāzānī's *Commentary* on Nasafī's *Creed of Islam*, trans. E. E. Elder (New York, 1950), pp. 116.

[5] Ḥillī, *Al-Bābu'l-Ḥādī 'Ashar*, trans. W. M. Miller (London, 1928), pp. 7-8; Qāḍī Nu'mān, *Da'ā'im al-Islām*, ed. Āsif A. Fayḍi (Fyzee) (Cairo, 1950), Vol. I, pp. 3, 17; Shahrastānī, *op. cit.*, p. 108 f.

[6] Baghdādī, *Kitāb Uṣūl al-Dīn* (Istanbul, 1928), Vol. I, pp. 247-51; Wensinck, *op. cit.*, pp. 103-6.

tion of the law punishable both in this world and the next. Not only is the person denied salvation in the next world, but he is also liable to capital punishment by the state. This is based on several Qur'ānic injunctions which run as follows:

1. Whosoever of you apostatize from his religion and dies while still a misbeliever; these are those whose works are vain in this world and the next; they are the fellows of the fire, and they shall dwell therein for aye. Q. II, 214.

2. Why are ye two parties on the subject of the hypocrites, when Allah has cast them off for their doing? . . . Take therefore none of them for friends, till they have fled their homes for the cause of Allah. If they turn back, then seize them, and slay them wherever ye find them. . . . Q. IV, 90-1.

3. O ye who believe! should any of you apostatize from his religion, Allah will then raise up a people loved by Him, and loving Him, lowly towards the faithful, haughty towards the unbelievers. For Allah's path will they make jihād, and not fear the blame of the blamer. That is Allah's grace. He gives it unto whom He pleases, for Allah both comprehends and knows. Q. V, 59.

4. Whoso disbelieves in Allah after having believed, unless it be one who is forced and whose heart is quiet in the faith—but whoso expands his breast to misbelieve—on them is wrath from Allah, and for them is mighty woe! Q. XVI, 108.

Although only the second of these four verses specifically states that death sentence should be imposed on those who apostatize or turn back from their religion, all the commentators agree that a believer who turns back from his religion (irtadda), openly or secretly, must be killed if he persists in disbelief. The traditions are more explicit in providing the death penalty for everyone who apostatizes from Islam. The Prophet Muḥammad is reported to have said: "He who changes his religion must be killed."[8] Cases of those who apostatized and escaped

[8] Abū Dā'ūd, *Sunan* (Cairo, 1935), Vol. IV, p. 126. The same authority reports cases of apostasy in which the apostates were punished by having their hands and feet cut off and finally put to death.

punishment are few, but the rule was certainly more strictly enforced after Muḥammad's death as a result of the victories won during the wars of the ridda (secession).[9] The law of apostasy endorsed by the practice of early caliphs has been sanctioned by ijmā' (i.e., unanimity), and there is no disagreement as to its validity.[10]

The murtadd, however, is not to be executed at once; he is warned and given three days of grace to afford him time to choose between Islam and death.[11] Except the Ḥanafī and Ḥanbalī jurists, the authorities treat women on the same footing as men. Abū Ḥanīfa maintained that women should be forced to return to Islam by such punishment as beating or imprisonment.[12] Children and the insane are not liable to be killed until the latter recover and the former come of age. The killing of the murtadd must be done by the sword, not by burning, since only God punishes by fire. The execution must be done by an order of the imām, although some jurists, including Shāfi'ī, permit the master to kill his slave if he apostatizes.[13]

If a group of apostates constituted a threat to authority, the imām may wage a jihād and enforce its rules. The law governing such a situation has been discussed under the law of war.[14]

The law of apostasy did not prevent a few believers, during Muḥammad's career, from reverting to polytheism. In his

[9] See Balādhurī, *Kitāb Futūḥ al-Buldān,* ed. de Goeje (Leiden, 1866), pp. 94-107.

[10] See S. M. Zwemer, *The Law of Apostasy in Islam* (London, 1924), Chapter 2.

[11] Mālik, *al-Muwaṭṭa',* Vol. II, p. 117.

[12] Abū Yūsuf, *op. cit.,* pp. 179-80; Shaybānī, *al-Siyar al-Kabīr,* Vol. IV, p. 162.

[13] Shāfi'ī, *Kitāb al-Umm,* Vol. VI, pp. 145-65; Ibn Qudāma, *al-Mughnī,* Vol. VIII, pp. 123-50.

[14] See pp. 76-7, above.

treaty with the Makkans (A.D. 630) Muḥammad permitted the return of those Makkans who had joined his congregation before the peace settlement.[15] Cases of apostasy became less frequent after the wars of secession since Islam had become firmly established in the Arabian Peninsula. It was from that time that the rule of execution, based on Muḥammadan traditions, was formulated as a law to be enforced by the imām.

The Head of State: The Imām

Perhaps no other issue in Islam proved to be as controversial as the caliphate; few others have in practice so radically deviated from theory. Because the issue was one which caused schism and endless controversy, the jurist-theologians were more inclined to speculate on what the nature and functions of the imāmate (caliphate) should be in theory—each stressing or defending his own schismatic viewpoint—rather than to reflect its actual historical development.

In the Islamic legal theory, God—not the imām—is the head of the state;[16] but in practice the imām, to all intents and purposes, acts as the actual head of the state. He is enthroned, by election or designation, to enforce the law in his realm as well as to act as the spokesman for his people in foreign relations. Since a study of the nature and functions of the imāmate essentially belongs to constitutional theory, the subject will be dealt with only insofar as it relates to the conduct of foreign relations.

The imām is under obligation to see that Islam's ultimate mission, namely, the supremacy of Allah's word over this world, is carried out by the jihād. To achieve this end, the imām enforces the law that regulates the relations of believers with nonbelievers during war and peace: he issues orders for

[15] See p. 212, below.

[16] See p. 10, above.

the conduct of fighting, enforces the law in newly occupied territories and punishes Muslims and non-Muslims in his territory if they violate the law. He decides when the jihād should be continued or stopped, and he advises when the Muslims should accept peace and come to terms with the enemy, even on their own terms.

These extensive powers are not without limitations; they must be exercised within the bounds of the law, that is, in fulfillment of the objectives of the law. If the imām exercises his powers in conformity with Islam's objectives, he is fully entitled to obedience; if he fails to do so, opinion differed as to the possibility of removing him.

In the conduct of foreign relations, the imām may delegate his powers to the commanders in the field or to provincial governors: these were often given full powers to negotiate, to conduct a jihād and to divide the spoil.[17] But the imām retains a veto by his right to refuse to ratify a treaty or by his right to repudiate any arrangement, should it prove harmful to Muslim interests. He may even punish his deputies if they act contrary to what is deemed to be Islam's interests.

As God's representative on earth, charged with the enforcement of His law, the imām's rule, except perhaps to the Khārijīs, is by nature necessary; if he dies, is incapacitated, or abdicates, the Muslim community is under obligation to enthrone a new imām. If, however, the imām falls into the hands of the enemy and is not killed but is detained or imprisoned, he remains the lawful imām and the Muslim community is under obligation to seek his release by war or diplomacy.[18]

More serious situations had arisen, however, namely, the enthronement of more than one imām in different regions

[17] Ṭabarī, *Kitāb al-Jihād*, pp. 66-7.

[18] Māwardī, *Kitāb al-Aḥkām al-Sulṭāniyya*, ed. Enger (Bonn, 1853), p. 31.

within the dār al-Islām. The most important legal problem that remained unresolved was not the question of securing recognition by one of the non-Muslim rulers, since Muslim law refuses to derive validity by the recognition of a non-Muslim State, but the legal status of one imām vis-a-vis another under Muslim law. The classical theory, of course, stressed the rule that, since there was one God and one law, there must be only one ruler.[19] Some jurists, like al-Bāqillanī, Ibn Rushd (Averroes) and Ibn Khaldūn, offered a formula that if the regions of dār al-Islām had become very extensive and some of them widely separated by sea, two or more imāms might be enthroned, and each was to enforce the law in his own dominion in a manner fulfilling the ultimate objectives of Islam.[20] But neither Ibn Rushd nor Ibn Khaldūn carried the argument beyond justifying the existence of more than one caliphate; both failed to define the legal obligations of one imām toward another. Thus, the law remained inadequate regarding the pluralistic doctrine of the imāmate. Non-recognition, if not even the unlawful existence, remained the dominating rule which reflected the refusal of the Muslim jurist-theologians to recognize existing realities. It should be remarked, however, that perhaps the jurists of Western Islamdom were more inclined than their Eastern contemporaries to give legal justification to the coexistence of a separate caliphate or caliphates side by side with the 'Abbāsid caliphate. Jurisdiction over non-Muslims, whether subjects of the imām or aliens, will be treated in the following two chapters.

19 Q. XXI, 22. See p. 7 f., above.

20 See Baghdādī, *Kitāb Uṣūl al-Dīn* (Istanbul, 1928), Vol. I, pp. 274-5; *idem, Kitāb al-Farq Bayn al-Firaq* (Cairo, 1948), p. 211. Ibn Khaldūn goes so far as to admit secular rulership (*al-Muqaddima*, ed. Quatremère [Paris, 1858], Vol. I, pp. 342-55, 364-76).

Muslim Territory: Dār al-Islām

Although references to dār al-Islām and dār al-ḥarb have previously been made, no precise definitions have yet been given. It has been remarked that Muslim law binds individuals with respect to the Muslim community they belong to, not to the territory they live in. The Muslims, however, must live in a certain territory. The law, accordingly, is bound to take into consideration the relation of the territory to the individuals. But the law defines the status of the territory with respect to the Muslim community, not the status of the Muslim in relation to the territory. It follows that the legal position of a territory would depend on the allegiance of its people to Islam, not on mere proclamation that it belongs to Islam. It follows, accordingly, that any territory whose inhabitants observe Muslim law is called a Muslim territory or dār al-Islām.

This, however, is too broad a definition. Must the law be observed by the majority of the people, by a considerable number of them, or must there be certain other conditions? 'Abd al-Qāhir al-Baghdādī maintained that any territory in which Islam is accepted by its people without restrictions and Muslim authority prevails over dhimmis is dār al-Islām.[21] Others held that, in order that a Muslim territory may be regarded as dār al-Islām, the believer should be able to fulfill freely the obligations of his religion. One of the tests was whether prayers on Fridays and Īds (feast-days) could be held in the territory. The jurists maintained that such prayers could be said only where there was a wāli (representing the caliph) in whose name they were authorized, and a qāḍī who administered the law.

The territory constituting dār al-Islām may either be acquired by force ('anwatan) or by peace.[22] A sign to this effect

[21] Baghdādī, *Kitāb Uṣūl al-Dīn*, p. 270.

[22] See p. 125, above.

was placed on the pulpit of the speaker on Fridays which, if it were a sword, indicated that the city or country was taken by force; if it were a wooden staff, the city or the country was taken by peace, such as Cairo. There was a difference of opinion about Damascus, some say that half of the city was taken by force and half by peace; therefore the practice was to adopt a sword of wood to combine both signs. In the city of Madīna, which voluntarily adopted Islam, no sign is placed on the pulpit.[23]

If, however, the prayers could not be said, the Muslim territory ceased to be part of the dār al-Islām. The Ḥanafī jurists laid down three conditions under which a Muslim territory reverts to dār al-ḥarb: first, the law of the unbelievers is enforced; second, it becomes separated from dār al-Islām by non-Muslim territory; and third, no believer or dhimmī could safely reside in the territory. Some of the Ḥanafī jurists insisted that once the law of the unbelievers was enforced in place of the sharī'a, the territory ceased to be a dār al-Islām. As a result, if the believers find it difficult to reside in the territory, they must migrate to dār al-Islām. If, however, the believer found that he could safely reside and say his prayers, even though the law of the unbelievers was enforced, the territory might still be regarded, at least in theory, as a Muslim territory, on the assumption that either the Muslims might return to it or that those who stayed might have the opportunity of persuading the unbelievers to join Islam.[24]

It follows that in Muslim legal theory a territory becomes dār al-Islām or dār al-ḥarb depending on the expansion or the shrinking of the area of the validity of Muslim law in that

[23] See Sayyid Murtaḍa al-Zahīdī, *Itḥāf al-Sāda Sharḥ Iḥyā' 'Ulūm al-Dīn* (Cairo, A.H. 1311), Vol. III, p. 229. See also Edwin E. Calverley, *Worship in Islam* (Madras, 1925), p. 148.

[24] Shawkānī, *Nayl al-Awṭār* (Cairo, 1952), Vol. VIII, pp. 28-9.

territory; if the law was observed even by a few believers, the territory remained in theory a Muslim territory. This definition was endorsed by leading Muslim scholars during the latter part of the nineteenth century with regard to India. Although India was controlled by Great Britain, the jurists maintained that the ruler should not necessarily be himself a Muslim, if the sharī'a—most of it, if not all—is enforced. Since the qāḍī is a Muslim, even if he were appointed by a non-Muslim (but such an appointment was made by the consent of the Muslims) and can see that the prayers are said and the sharī'a is administered, the territory remains a Muslim territory.[25]

Classification of Muslim Territory

Muslim publicists have classified the territory of Islam into a variety of divisions and subdivisions, depending on the approach and purpose of each one of them. Some writers have stressed the tribal distribution, others the dynastic division (according to the dynasty ruling a certain region, such as the Aghlabids in North Africa, the Fāṭimids in Egypt, the Būwayhids in Persia, etc.); and still others, especially the geographers, have based their division on regional grounds. For instance, al-Muqaddasī divides the dār al-Islām into Arab and 'Ajam (Persian) zones; the latter was subdivided into eight regions and the former into six.[26] The author of *Ḥudūd al-'Ālam,* who describes not only Muslim but also non-Muslim territory, divides the world into three parts—Asia, Europe, and Libya—subdivided into fifty-one regions. The territory of Islam, following the same pattern, is classified on regional grounds.[27]

[25] Abdur-Rahim, *Principles of Muhammadan Jurisprudence* (Madras, 1911), pp. 396-7; W. W. Hunter, *The Indian Musalmans* (London, 1871), pp. 120-5.

[26] Muqaddasī, *Kitāb Aḥsan al-Taqāsim fī Ma'rifat al-Aqālim,* ed. de Goeje (Leiden, 1876), Vol. I, pp. 9-10.

[27] V. Minorsky (ed.), *Ḥudūd al-'Ālam* (London, 1937), p. 33.

In Muslim law, however, these divisions have no validity whatsoever, since the law recognizes neither division in Muslim authority nor differentiation among Muslims on racial or cultural background. The law recognizes one umma[28]—ummat Muḥammad—to whom belongs every one who professes the religion of Islam, regardless of the ruler or dynasty that enforces the law and the region (provided it lies within dār al-Islām) in which he resides. And in practice many a Muslim moved from one region governed by one ruler into the territory of another with perfect freedom without the question of loyalty ever arising, since all Muslim rulers were in theory charged to enforce the same law and practice the same religion, each in his own territory. The fact that distinguished Muslims such as the historian Ibn Khaldūn (A.D. 1406), the mystic-philosopher Ibn al-ʻArabī (A.D. 1240) and such travelers as Ibn Jubayr (A.D. 1217) and Ibn Baṭṭūṭa (A.D. 1377) have traveled extensively and changed their residences with perfect freedom demonstrates that the cultural milieu proved to be a permanent unifying factor in spite of the political division of authority and the geographical differentiation of Muslim territory.

The jurist-theologians, although recognizing no division within the dār al-Islām, have differentiated certain territories from others on the basis of sacredness and religious significance. Al-Māwardī divides the dār al-Islām into three divisions: the ḥaram; Ḥijāz; and the rest of the Muslim territory.[29] The sharīʻa provided certain rules applicable to each one of these three divisions with regard to the taxes imposed by the state, accessibility to non-Muslims and land ownership.

The ḥaram, which means the place of security, includes Makka and its suburbs, according to some jurists, and Makka

[28] See pp. 7-8, above.

[29] Māwardī, *Kitāb al-Aḥkām al-Sulṭāniyya,* ed. Enger (Bonn, 1853), p. 272.

and Madīna, according to others.[30] The latter view, however, has prevailed, and the later jurist-theologians used the term "the two ḥarams" (al-ḥaramayn al-sharīfayn), Makka and Madīna, the protection of which is a prerogative of the caliph.[31] According to traditions these two cities have been erected on the best two spots on earth, and to some, who assume the earth to have the shape of a bird, Makka and Madīna occupy the places of the bird's eyes.[32]

The ḥaram is a territory which only Muslims can visit or live in; non-Muslims, whether Scripturaries or polytheists, are denied the right of residence or transit. While Abū Ḥanīfa permitted Scripturaries to pass through this territory, though not to reside in it, all others made no exception to the rule.[33] The inhabitants of the ḥaram are ordinarily immune from war, for the Prophet Muḥammad prohibited bloodshed in this territory. Even if the inhabitants of Makka raised a rebellion against the imām, they were not, according to some jurists, liable to be punished, although most jurists permitted the imām to fight them as bughāt (dissenters).[34] It is not permitted to cut, destroy, or kill plants and animals of the ḥaram territory which are in the state of nature; but domesticated animals and agricultural products planted by man may be cut or killed. Although these rules have not been observed in practice, they reflect the degree of reverence towards the territory in which Islam had originally arisen.

30 Māwardī, p. 272, 286-90; Abū Ya'la, *al-Aḥkām al-Sulṭāniyya*, ed. al-Fiqqy (Cairo, 1938), p. 181.

31 Among the arguments put forth by the Ottoman sultans in their claim to the caliphate, in addition to its possession by force, was the fact that they were the guardians of the two ḥarams.

32 See Ibn 'Abd al-Ḥakam, *Kitāb Futūḥ Miṣr*, ed. Torrey (New Haven, 1922), p. 1.

33 Māwardī, p. 290; and Abū Ya'la, p. 179.

34 See p. 77, above; Māwardī, p. 289.

The Ḥijāz forms the second category of Muslim territory, and it occupies in the eyes of the Muslims a place next in importance to the ḥaram territory. Non-Muslims are not allowed to live, although they are permitted to travel, in this territory. This rule is based on a ḥadīth which Muḥammad is reported to have said: "expel the unbelievers from the Arab Peninsula."[35] Some jurists have narrowly interpreted this ḥadīth to cover only Makka and Madīna, others to include the Ḥijāz, and still others the whole of the Arabian Peninsula.[36] Should an unbeliever die while on travel in the Ḥijāz, his body must be removed and buried outside this territory, for the burial would constitute permanent residence which is not permitted by the law.

Finally the Ḥijāz is revered because it is the territory in which the Prophet Muḥammad received his ministry, preached Islam and passed all the years of his political career. His own property, movable and immovable, remained there, although some of his relics, such as the mantle and robe, were taken out of the Ḥijāz. Muḥammad's successors preserved and carried as symbols on the occasion of their installation as caliphs.

The rest of the dār al-Islām forms a third division which comprised all that had been occupied outside the Arabian Peninsula. In Muslim law no distinction was made regarding the various regions constituting this division. Scripturaries were permitted to live as dhimmīs; ḥarbīs could travel by amān; and even polytheists were not denied the right of residence provided they paid the poll tax. The land constituting this territory was divided into four types: (a) the land whose original owners became Muslims, called 'ushr (tithe) land; (b) occupied territory, which was divided among the Muslims,

[35] Dārimī, *Sunan* (Damascus, A.H. 1349), Vol. II, p. 233.

[36] Māwardī, p. 291; Abū Ya'la, p. 179-81; Ibn Qudāma, *al-Mughnī*, ed. Rashīd Riḍa (Cairo, A.H. 1367), Vol. VIII, p. 529.

and became also 'ushr land; (c) occupied territory which was left in the hands of its original owners, but these were required to pay the kharāj; (d) mawāt (waste) land which Muslims revived and became 'ushr land. The detailed rules governing the categories of land belong to the field of fiscal and constitutional theory which is outside the scope of this study.[37]

[37] The rules governing lands of occupied territory is treated in chapter 17. For a study of land under Islamic law, see A. N. Poliak, "Classification of Lands in Islamic Law and its Technical Terms," *American Journal of Semitic Languages and Literatures,* Vol. LVII (1940), pp. 50-62; and Frede Løkkegaard, *Islamic Taxation in the Classic Period* (Copenhagen, 1950), chaps. 1-3.

"If any one of the polytheists ask an asylum of thee, grant him an asylum, that he may hear the word of Allah, and then let him reach his place of safety." Qur'ān IX, 6.

CHAPTER XV

FOREIGNERS IN MUSLIM TERRITORY: ḤARBĪS AND MUSTA'MINS

Foreigners and Muslim Law

Although Muslim law recognizes only Muslims as persons with full legal capacity, non-Muslims have a certain legal claim to the protection of Muslim authorities if they were permitted to enter Muslim territory. A Muslim is the natural person under Muslim law who enjoys full citizenship rights; all others enjoy varying degrees of rights, depending on the type of relationship they have established with the Muslims. Three types of persons might be distinguished who do not possess full legal capacity: the ḥarbī; the musta'min; and the dhimmī. The last category, forming the subject of the next chapter, will not be dealt with here.

The Ḥarbī

The ḥarbī, whether a Scripturary or a polytheist, is a person who belongs to the dār al-ḥarb, regardless of his country of origin. Since dār al-ḥarb is legally at war with dār al-Islām, the ḥarbī is a foreigner with whom the Muslim is at war too. If the ḥarbī is a polytheist, he is liable to be killed if he encounters a Muslim in accordance with a Qur'ānic injunction which runs as follows: ". . . slay the polytheists wherever ye may find them."[1] If the ḥarbī is a Scripturary, his life can be spared, but he may be taken as a prisoner of war and enslaved.[2] The ḥarbī, however, might enter the dār al-Islām without molestation if he obtained a special permission called the amān (safe conduct) which would permit him, with his family and property, to travel or reside in the dār al-Islām for a limited period.

The Amān

The amān is a pledge of security by virtue of which the ḥarbī would be entitled to protection while he is in the dār al-Islām by Muslim authority. No longer at war with Islam during his sojurn, the ḥarbī would become a musta'min (secured). The duration of the amān must by necessity be less than a year: for if the ḥārbī requests a period which exceeded one year, he must pay the poll tax and become a dhimmī.[3]

The amān may be either given by the imām (or his representative) by virtue of muhādana or muwāda'a (truce), or by

[1] Q. IX, 5.

[2] See p. 126 ff., above.

[3] Māwardī, *al-Aḥkām al-Sulṭāniyya*, ed. Enger (Bonn, 1853), 252. Only the Ḥanbali school permits giving amān for as long a period as ten years, the full period of a truce with the unbelievers. See Buhūtī, *Kashshāf al-Qinā'* (Cairo, 1936), Vol. III, p. 82.

individual believers. The first type may be called the official amān and the other the unofficial amān.[4]

The official amān is usually given by the imām or one of his representatives either to the entire population of a territory or a city, or to a few individual ḥarbīs.[5] This type of amān is either implied in a treaty of peace, by the terms of which the ḥarbīs enjoy safe conduct, or granted by the imām or by the commander of an army to one or a few ḥarbīs for purposes of negotiations. The ḥarbīs were entitled to protection by Muslim authorities so long as they enjoyed the benefits of the amān.[6] When the purpose of the amān was achieved, the musta'min would be conducted until he returned safely to his place of origin.

The unofficial amān may be given to the ḥarbī upon request by any adult believer, free or slave, a man or a woman. There is, however, disagreement among the jurists as to the capacity of the believer who can give the amān. The Mālikī, Shāfi'ī, and Ḥanbalī jurists approve of giving slaves, men and women, the right to give amān; the Ḥanafī jurists deny the slave this right, unless he be a jihādist or be empowered by his master to do so.[7] Awzā'ī permits even Khārijīs to give amān.[8] Children

[4] Cf. N. P. Aghnides, *Mohammedan Theories of Finance* (London, 1916), p. 355.

[5] The Ḥanbalī school is averse to giving amān to the population of a whole country or a big city; only to small cities and towns should the amān be given (Buhūtī, *op. cit.,* Vol. III, pp. 82-3.)

[6] Mālik reports disapprovingly a case where a commander in the field had given an amān to a ḥarbī and then killed him. When the news reached Caliph 'Umar, he wrote to the commander calling his attention to the necessity of living up to one's own pledge of security. See Mālik ibn Anas, *al-Muwaṭṭa',* with commentary of Jalāl al-Dīn al-Suyūṭī (Cairo, 1939), Vol. I, p. 298.

[7] Ṭabarī, *Kitāb al-Jihād,* ed. Schacht (Leiden, 1933), p. 29.

[8] *Ibid.,* p. 26.

and the insane are as a rule denied the right of giving amān.[9] Abū Ḥanīfa and Shāfi'ī permit the child to give amān only when he comes of age; Awzā'ī permits him to do so when he reaches his tenth year. The dhimmīs, as a rule, are denied the right of granting amān by all schools.

The procedure of granting amān is very simple and there is no disagreement among the jurists on it. Once the ḥarbī's intention of requesting the amān was known, regardless of the language he spoke, any word or sign of approval was enough to constitute granting it. Even a hint or mere salutation are enough to grant the ḥarbī protection, provided this carried with it the intention of giving amān.[10] If the believer did not mean to give amān, but his sign or hint was understood by the ḥarbī to constitute amān, this was considered a valid amān. The case of al-Hurmuzān, it will be recalled, illustrates the giving of amān by inference, if not by a trick, without the intention of giving it.[11]

If the ḥarbī entered dār al-Islām without amān, or was unable to obtain one, he was liable to be killed unless he adopted Islam.[12] Shāfi'ī advised giving him a period of four months, at the end of which he had either to leave (conducted safely to the frontiers), pay the jizya and become a dhimmī, or adopt Islam.[13] Other jurists advise that he should be expelled, provided he is given protection until he reaches dār al-ḥarb.[14] If the ḥarbī claimed he was on a mission, carrying a message to the imām,

[9] Mālik approves of children giving amān if they understood what they were doing. See Saḥnūn, *al-Mudawwana al-Kubra* (Cairo, A.H. 1323), Vol. III, p. 41.

[10] Bukhārī, *Kitāb al-Jāmi' al-Ṣaḥīḥ*, ed. Krehl (Leiden, 1864), Vol. II, p. 296; and Buhūtī, Vol. III, p. 83.

[11] See pp. 128-9, above.

[12] Abū Yūsuf, *Kitāb al-Kharāj* (Cairo, A.H. 1352), p. 188.

[13] Shāfi'ī, *Kitāb al-Umm*, Vol. IV, p. 201.

[14] Buhūtī, Vol. III, p. 84.

he was permitted to proceed to the imām without amān, since he possessed diplomatic immunity, but if the imām found that the messenger lacked the letters of credence or that he had no message to deliver, he was liable to be killed.

The ḥarbī may enter the dār al-Islām by a mistake, or as a result of shipwreck, whereby he finds himself among the Muslims without amān. The majority of jurists advise giving the imām the choice of setting the ḥarbī free, or ordering his immediate execution, or releasing him after payment of ransom.[15]

The Musta'min's Rights and Obligations

Once the ḥarbī becomes a musta'min, he is allowed to bring with him his family and children; to visit any city of dār al-Islām except the holy cities of the Ḥijāz; to reside permanently in dār al-Islām, if he accepted the status of dhimmī and paid the jizya; and to marry a dhimmī woman and take her back with him to dār al-ḥarb (conversely, if the ḥarbī were a woman and married a dhimmī man, she had no right to take him with her to dār al-ḥarb since this might constitute potential power for use against dār al-Islām).[16] While he is enjoying his right of safe conduct, the musta'min can enter into business transactions within the limitations of the law.[17]

The musta'min, on the other hand, is expected to respect the religious beliefs and practices of the Muslims and to abstain from saying or doing anything which might be construed as lack of respect for Islam. His activities should in no way lead to harm or endanger Islam's interests. If he were a spy who entered dār al-Islām in the guise of a musta'min, he is liable to be

[15] Ṭabarī, p. 32.

[16] Marghīnānī, *al-Hidāya* (Cairo, 1936), Vol. III, p. 131-2.

[17] The ḥarbī's commercial relations with the Muslims will be discussed in chapter XXIX.

killed.[18] He is, likewise, not allowed to buy war weapons or slaves or any other kind of instruments useful in war, since all of these, regarded as contraband, might result in strengthening the dār al-ḥarb against dār al-Islām. The purchases of contraband were considered void, and the musta'min was given back his money and the weapons returned.[19] Under no circumstances, however, was the ḥarbī allowed to take them to dār al-ḥarb, if the transaction was not dissolved. Usury contracts were also prohibited.

If the Musta'min, however, violated certain rules of conduct or even committed a crime, his amān remained valid, but he was liable to be punished. Shāfi'ī distinguished between violation of devotional rules—for which the musta'min was not punished but warned that his amān might be terminated—and other rules of civil or criminal nature for which he was punished, such as other persons, believers or dhimmīs.[20] Abū Ḥanīfa and Abū Yūsuf contended that the musta'min was not liable for punishment: if he committed adultery, nothing was to be done to him; but if he stole or robbed someone, the property was taken from him. If, however, he killed a Muslim or cut his hand, he was liable to be killed or to have his own hand cut off.[21] If two or more musta'mins chose to adjudicate before a Muslim judge and apply the sharī'a, they were allowed to do so. But if a Muslim attacked the musta'min, the Muslim was punished by the imām or his representatives.[22] The Muslim,

[18] Abū Yūsuf, p. 189.

[19] Abū Yūsuf, p. 188.

[20] Shāfi'ī, *Kitāb al-Umm* (Cairo, A.H. 1321), Vol. VII, p. 326. Awzā'ī agrees with Shāfi'ī on punishing the musta'min. See Ṭabarī, p. 54.

[21] Ṭabarī, p. 56.

[22] Shaybānī, *al-Siyar al-Kabīr,* with Sarakhsi's Commentary (Hyderabad, 1335), Vol. IV, pp. 108-9. Opinions of jurists vary as to whether the Muslim is to be killed, if he killed the musta'min, or merely to pay the diyya. See Ṭabarī, pp. 56-7.

likewise, was denied the right to enter into business transactions not permitted under the sharī'a or to make certain purchases which were considered as invalid.

Termination of Amān

The amān normally terminated either when its period (not exceeding a year) expired or when the musta'min left the dār al-Islām. If he wanted to return to the dār al-Islām he had to obtain another amān.

The amān might be repudiated and the musta'min expelled by the imām at any time it was discovered that the musta'min had either concealed harmful purposes or if the imām thought that it was inconsistent with Muslim interests. The imām might even punish the Muslim who gave an amān that proved to be harmful to Islam.[23]

If the musta'min, after he returned to dār al-ḥarb, leaving his property in the dār al-Islām, suddenly died; his property could not be taken out from dār al-Islām by his heirs; instead, it would be confiscated by the State. But if the musta'min died while he was in the dār al-Islām, the amān granted was still valid for his property; his heirs could therefore take it out of the dār al-Islām if they wanted to do so.[24]

Importance of Amān

The amān served a very useful purpose for both Muslims and non-Muslims in making possible the establishment of temporary peace relations among them, which otherwise would have been impossible, owing to the rule that normal relations between Muslim and non-Muslim territories were not peaceful, but hostile. The amān may therefore be regarded as a qualify-

[23] Buhūtī, Vol. III, p. 83, 85.

[24] Shāfi'ī, Vol. IV, p. 191; Buhūtī, Vol. III, p. 86.

ing principle which permits Muslims and non-Muslims to travel in the country of the other. Thus the amān served as a passport which a foreigner obtained during his sojourn in a Muslim territory. For without such a passport no exchange of goods was possible if Muslims and non-Muslims were not allowed to leave or enter the dār al-Islām. The amān regularized the inevitable crossing of frontiers, without which illegal movements would have aggravated the tension between the two dārs, which were legally not at peace with one another. The frequent grant of amān, especially when fighting was in suspense, facilitated the establishment of normal trade relations between Muslim merchants and those beyond the frontiers of Islam.

"Fulfill Allah's covenant when ye have covenanted, and break not your oaths after asservating them, for ye thereby make Allah your surety." Qur'ān XVI, 93.

CHAPTER XVI

MUSLIMS IN NON-MUSLIM TERRITORY

Non-Muslim Territory: Dār al-Ḥarb

The dār al-Islām, it will be recalled, has been defined as the territory in which Muslim law is enforced by a Muslim authority or in which the Muslim, even if the territory falls under non-Muslim rule, can observe Muslim law with relative freedom.[1] Conversely, a territory in which non-Muslim law is enforced, and in which the Muslim cannot possibly observe his own law, is a non-Muslim territory. Thus the dār al-ḥarb, in contrast to the dār al-Islām, may be regarded as a territory outside the pale of Muslim law; it lacks the legal competence to enter into relations with dār al-Islām on the basis of equality. It follows that any arrangement made between the two dārs is, by necessity, of short duration, since it carries with it no implied recognition or change in the war status.

[1] See p. 155, above.

The dār al-ḥarb, however, although outside the pale of Muslim law, is not regarded as a no-man's land. The fact that a state of war exists between the two dārs implies that the dār al-ḥarb is entitled, under Muslim law, to conduct its hostile relations with Islam in accordance with the Muslim law of war. Thus the Muslim is under obligation to respect the rights of non-Muslims, both combatants and civilians, as prescribed by his own law, while fighting is in progress.[2]

During the short intervals of peace, when the jihād is in suspense, Islam takes cognizance of the authority or authorities that exist in countries which are not under Muslim rule. But this cognizance of the need of authority does not constitute recognition, in the modern sense of the term, since recognition implies approval of the conduct of non-Muslim authorities by Islam. Islam's cognizance of non-Muslim rule merely means that authority is, by nature, necessary for the survival of society. It follows that, if a Muslim happens to travel or reside in a non-Muslim territory, he is not, in principle, expected to undermine or oppose the authority of that territory, unless charged with such a duty by the imām. He is under an obligation to respect, if he entered by amān, the law of this territory as well as that of his own. Should he find there is a conflict between the law of this country and his own law, there is no doubt as to what his choice must be.

Conduct of the Muslim in a Non-Muslim Territory Under Amān

In the same way as the non-Muslim enters Muslim territory by amān, the conditions of which require certain limitations upon the freedom and conduct of the non-Muslim, so should the Muslim enter non-Muslim territory with similar limitations

[2] See chaps. 9-11.

in mind even if they were not specifically stated.[3] The Muslim is under obligation to abstain from doing any harm or injury to non-Muslims as long as he enjoys the benefits of their amān. Moreover, he is under obligation to observe the rules of his own law in such matters as usury or the sale of wine and pork, even though permitted by the law of the country of his sojourn, in his relations with non-Muslims.[4] For Muslim law, as has been repeatedly stated, is binding on the Muslim regardless of the territory he lives in. He is also under obligation to live up to his promises as well as to fulfill all contractual arrangements even after he has returned to dār al-Islām.[5] For instance, if he has borrowed or stolen certain property, it must be returned even after he has left dār al-ḥarb. But during his stay in dār al-ḥarb, the Muslim should by no means engage in strengthening that territory against dār al-Islām. Thus he should neither give intelligence nor should he help in the manufacturing of weapons and war materiel which might be used against Islam.[6] The Muslim is also advised to abstain from marrying a ḥarbī woman, even if she were a Scripturary, for such a marriage might result in leaving his children in the service of dār al-ḥarb.[7]

The Muslim is liable to punishment after he returns to dār al-Islām if he has encroached (while still in enemy territory) upon the rights of another Muslim or committed a crime

[3] Buhūtī, *Kashshāf al-Qinā'* (Cairo, 1947), Vol. III, p. 85.

[4] He is also prohibited from carrying with him the Qur'ān to the dār al-ḥarb, as both the Prophet Muḥammad and the jurists did not like to see the unbelievers show disrespect to the Book of the believers. See Bukhārī, *Kitāb al-Jāmi' al-Ṣaḥīḥ*, ed. Krehl (Leiden, 1864), Vol. II, p. 245.

[5] Buhūtī, Vol. III, p. 85; Marghinānī, *al-Hidāya* (Cairo, 1936), Vol. III, pp. 130-1; Shaybānī, *al-Siyar al-Kabīr*, with Sarkhasī's Commentary (Hyderabad, A.H. 1335), Vol. I, p. 165.

[6] Shaybānī, Vol. III, pp. 217-9.

[7] *Ibid.*, Vol. IV, p. 99.

against him, provided that sufficient evidence is supplied by eye-witnesses.

Conduct of the Muslim in Non-Muslim Territory Without Amān

If the Muslim entered dār al-ḥarb without amān, he is under no obligation to observe its laws and regulations as others do under amān. In Muslim legal theory, the Muslim in a non-Muslim territory without amān is at war with that territory. He is, therefore, under no obligation to submit to the law of non-Muslim territories, although in the meantime he is not expected to engage in hostile actions. If the Muslim, however, enters ḍār al-ḥarb by permission of the imām he may seize property or take prisoners of war in the same way as the jihādists are permitted during actual fighting. He is also required to refrain from acts prohibited by law. Thus, if the Muslim commits adultery, or eats pork and drinks wine, or if he encroaches upon the rights of another Muslim, he is liable to punishment after he returns to dār al-Islām. Only the Ḥanafī jurists relax the limitations of the law, except in matters related to usury and debt.[8] Abū Ḥanīfa is an advocate of the doctrine that the law of Islam is not binding upon Muslims in non-Muslim territory.[9]

Muslim Prisoners

Muslim warriors who fall into the hands of the enemy and are taken to dār al-ḥarb are under obligation to live up to their promises if they are set free on parole. If the Muslim prisoner is permitted to return to his country in order to obtain funds for ransom, he must fulfill his promise and return to the enemy

[8] Shaybānī, Vol. II, p. 223.

[9] Ṭabarī, *Kitāb al-Jihād*, ed. Schacht (Leiden, 1933), p. 62; Shaybānī, Vol. IV, pp. 107-8.

if he fails to obtain them.[10] Some jurists, however, including Shāfi'ī, maintain that Muslim prisoners are under no obligation to live up to their promises in such matters as returning to the country, even if they gave such promises.[11] If, on the other hand, the prisoners gave no promises, they were not only free to flee but also free to destroy enemy property or kill non-Muslims on their way back to dār al-Islām.

While Muslim prisoners are residing in dār al-ḥarb they are under obligation not only to observe Muslim law, unless circumstances prevent them from so doing, but also to observe the law of that territory, provided it does not conflict with their own law. They are, however, under no obligation to take part in fighting with enemy warriors, even if promised a share in the spoils of war.[12] They are also under obligation not to pass on intelligence useful for the enemy against Islam. If the prisoner, under duress, is compelled to commit acts prohibited by Muslim law, including even the renunciation of Islam, he is not liable to punishment.[13] If the prisoner is a woman who is subjected to physical hardships, she must at first endure persecution; but if she fears death, she is permitted to submit to enemy demands unwillingly.[14]

[10] Ṭabarī, p. 183.

[11] *Ibid.*, pp. 188-9.

[12] *Ibid.*, pp. 194-6. Only Awzā'ī and Thawrī saw no reason why Muslim prisoners could not take part in fighting with enemy warriors, if fighting were not directed against Islam. *Ibid.*, p. 195; Shaybānī, Vol. III, pp. 234-7.

[13] Ṭabarī, p. 197-8.

[14] *Ibid.*, pp. 196-7.

"Whoever wrongs one with whom a compact has been made [i.e., a dhimmī] and lays on him a burden beyond his strength, I will be his accuser." a ḥadīth.

CHAPTER XVII

STATUS OF THE DHIMMĪS

Islam and Non-Muslim Subjects

The status of minority groups has been dealt with differently under the different systems of law, varying from permanent social servitude to temporary penalization as long as the group persisted in its attachment to a certain religious or cultural exclusiveness. Islam provided an interesting experiment in the treatment of subject races that had originally entered into compacts with the Muslim authorities, the provisions of which became later part of the law of Islam. This law provides that it is in the competence of any member of the protected communities, in contrast to other penalized groups, at any moment to join the dominant community by merely pronouncing the shahāda, the Muslim formula of professing the faith. As long as they remained attached to their own religion, the dhimmīs were allowed to enforce their own law (except when Muslim interests were involved), but if they wanted to avail themselves of Muslim justice, they were not denied access to Muslim courts. The canon laws and judicial organizations of the dhimmī communities constitute a separate field of research, but this is obviously outside the scope of our present study.

Meaning of Dhimmī

The tolerated communities within Islam included not only the so-called ahl al-Kitāb (people of the Book) or Scripturaries, but also idolaters ('abadat al-aṣnām) and fire-worshippers, provided they have accepted residence in any Muslim territory except the Arabian Peninsula.[1] The Scripturaries include Christians, Jews, Magians (Zoroastrians), Samaritans, and Sabians. Polytheists (mushrikūn) were, as a rule, denied the status of dhimmīs (especially in Arabia), since they had to choose between Islam and the sword.

Strictly speaking, the Magians were not a Scripturary community, for, according to traditions, they neither believed in Allah nor did they possess a Scripture; but since they believed in a certain deity, the Prophet Muḥammad and the early caliphs considered them in the same category as the Scripturaries and treated them as a protected community.[2]

The term ahl al-Kitāb was applied to all non-Muslims who possessed a scripture whether they resided within or without the dār al-Islām. The ahl al-Kitāb who resided in the dār al-Islām and accepted Muslim rule were called dhimmīs. Literally the word dhimma means a compact which the believer agrees to respect, the violation of which makes him liable to dhamm

[1] Abū Yūsuf, *Kitāb al-Kharāj* (Cairo, A.H. 1352), pp. 128-9. The idolaters were probably included after Muḥammad's time as a matter of expediency.

[2] On the authority of 'Ali the Muslims accepted the view that the Magians were at one time in possession of a scripture which was lost. See Abū Yūsuf, *op. cit.*, p. 130.

(blame).[3] Legally, the term refers to a certain status, the acquisition of which entitles the person to certain rights which must be protected by the state. These rights include, in addition to security of life and property, an indefinite amān, but it does not confer full citizenship, since the Scripturary, although believing in Allah, fails to believe in His Apostle; he is therefore not a true believer and is not entitled to the full membership in the Muslim brotherhood. Punishment for disbelief in the Qur'ān and Allah's Apostle is implied in certain disabilities; at the same time the dhimmī, by paying the poll tax is entitled to full protection against any possible encroachment or molestation.

The question has been raised as to whether it is not inconsistent with Islam's objective, seeking ultimate supremacy of the true religion, to accept payment in money for persistence in unbelief. Sarakhsī held that the object is not pecuniary consideration, but the invitation of unbelievers to Islam in the most gentle manner. By being allowed to live among Muslims, the dhimmīs will be attracted by the beauties of the Muslim faith, and they may willingly accept it.[4]

Dhimmī Compact with Muḥammad

The text books of the classical jurist-theologians provide an elaborate set of rules governing the relations of the dhimmīs with Muslims. The restrictive character of the rules raises the query as to whether some of them have not been the product of an age of intolerence and oppressive rule. A study of the early Muslim theory and practice regarding the treatment of non-Muslim communities might throw light on the subsequent changes it had undergone in later periods.

[3] Jurjānī, *Kitāb al-Ta'rīfāt*, ed. Flügel, p. 112; and Najm al-Dīn al-Nasafī, *Ṭalibat al-Ṭalaba* (Istanbul, A.H. 1311), p. 80.

[4] Sarakhsī, *Kitāb al-Mabsūṭ*, (Cairo, A.H. 1324), Vol. X, p. 77.

Muḥammad's relations with Scripturaries who were willing to come to terms with him showed both religious tolerance and prudence in his early political career. This is clearly reflected in the Madīna Treaty (circa A.D. 623), concluded between the Aws and Khazraj tribes, to which the Jews were allowed to adhere. With regard to the relations of the Jews to the Muslims, the Treaty provided:[5]

> The Jews of Banū 'Awf form a nation with the believers. The Jews shall have their own religion, and the Muslims their own religion. . . .
>
> No Jew is allowed to join [the Muslims in battle] without the authorization of Muḥammad. . . .
>
> The Jews shall contribute to expense for battle so long as they fight with believers.

This treaty imposes no restrictions on the Jews save their maintenance as a separate religious group within Muḥammad's larger community. They were not bound to take part in war, unless invited to do so, but if they did they must contribute their share of expenses in the joint action. No tribute or any other disability was yet imposed; indeed, the Jews were treated almost on equal footing with the Muslims. The need for allies was, perhaps, the compelling reason for a compromise with Scripturary communities; but it is also true that after Islam had been firmly established, especially after the capture of Makka (A.D. 630), Muḥammad required no more than the paying of tribute, a pre-Islamic practice, which was formalized in a Qur'ānic injunction (probably about the year A.D. 631) which runs as follows:

> Fight against those to whom the Scriptures have been given who believe not in Allah nor the Last Day, and who forbid not that which Allah and His Apostle have forbidden, and who profess not the profession of the truth, until they pay the jizya out of hand, and they be humbled.[6]

[5] The order of the foregoing provisions is rearranged for purposes of clarity. For full text of the treaty, see pp. 206-9, below.

[6] Q. IX, 29.

Except perhaps certain warnings against possible Scripturary intrigues, the Qur'ān imposes no other restrictions; indeed the Qur'ān and the ḥadīth stress Muslim obligations not only to tolerate but also to protect the Scripturaries from possible attack and molestation if they maintained peaceful relations with Islam.[7] Abū Yūsuf and Balādhurī report several charters issued by Muḥammad to the Scripturaries of Tabāla, Jarash, Adhruḥ, Maqna, Khaybar, Najrān, and Ayla, in which they were promised the protection of their lives, property, and beliefs in return for paying the jizya. The text of the compact with Najrān, a typical example, is as follows:

> In the name of Allah, the Compassionate, the Merciful. This is [the pact] which has been issued by Muḥammad, the Apostle of Allah, to the people of Najrān, to whom his authority shall extend—their fruit, their money and their slaves. All these are left to them except the payment of 2,000 uncial dresses (ḥulal al-awāqī), of which 1,000 to be paid in the month of Rajab and 1,000 in the month of Safar together with an ounce of silver on each payment. If the produce exceeded, or became less than [the tribute], the latter will be estimated in proportion to the former. The people of Najrān are expected to lend [the Muslims] shields, horses, animals and other objects. They must also entertain and provide supplies for my messengers for a maximum period of twenty days, but these must not be kept with them more than a month. If there were war in al-Yaman or in Ma'arra, they must supply clothes for thirty persons, thirty horses and thirty camels. If some of what was lent to my messengers had been destroyed or perished, [the people of Najrān] shall be compensated. They shall have the protection of Allah and the promise of Muḥammad, the Apostle of Allah, that they shall be secured their lives, property, lands, creed, those absent and those present, their families, their churches, and all that they possess. No bishop or monk shall be displaced from his parish or monastery and no priest shall be forced to abandon his priestly life. No hardships or humiliation shall be imposed on them nor shall their land be occupied by [our] army. Those who seek justice, shall have it: there will be no oppressors nor oppressed. Those who practice usury, shall seek

[7] Q. II, 62; V 82; XXXIX, 46; Bukhārī, *Kitāb al-Jāmi' al-Ṣaḥīḥ*, ed. Krehl (Leiden, 1864), Vol. II, pp. 291-301.

no protection from me. No one shall be taken as responsible for the fault of another. For the continuation of this compact, the guarantee of Allah and the assurance of Muḥammad, Apostle of Allah, sanction what has been written until Allah manifests his authority so long as [the people of Najrān] remain faithful and act in accordance with their obligations, giving no support to oppression. Done in the presence of the following witnesses: Abū Sufyān Ibn Ḥarb, Ghaylān Ibn 'Amr, Mālik Ibn 'Awf of [the tribe of] Banū Naṣr, al-Aqra' Ibn Ḥabīs al-Ḥanzalī, and al-Mughīra Ibn Shu'ba. 'Abd-Allah Ibn Abū Bakr acted as secretary.[8]

A similar pact was issued by Muḥammad to the Christians of Ayla ('Aqaba). Muḥammad sought to bring the last of the Scripturary communities in line with others, thus making Islam supreme over Arabia. He addressed a letter to Yūḥanna (John), the Christian chief of Ayla, inviting him to come to terms with Islam. The text of the letter follows:

To Yūḥanna Ibn Ru'ba and the chiefs of the people of Ayla. Peace be on you. Praise be to Allah, besides whom there is no god. I shall not fight you until I have written to you. Accept Islam or pay the jizya, and obey Allah and His Apostle and the messengers of the Apostle. Honor the messengers and clothe them with good clothing, but not clothing of conquerors.[9] Clothe Zayd with good clothing for so long as my messengers will be pleased, so am I. . . . If you desire security by land and by sea, obey Allah and His Apostle and you will be defended from every attack by Arab or 'ajam [foreigner]. If you refuse, I will not accept anything from you until I have fought against you, and have slain your men, and have taken captive [sabī] your women and children. I am the Apostle of Allah; I believe in the truth, in Allah, His Books, His Apostles, and in Jesus son of Mary, who is the word of Allah, and I believe in him as an Apostle of Allah.

[8] Abū Yūsuf, *Kitāb al-Kharāj*, pp. 72-3; Balādhurī, *Kitāb Futūḥ al-Buldān*, ed. de Goeje (Leiden, 1866), p. 65. For an English translation, see Philip K. Hitti, *The Origins of the Islamic State* (New York, 1916), pp. 101-2; for a French translation, see M. Ḥamidullah, *Documents sur la diplomatie Musulmane* (Paris, 1935), pp. 47-8 (Corpus).

[9] Clothing given to conquerors was taken by force, and consequently the conquered people were not willing to give the best they had.

Come before evil will touch you! I have commanded my messengers to you. Give Ḥarmala three wasqs [measure] of barley. For Ḥarmala has interceded for you. As for me, if it were not for Allah and for that [intercession], I would not have communicated with you until you have been brought face to face with my army. If you obey my messengers, Allah will be your neighbor and so is Muḥammad and his followers. My messengers are Shurḥabīl, Ubay, Abū Ḥarmala, Ḥurayth Ibn Zayd al-Ṭā'ī.

Whatever they will agree upon with you, I shall accept. Upon you is the protection of Allah and His Apostle. If you submit, then peace be on you.

Send the people of Maqna to their land.[10]

Yūḥanna hastened to Muḥammad's camp; he was received as a guest with kindness and was given a mantle. The negotiations resulted in the following pact:[11]

In the name of Allah, the Compassionate, the Merciful;

This is a guarantee from Allah and from the Prophet Muḥammad, the Apostle of Allah, to Yūhanna Ibn Ru'ba and the people of Ayla;

For their vessels and their travelers is the security of Allah and Muḥammad, the Apostle of Allah, and for all who are with them, whether from al-Shām [Syria] or al-Yaman or from the sea-coast;

Those who cause a grave event [ḥadath],[12] their wealth will not save them; they will be the fair prize of whosoever captures them;

It will be unlawful to prevent them [the people of Ayla] from going to the springs of water, or to stop them from the road they follow, by land or by sea;

This is written by Juhaym Ibn al-Ṣalt and Shuraḥbīl Ibn Ḥasana by the permission of the Apostle of Allah.

The foregoing instruments are of particular interest for indicating not only the early character of Muslim-Scripturary relations but also the simplicity and lack of social differences between Muslims and non-Muslims. It might be argued that

[10] Ibn Sa'd, *Kitāb al-Ṭabaqāt al-Kabīr,* ed. Edward Sachau (Leiden, 1917), Vol. I, pp. 28-29.

[11] Ibn Hishām, *Kitāb al-Sīra,* ed. F. Wüstenfeld (Göttingen, 1859), Vol. II, p. 902; Ibn-Sa'd, *op. cit.,* Vol. I, Part 2, p. 37.

[12] Ḥadath may mean a serious event or a calamity.

perhaps prudence dictated a policy of conciliation, but it is also true that inherent in Muḥammad's teaching was the toleration of those who possessed a scripture. For the main purpose of his mission was, in the first place, the belief in Allah; the recognition of his being the Apostle of Allah, which meant the tacit admission of his authority, was subordinate to the first. The Scripturaries, however, although believing in Allah but not in His Apostle, had, by the very fact of their submission to Muḥammad's pacts, recognized his overlordship (i.e., his divinely ordained authority) without the appellation Apostle of Allah. Realistic in his approach to a practical problem, Muḥammad accepted this compromise with the hope, perhaps, that toleration might have a better effect in persuading these half-believers to embrace the true belief.[13] It was therefore in pursuance of this policy that no social or other discriminatory measures were imposed beyond the jizya, paid in the form of tribute, not unlike the payment of zakāt by Muslims. If Muḥammad ever resorted to crushing his opponents, such actions were dictated by *raison d'état*—for failure to obey authority—not for lack of religious tolerance.

The Legislation of 'Umar

In addition to the Qur'ānic injunctions and the practice of Muḥammad, the jurist-theologians often refer to a covenant issued by the Caliph 'Umar I in which the position of Scripturaries, after the expansion of the Muslim Empire, has been redefined. It is unnecessary at this stage to touch the content of the Covenant, which will be dealt with later. But it is important to state at the outset whether the detailed provisions of the Covenant were, as is generally accepted, laid down by 'Umar in a single document. Whether 'Umar had laid down a consistent policy or dealt with Islam's problem from time to time is an

[13] Q. II, 255; III, 61-64; XXIX, 45.

important matter which has bearing on the position of dhimmīs in early Islam. A study of the formulation of 'Umar's policy will therefore help to indicate the development of the position of the dhimmīs after Muḥammad's death and the various stages it passed through before it reached the form reproduced in the jurists' textbooks.

Abū Yūsuf and Balādhurī report that the initiative to come to terms with the Christians of Iraq and Syria by signing treaties of peace was taken by Khālid ibn al-Walīd and Abū 'Ubayda. The Caliph 'Umar ratified these treaties. Since Balādhurī's texts agree in general with those of Abū Yūsuf, and since Abū Yūsuf's texts provide the earliest recorded sources for later juridical formulations, these are the texts which will be reproduced hereunder. Abū Yūsuf states that the forces under Khālid, the commander-in-chief in Iraq, took many towns by force ('anwatan); but he met stiff resistance at Ḥīra. Negotiations took place which resulted in an agreement between him and the people of this city. This is the first treaty we have on record defining the relations between the Christians of Ḥīra and the Muslim authorities. The text of the treaty follows:[14]

> In the name of Allah, the Merciful, the Compassionate. This is the agreement between Khālid ibn al-Walīd and the people of Ḥīra. The Caliph Abū Bakr has ordered me to proceed from Yamāma to the people of 'Iraq—Arabs and Persians—to call them first to believe in Allah and His Apostle and to promise them Paradise [if they accepted Islam] and to warn them with the Fire [if they refuse]. If Islam is accepted, they shall have the same rights and obligations as the Muslims. I have arrived finally at Ḥīra and met Iyās ibn Qabīṣa al-Ṭā'ī with a few of the leaders of the city. I invited them to believe in Allah and His Apostle, but they refused. I have therefore offered them either to accept the jizya or fighting. They replied: "we do not want to fight; we want peace with the same conditions as those accepted by other People of the Book, namely, the paying of the jizya." [I have accepted this] and counted them; they were seven thousand:

[14] Abū Yūsuf, *op. cit.*, pp. 143-4.

one thousand of them of old age were exempted; those who have to pay the jizya were six thousand. Our agreement was accordingly based on paying sixty thousand [dinārs].

It was therefore agreed that [the people of Ḥīra] will not violate their compact; that they shall not support an unbeliever against an Arab or Persian Muslim, and that they shall not pass on any intelligence to them. . . . If any of their men become weak and old, or inflicted with a disease, or was rich and had become poor, the jizya shall be lifted from him and he and his family shall be supported by the Public Treasury [bayt māl al-Muslīmīn] so long as he resides in the dār al-Islām. If they [the men] leave the dār al-Islām, their families shall not be supported by the Muslims. If any of their slaves adopt Islam, they are to be sold with the highest possible price and paid to their [Scripturary] masters. They [the Scripturaries] shall have the right to wear any kind of clothes save military uniforms, provided their clothes shall not be similar to those of the Muslims. If any one of them is found to wear a uniform, he is to be arrested and to give reasons for so doing; if [his answer is unsatisfactory] he is to be punished by a fine equivalent to the price of his uniform. It was agreed that their payment [of the jizya] shall be made to the Public Treasury; if they ever needed support, it is to be given from that Treasury.

The significance of this agreement, the first in a series of treaties signed between the Muslims and the Christians of the occupied territory, lies in the character of obligations assumed by both parties: the Christians agreed to lead a civilian life, to give up the wearing of military uniforms, and to refrain from supporting the enemy or giving him intelligence. The Muslim authorities were to receive the jizya, in the form of a collective tribute estimated on the number of those eligible for payment, in exchange for security and protection. Abū Yūsuf said that this was "the first jizya collected from the East,"[15] which clearly indicates that this agreement provided the earliest stipulations which the Christians of the Fertile Crescent accepted from the Muslim authorities. There is nothing in this arrangement

[15] Abū Yūsuf, p. 145.

which might be construed as humiliating, whether in the payment of the jizya or in giving up rights of engagement in military activities: for the capitulation of any people would entail giving up civil and military powers to the conquering authority who undertakes the responsibility of defense, the jizya or tribute might be construed as payment for the enjoyment of the right of protection and security which the Muslim authority conferred. It should be noted that no land tax (kharāj) was imposed nor was the jizya in the sense of a poll tax on every individual required: only a jizya in a collective form—a tribute—was imposed, whose payment carried no humiliating stigma. The treaty makes no reference to the possibility of increasing the jizya; rather it stresses the stipulation that if the rich were no longer able to pay, they were to be relieved of it and would be supported by the Muslim treasury. In this, it is significant to note, the Scripturary was put on the same footing as the Muslim poor in becoming the benefactor of the Muslim state.

Abū Yūsuf, supported by Balādhurī, reports that a number of other towns such as Bānīqiya and 'Ayn al-Tamr, capitulated on similar terms. In the case of Syria, however, additional stipulations were made, apparently at the suggestion of Abū 'Ubayda, which Caliph 'Umar approved, and were later extended to cover all Scripturaries under Muslim rule. Here again Balādhurī, as well as Ṭabarī and Ya'qūbī, on the whole agree with Abū Yūsuf's account, although certain variations may be noted in the texts of the treaties. Abū Yūsuf's text, reported on the authority of Makḥūl (who witnessed the military operations in Syria), may be summarized as follows: peace between the Muslims and the people of Damascus was concluded on their paying the jizya, provided that the Muslims promised them security of their lives, property, and churches. It was also stipulated that no new churches were to be built, although repair or rebuilding was permitted. The people of Damascus were under obligation to build bridges, freely, to act as hosts for three days to believers when passing their places, as well as to guide them if this was needed, and to light beacons for those who fight in Allah's path. They were not allowed to beat or show disrespect to a believer, nor to ring their bells at the time of the call to prayer, nor to display their crosses or take their pigs to Muslim gatherings. They were not allowed to wear uniforms or carry arms, nor to take out their banners during their feasts, except during holidays.[16]

These terms, favorably received by the people of Damascus, induced others to surrender on similar terms. When they were communicated to Caliph 'Umar for approval, he replied:[17]

> I have examined . . . the terms of peace reached with the people of the towns and cities [of Syria] and I have consulted the Companions of the Apostle of Allah, each giving his own opinion. My own opinion [based on these] and on the Book of Allah [citing Q. LIX, 6-8] is that you should keep what has been given by Allah to you [of the land] in the hands of its people, since they are the best fitted for its cultivation, and to impose on them the jizya in accordance with their ability . . . as stated in Allah's Book [Q. IX, 29]. If the jizya is paid by them [the dhimmīs] you should require no more of them. . . . For if we divide the land [among us] nothing will be left for our descendants. . . . [If the land is left with its people] the Muslim will be able to live on its produce.
>
> You may therefore impose on them [the dhimmīs] the jizya, never to take them as prisoners, nor to do any injustice or harm to them or to take any of their property unless you have a claim to it. You must fulfill the obligations you accepted in accordance with your agreement with them.
>
> As to the request of taking out their crosses during their holidays once a year, you should not prevent them from so doing outside the city, provided they agree not to take with them their banners and standards.

Although Abū Yūsuf reproduces only 'Umar's letter approving the policy proposed by Abū 'Ubayda, it is understood that

[16] Abū Yūsuf, pp. 138-9.
[17] *Ibid.*, pp. 140-1.

'Umar had approved of Khālid's policy, too, and that all the treaties signed with the Scripturaries were to remain in force to the Day of Resurrection.[18]

In 'Umar's letter to Abū 'Ubayda we note not only a new stipulation regarding the crosses and churches, which were later enforced upon all the dhimmīs (although Khālid's treaty with the Christians of Iraq carried no such stipulation) but also a statement of policy regarding the treatment of land acquired from enemy territory. 'Umar insisted that the land—presumably rural, not in towns and cities—should not be divided as a spoil (ghanīma) among the warriors (the jihādists), but was to be immobilized and kept in the hands of the dhimmī peasants ('ulūj) who were to till it and pay the jizya, "in accordance with their ability to pay," for the benefit of all Muslims and their descendants, not only for those who took the field. It will be noted that both Khālid's treaty and that of Abū 'Ubayda use the term jizya in the sense of tribute to be paid by the dhimmīs, regardless of the source of income; 'Umar's letter refers only to the land which the dhimmīs were permitted to retain and pay the jizya. The question might be raised whether 'Umar required an additional rental (in the form of a land tax), or such a tax was not required, since most of the dhimmīs were peasants living on the land. No satisfactory answer could be given by a mere examination of the texts of the treaties given by Abū Yūsuf and Balādhurī, although both state that a poll tax (jizya) as well as a land tax (kharāj) were required in accordance with 'Umar's order.

Jizya and Kharāj

The uncertainty about jizya and kharāj has led several scholars to formulate a number of theories as to what the early juridical rules were regarding the taxation system in occupied

18 Abū Yūsuf, p. 147.

enemy territory. Julius Wellhausen contended that the jizya imposed at the time of conquest was in the form of a collective tribute, consisting of a fixed sum of money and a fixed amount of agricultural products. This tribute included a tax on land (kharāj) and a tax on the individual (jizya), but the Muslim authorities were not concerned with the way the taxes were collected. If at times only one of the two terms was used, it was because the two terms were then synonymous and signified merely tribute. The distinction between these two taxes as poll tax (jizya) and land tax (kharāj) was a later distinction made by the jurists and applied to early Muslim practice. Thus, to Wellhausen, a dhimmī who adopted Islam was entitled to be free from all tribute, not only the jizya. The practice of preventing Muslims from buying land or converts from paying land tax was introduced by the Caliph 'Umar Ibn 'Abd al-'Azīz and then formulated into a general rule to collect kharāj from all land, regardless of the person who owned it, whether a dhimmī or a convert.[19]

Wellhausen's theory has been accepted by several scholars, such as Carl Becker and Prince Caetani,[20] and rejected by Daniel C. Dennett.[21] Except for differences on certain particular points, Becker and Caetani support Wellhausen. Dennett, however, offers an improvement on Wellhausen's theory, which answers certain questions hitherto unanswered. He rightly makes the observation that there was no uniform rule of taxation. This answers the question as to why there are certain conflicting passages in the early Muslim authorities,

[19] J. Wellhausen, *The Arab Kingdom and Its Fall,* trans., M. G. Weir (Calcutta, 1927), pp. 276-81.

[20] L. Caetani, *Annali Dell' Islam* (Milano, 1912), Vol. V, pp. 280-532; and C. H. Becker, *Beitrage zur Geschichte Agyptens unter dem Islam,* Strassburg, 1903, Vol. II, pp. 81 ff.

[21] Daniel C. Dennett, *Conversion and Poll Tax in Early Islam* (Cambridge, Massachusetts, 1950).

because these passages refer to various parts of the Muslim State. While Dennett agrees with Wellhausen that the terms jizya and kharāj were used interchangeably; he rejects Wellhausen's interpretation that these merely meant tribute. Dennett contends that in a general sense both jizya and kharāj simply meant tax, since the general sense of tax existed from earliest times.

Dennett's thesis offers considerable improvement on that of Wellhausen, but it suffers from certain defects. His contention that jizya and kharāj were used interchangeably (following Wellhausen, Becker, etc.) for the term tax, not for tribute (as Wellhausen asserted), is only partially correct. As we pointed out in the case of Khālid's treaty,[22] the jizya was estimated on the population of Ḥīra (6,000 dinārs on 6,000 eligible out of 7,000 of the inhabitants of the town); its nature, however, was more of a collective tribute than a poll tax paid by each individual to the Muslim authorities. Wellhausen is not far from the truth in using the term tribute, but it should be kept in mind that it was based on the population of a certain town. Nor is Dennett right in asserting that both jizya and kharāj were used in the sense of tax: only kharāj, not jizya, was used in the general sense of tax. For the term jizya had acquired the special sense of poll tax (not merely tax) long before the time of Muslim conquest both within and without Arabia. Dennett himself states, on the authority of Christensen and Lot,[23] that there existed in Syria and Mesopotamia a poll tax at the time of the Muslim conquest. The term jizya, Aramaic gzīthā, signified a difference between believers and unbelievers. Since the Qur'ān (Q. IX, 29) stresses this specific meaning, it would

[22] See p. 183, above.

[23] Arthur Christensen, *L'Iran sous les Sassanides* (Paris, 1936), p. 118, 362; Ferdinand Lot, *L'Impot foncier et la Capitation personnelle* (Paris, 1928), pp. 26-40; Dennett, *op. cit.*, pp. 14-16, 51-5.

seem unnecessary to assume that jizya meant tax, in order to fit the hypothesis that jizya and kharāj were used interchangeably.

The term kharāj (Greek *choregia*), however, was used in the general sense of tax. The Qur'ān refers to kharāj as an income tax favored by God.[24] Abū Yūsuf, Balādhurī, Ya'qūbī and Ibn Sallām speak of the "kharāj on land" and the "Kharāj on the head" or the neck, which obviously mean merely tax; as for poll tax, they as a rule use the term "jizya on the head" or the neck. Virtually without exception these jurists have never used the term "jizya on the land" in the general sense of tax; only Ibn 'Abd al-Ḥakam does so, and this may refer to an Egyptian usage.[25]

In the absence of a general term for tax, for which Ibn Sallām (died A.H. 224) uses the word ḍarība, early jurists such as Abū Yūsuf, Yahya Ibn Ādam and Qudāma Ibn Ja'far, entitled their works on the fiscal and taxation systems as *Kitāb al-Kharāj*, but no one called his book *Kitāb al-Jizya*.[26] In both the *Lisān al-'Arab* and *Tāj al-'Arūs* the general sense of tax (itāwa) is stressed, in addition to land tax.[27] It follows that kharāj—not jizya—was used in the general sense of tax.

Although the initial Muslim practice of imposing the kharāj and jizya in the conquered territories varied from one region to another, a more uniform rule developed after a short time, especially under the Caliph 'Umar Ibn 'Abd al-'Azīz (died A.D. 720). This uniform rule became the basis for the classical jurists' formulation of the law of jizya and kharāj.

It will be recalled that the towns which originally sur-

[24] Q. XXIII, 74.

[25] Ibn 'Abd al-Ḥakam, *Kitāb Futūh Miṣr*, ed. C. C. Torrey (New Haven, 1922), p. 154.

[26] Ṭabarī's *Kitāb al-Jihād wa Kitāb al-Jizya* are merely fragments of *Kitāb Ikhtilāf al-Fuqahā.*

[27] *Lisān al-'Arab,* Vol. III, p. 76, 77; *Tāj al-'Arūs,* Vol. III, p. 28.

rendered by peace treaties—such as Ḥīra, Ullays, 'Ayn al-Tamr, and Bānīqiya, in the Sawād, and Damascus, Ba'labakk, Ḥims, and Jerusalem, in Syria—were required to pay jizya in the form of a tribute based on the total eligible population of the towns (such as Ḥīra to pay 6,000 dinārs; Ḥims, 170,000 dinārs). This tribute, which was at first to satisfy the general rule of jizya, became in practice the jizya paid by each individual dhimmī, the reason being that those who became Muslims in each town were freed of their jizya, while the sum total of the jizya as a tribute was paid by the remaining dhimmīs. This naturally raised protests, but the local authorities would not change the practice until 'Umar II enforced a uniform rule that all dhimmīs must pay the jizya, in accordance with the Qur'ānic rule, each on his own head. A case in point is that of the Christians of Najrān, in their new home of Najrāniyya in Iraq. Balādhurī reports that by death or conversion the population dwindled, but neither Mu'āwaiya nor others would reduce the tribute. 'Umar II reinterpreted their covenant with Muḥammad and changed their tribute to poll tax, on the basis of the uniform rule of "jizya on the head."[28]

The Caliph 'Umar I, in a similar way, dealt with the territories that surrendered by force ('anwatan) or by peaceful capitulation without a treaty. The land in the latter case, it will be recalled, is called fay' and in the former ghanīma. As a rule the fay' land must be regarded as state land, but the ghanīma land offered a difficulty to 'Umar. The practice of the Prophet Muḥammad varied from confiscation and division in the case of Banū Qurayza to that of regarding it as state land (permitting its people to till the land and pay part of the produce to the state, as in the case of Khaybar).[29] 'Umar de-

[28] Balādhurī, *op. cit.*, p. 67.

[29] Ibn Hishām, *Kitāb al-Sīra*, Vol. II, pp. 684-6 755f.; Balādhurī, *op. cit.*, pp. 21-2, 23-9; Yaḥya Ibn Ādam, *Kitāb al-Kharāj* (Cairo, A.H. 1347), p. 20; Abū Yūsuf, *op. cit.*, p. 51.

cided to immobilize the land and treated both categories alike by requiring the people to pay the kharāj or land tax.[30] This practice became the rule that was enforced by succeeding caliphs.[31] If the dhimmī peasant became a Muslim, he was freed of the jizya on his head but not of the kharāj on the land. The dhimmī was constantly reminded that conversion would free him of the discriminatory poll tax for unbelief, but he had to pay the land tax as a rental for the state land he was allowed to till, unless he gave it up. If the land were inherited by, or sold to, another dhimmī, he in turn had to pay the kharāj to the state. If, however, the land was sold to a Muslim, the early practice varied; some were freed of payment, others had to pay the kharāj, although Muslims were discouraged from acquiring land (not dwelling within the towns). The caliph exercised discretionary right: he had the choice either of lifting the kharāj and requiring the tithe ('ushr), as was the rule in Arabia, or of enforcing the kharāj rule.[33] The former practice, exceptional in the time of 'Umar I, became a rule under 'Uthmān and succeeding caliphs.

While it is not clear either from Khālid's treaty or Abū 'Ubayda's that both a land tax and a poll tax were imposed, it is clear from the writings of Abū Yūsuf, Balādhurī, Yaḥya Ibn-Ādam, and others that the jizya was collected, in addition to

[30] 'Umar sent 'Uthmān Ibn Ḥunayf to the Sawād and Ḥudhayfa Ibn al-Yaman to the area east of the Tigris to measure the lands. Upon the suggestions of these commissioners, 'Umar imposed the kharāj, about which there are conflicting accounts. According to one version, 'Umar decreed that each jarīb of land must pay one dirham in money and one qafīz of produce; the other version is that 'Umar imposed the tax according to crops grown, varying from 10 dirham per jarīb for vineyard to wheat and barley, paying four and two dirhams per jarīb. See Abū Yūsuf, *op. cit.*, pp. 28-39.

[31] Yaḥya Ibn Ādam, *op. cit.*, p. 19.

[33] Abū Yūsuf, *op. cit.*, p. 59-60; Yaḥya Ibn Ādam, p. 18.

kharāj, from all dhimmīs, except women, children, the poor, the blind, the sick, the insane, the unemployed, and monks (if they were poor).[34] Abū Yūsuf reports that each dhimmī paid according to his wealth and income, graded in Iraq in three categories of 48, 24, and 12 dirhams annually.[35] The rate in Syria varied; the payment of a dinār by each person in addition to a fixed amount of grain on each jarīb was stipulated in several treaties.[36]

The Covenant of 'Umar

It follows from the foregoing discussion that 'Umar I did not issue a set of uniform and well-defined rules fixing the status of the dhimmīs; rather, such rules evolved, partly on the basis of Muḥammad's practice, partly on 'Umar's instructions (issued on various occasions), and partly on the practice of succeeding caliphs. However, the classical jurist-theologians provide us with a text, consisting of an elaborate set of rules, alleged to have been issued by 'Umar I, governing the relations of the dhimmīs with Islam. This is the so-called Covenant of 'Umar, preserved in the form of a letter submitted by the Christians of Syria to Abū 'Ubayda, which 'Umar ratified. The translation of the text follows:[37]

When thou camest into our land we asked of thee safety for our lives and the people of our religion, and we imposed these terms on ourselves: not to build in Damascus and its environs church, convent, chapel, monk's hermitage; not to repair what is dilapidated of our churches nor any of them that are in Muslim quarters; not to withhold our churches from Muslims stopping there by night or day; to open their doors to the

[34] Abū Yūsuf, p. 122; Balādhurī, *op. cit.*, pp. 129-30; Māwardī, pp. 248-9.

[35] Abū Yūsuf, p. 122, 124; Yaḥya ibn Ādam, p. 23.

[36] Balādhurī, p. 124, 144, 147.

[37] Ibn 'Asākir, *Ta'rīkh,* Vol. I, p. 149. Translation is quoted from A. S. Tritton, *The Caliphs and Their Non-Muslim Subjects* (London, 1930), pp. 6-8.

traveller and wayfarer; not to shelter there nor in our houses a spy, not to hide one who is a traitor to the Muslims; to beat the nāqūs only gently in our churches; not to display a cross on them; not to raise our voices in prayer or chanting in our churches; not to carry in procession a cross or our book; not to take out Easter or Palm Sunday processions; not to raise our voices over our dead, nor to show fires with them in the markets of the Muslims, nor bring our funerals near them; not to sell wine nor parade idolatry in companies of Muslims; not to entice a Muslim to our religion nor invite him to it; not to keep slaves who have been the property of Muslims; not to prevent any relative from entering Islam if he wish it; to keep our religion wherever we are; not to resemble the Muslims in wearing the Qalansūwa, the turban, shoes, nor in the parting of the hair, nor in their way of riding; not to use their language nor be called by their names; to cut the hair in front and divide our forelock; to tie the zunnār round our waists; not to engrave Arabic on our seals; not to ride on saddles; not to keep arms nor put them in our houses nor wear swords; to honour Muslims in their gatherings, to guide them on the road, to stand up in public meetings when they wish it; not to make our houses higher than theirs; not to teach our children the Koran; not to be partners with a Muslim except in business; to entertain every Muslim traveller in our customary style and feed him in it three days. We will not abuse a Muslim, and he who strikes a Muslim has forfeited his rights.

The above is not the only version; others are cited in varying degrees of length, although all agreeing on the general terms.[38] It is hardly necessary to prove that the text of 'Umar's covenant was not the product of 'Umar's time, but the work of later generations; for, it will be observed, several of its restrictive provisions are not in accord with 'Umar's instructions to his commanders. For several of these clauses are the product of intolerance and oppression, not of toleration.

The Covenant, however, has juridical significance, because

[38] For other versions, see Tritton, *op. cit.*, p. 5-6. Shāfi'ī gives perhaps the most elaborate text, embodying the provisions of the Covenant of 'Umar, which he suggests should be the model treaty between a Muslim ruler and the Scripturaries. See Shāfi'ī, *Kitāb al-Umm*, Vol. IV, p. 118. For a translation of this text see Tritton, *op. cit.*, pp. 12-16.

it provides us with a law as codified by the classical jurists and was regarded by all (i.e., by ijmā') as the definitive law governing the relations of the dhimmīs with Islam. The juridical validity of this law superceded any possible doubt that might be cast as to its historicity.

Dhimmī Rights and Obligations

It is now fitting to sum up the various rights and obligations of the dhimmīs which have developed since the rise of Islam and which constituted the law governing the relations of the non-Muslim with Muslim subjects of the Islamic state. Some of these rules, it will be recalled, were derived from Qur'ānic legislation, others from decrees issued by succeeding caliphs from the time of 'Umar I thereafter. Some of the disabilities, such as wearing the ghiyār, zunnār, and the colored Qalansūwa, were instituted by 'Umar II. These had fallen into disuse by the time of al-Mutawakkil, but he, probably in response to popular demand, felt it necessary to re-enforce them more strictly. The same process was repeated, probably adding further restrictions, under other caliphs especially the Fāṭimid al-Ḥākim bī Amr-Allah.[39]

Generally speaking, the law provides that Muslim authorities must guarantee the security of lives, property, churches, crosses, and other religious rites and practices of the dhimmīs, provided they do not build new churches (but they can repair or renew the building of old ones) or display their crosses and pray or ring their church bells loudly. No dhimmī is to be coerced into changing his religion nor restricted in his movement within the dār al-Islām, save in the sacred land (ḥaram[40]).

[39] See Jack Tagher [Tājir], *Aqbāṭ wa Muslimūn* (Cairo, 1951), pp. 78-97, 118-152.

[40] For a discussion of denying the right for a dhimmī to reside in Arabia see p. 160, above.

The jurist-theologians have summed up twelve duties and disabilities, divided into two categories; six absolutely necessary the breach of which, in theory, revokes the compact, and six desirable, the violation of which entails penalties. The first six of the following are absolutely necessary; the others are desirable:

(1) Every male, adult, free and sane dhimmī is under obligation to pay the jizya, the amount of which is to be fixed by Muslim authorities. The Mālikī school maintained that the amount should be fixed by the wālī (governor); the Ḥanafī school classified the tax into three categories: (a) the well-to-do to pay 48 dirhams; (b) the poor 12 dirhams; and (c) those in between to pay 24 dirhams; the Shāfi'ī jurists held that its minimum should be one dinār per head.[41] The jizya is lifted if the dhimmī renounces his religion and becomes a Muslim, since it is a form of punishment for disbelief. The dhimmī who possesses land is also under obligation to pay the kharāj. Unlike the jizya, however, if the dhimmī becomes a Muslim he has to pay his tax as a rental on land, unless he was exempted by the imām.

The refusal of the payment of jizya, according to the Ḥanafī school, is not a breach of the obligation. The important matter, they held, is not the payment of the tax *per se* but the acceptance of the status of a dhimmī, which, in turn, leads to the requirement of paying the jizya. Thus the jurists advised the imām to treat the dhimmīs gently in collecting the jizya. "They should not be beaten," said Abū Yūsuf, "if they fail to pay the jizya nor should they be required to stay under the Sun . . . but be imprisoned until they pay it. . . ."[42] Since the dhimmīs were not required to take part in the jihād, the jizya might be

[41] Abū Yūsuf, p. 122; Māwardī, p. 249; Ibn Rushd (al-Ḥafīd), *Bidāyat al-Mujtahid* (Istanbul, A.H. 1333), Vol. I, pp. 238-9.

[42] Abū Yūsuf, p. 123.

construed as payment in lieu of military service as well for the protection they received under Muslim rule.[43]

(2) The dhimmīs should not attack the religion of Islam nor show any disrespect to Muslim practices.

(3) They should not revile or show any disrespect to the Prophet Muḥammad or to the Qur'ān.

(4) They should not injure the life or the property of a Muslim, nor should they abjure his belief or induce him to apostatize, as this would amount to an increase in unbelief.

(5) The dhimmī is not permitted to marry a Muslim woman or to enter into sexual connection with her (zinā). (A Muslim can, however, marry a Scripturary woman, but not a Magian or polytheist).

(6) They are not permitted to assist the enemy nor give refuge to a ḥarbī (foreigner) nor harbor spies. Nor are they allowed to disclose the secrets of Islam to the enemy or pass on intelligence to them.

(7) While they are permitted to enter into business transactions with Muslims, they are not allowed to sell wine or practice usury. They, likewise, are not permitted to drink wine or eat pork in public.

(8) They are required to wear distinctive clothing such as the ghiyār, a yellow patch on their dress, the zunnār (girdle), and a tall and colored qalansūwa (headgear).

(9) They are not permitted to ride on horseback or carry weapons. They are allowed, however, to ride on donkeys and mules, distinguishing them by hanging a wooden ball on the saddle.

[43] See T. W. Arnold, *The Preaching of Islam* (London, 3rd. ed., 1935), pp. 60-1. Balādhurī reports that al-Jarājima who were exempt from the poll tax were required to take part in the jihād. Al-Jarājima were the inhabitants of the city of Jurjuma in the Amanus mountain. See Balādhurī, *Futūḥ al-Buldān*, pp. 160, 162.

(10) Their houses should not be higher than Muslim houses, preferably lower.

(11) They should not ring their church bells loudly nor should they raise their voices loudly in prayer.

(12) Their dead should not be wept over loudly; they must be buried in places away from Muslim quarters.

Although the foregoing stipulations hardly left a respectable position for the dhimmīs, it gave self-rule to each of the communities that professed its own religion to govern itself under its acknowledged religious head, who, in turn, was responsible to the Muslim authorities. Thus the dhimmī was bound to owe allegiance to two social orders, his own and the superstructure within which his community existed. His rights were fully protected within his own community, but, as a subject of the Muslim state, he suffered certain disabilities which reduced him to the status of a second-class citizen. For instance, he was under legal disability with regard to testimony, criminal law, and marriage. He could not inherit from a believer. If his wife were converted to Islam he had either to adopt her new religion or divorce her. He had no legal share in the ghanīma (spoil); he could receive allowances if his services in fighting were sought.[44]

The Christian Arabs of Banū Taghlib attained the highest status among the Scripturaries; they even refused to be called dhimmīs or pay the jizya. The caliph 'Umar I demanded at first that they should pay the jizya as long as they remained non-Muslims, but they refused and argued that they were Arabs and could not tolerate a different treatment from their compatriots. When 'Umar insisted that they should pay the jizya, they threatened to leave dār al-Islām. In the circumstances 'Umar, acting upon the advice of 'Ubāda Ibn al-Nu'mān (of the Taghlib tribe), decided to lift the jizya on

[44] Shāfi'ī, *op. cit.*, Vol. IV, p. 177; Māwardī, pp. 250-1.

condition that they pay double alms (ṣadaqa) and refrain from baptizing their children.[45] The Christians of Tanūkh were accorded similar status by 'Umar.

The case of Jabala Ibn al-Ayham, the king of the Christian Arabs of Ghassān, was decided differently. After the Muslim conquest, Jabala retired to his home; but shortly afterward he was asked to pay the jizya. He refused arguing that he was an Arab and went over to Byzantine territory. Another version of the story gives a different reason for Jabala's emigration. According to Balādhurī, Jabala was offended by a Muslim, but when the case was brought to 'Umar, the Caliph's decision did not satisfy him, and consequently he left the dār al-Islām. The various versions of the story agree that 'Umar was not willing to give a privileged position to Jabala as he did in the case of Banū Taghlib.

Conclusion

Practice differed considerably from the jurists' exposition of the law. Since the law made a distinction between the desirable and the necessary conditions, the degree of toleration depended largely on the whims of the rulers and their lieutenants. There are evidences which indicate that both sides tended at times to ignore and even to violate the law with regard to the employment of dhimmīs in government, the payment of the jizya, and the building of churches and synagogues. The Caliph al-Manṣūr removed all the dhimmīs from the administration, and al-Mutawakkil, reputed for his hostile attitude towards them, ordered all the churches and synagogues built after the Islamic conquest to be pulled down.[47] The dhimmīs, in order

[45] Abū Yūsuf, pp. 120-1; Balādhurī, pp. 181-3.

[47] Ṭabarī, *op. cit.*, Series III, Vol. III, p. 1390, 1392; and Richard Gottheil, "Dhimmīs and Moslems in Egypt," in Robert Harper *et al.*, *Old Testament and Semitic Studies* (Chicago, 1908), p. 359.

to obtain more concessions, made unfounded claims. A case in point is that of Mount Sinai. A false document is alleged to have been made between the Prophet Muḥammad and the monks in the year A.H. 2 for the purpose of keeping possession of a church.[48] Some of the Muslim governors, on the other hand, went so far as to declare that the early compacts with the dhimmīs had become obsolete and should be cancelled; and some jurist-theologians, including al-Ghazzālī, advocated a humiliating treatment of the dhimmīs for persistence in disbelief.[49]

These vexatious measures and practices, however, hard as they must have been on many individuals, should not obscure the original objective of the law which reflected a genuine spirit of toleration and provided safeguards for the non-Muslim subjects who preferred to follow their own Scriptures and practice their own rites. If a spirit of intolerance had at times been shown, it was the symptom of a growing oppressive rule which caused the Muslim populace at large to suffer no less than the non-Muslims. Mob violence may have been at times focused against non-Muslims, but mob violence indicates a dissatisfaction and unjust rule under which neither Muslims nor the dhimmīs could live with prosperity and security.

If certain caliphs and governors were harsh and brutal, others were inclined to show magnanimity and generous spirit.[50] Under reckless rule the dhimmīs may have suffered

[48] Gottheil, *op. cit.*, p. 356. See similar cases in 'Abd-Allah Muṣṭafa al-Marāghī, *al-Tashrī' al-Islāmī li-Ghayr al-Muslimīn* (Cairo, n.d.), pp. 122-36.

[49] Ghazzālī, *Kitāb al-Wajīz* (Cairo, A.H. 1317), Vol. II, p. 200; Jack Tājir, *op. cit.*, p. 164.

[50] In contrast to Mutawakkil's decrees see the Charter of al-Muktafī II (A.D. 1136-1160) issued to the Nestorian Patriarch in which a generous spirit of toleration is reflected. See A. Mingana (ed.), *A Charter of Protection granted to the Nestorian Church in A.D. 1138 by Muktafi II* (Manchester, 1925), pp. 3-7.

persecution, but the Muslims were not much better off. The harsh treatment of the dhimmīs may provide us with a test to indicate the degree of oppression suffered under a certain regime or in a certain age. The general treatment of the dhimmīs under Muslim rule, however, must be measured not in terms of such a suffering at the hands of careless caliphs and individual Muslims but in the spirit of tolerance embodied in the law and in the general spirit prevailing in each age and generation, and this must also be judged in terms of the relative prosperity and security enjoyed by the majority.[51]

[51] For a historical exposition of the life of the dhimmīs under Muslim rule, see Tritton, *op. cit.;* W. J. Fischel, *Jews in the Economic and Political Life of Medieval Islam* (London, 1937); Tājir, *Aqbāṭ Wa Muslimūn* (Cairo, 1951).

". . . . fulfill the covenant of Allah when you have made a covenant, and do not break oaths after making them . . . . be not like her who unravels her yarn, disintegrating it into pieces after she has spun it strongly." Qur'ān XVI, 93-94.

CHAPTER XVIII

TREATIES

Treaty-Making Power

Although the normal relationship between Islam and non-Muslim communities is a state of hostility, it is not considered inconsistent with Islam's ultimate objective if a peace treaty is concluded with the enemy, whether for purposes of expediency or because Islam suffered a setback.[1] Making treaties with non-Muslims is permitted by a divine legislation which runs as follows:

> How can there be for the polytheists a treaty with Allah and with His Apostle, save those with whom ye have made a treaty at the Sacred Mosque! So, as long as they act uprightly by you, do ye act uprightly by them; verily, Allah loves those who fear.[2]

[1] Abū Yūsuf, *Kitāb al-Kharāj,* p. 207; Shāfi'ī, *Kitāb al-'Umm.* Vol. IV, p. 110; Ṭabarī, *Kitāb al-Jihād,* pp. 14-15; Hans Kruse, "al-Shaybani on international instruments," *Journal of the Pakistan Historical Society,* Vol. I (1953), pp. 90-100.

[2] Q. IX, 7.

This Qur'ānic injunction is supported by precedent. The Prophet Muḥammad has set the classic example by concluding a treaty with the Makkans, known as the Ḥudaybiya Treaty, the terms and duration of which the Muslim jurists have regarded as a model for subsequent treaties. There is also a ḥadīth in which the Prophet is reported to have said: "The Byzantines will be making a secure peace with you [Muslims]."[3] Thus on the basis of the Qur'ān and ḥadīth, the jurists are agreed that a peace treaty with the enemy, if it serves Muslim interests, is a valid instrument, the provisions of which must be binding upon all Muslims. The jurists' agreement, constituting an ijmā', in addition to the early practice of the caliphs, rendered treaty-making an integral part of the sharī'a.

The treaty-making power rested in the hands of the Prophet Muḥammad and in his successors after him; but this power was frequently delegated to the commanders in the field, who were empowered to negotiate treaties with the enemy if he were willing to come to terms with Islam. The Prophet and his successors, however, always reserved their right to repudiate any treaty or arrangement which they considered as harmful to Islam; their approval or ratification was, accordingly, a prerequisite for making them binding upon the Muslim community.

Legal Nature of Treaties

A treaty (muhādana or muwāda'a) is a form of 'aqd (literally, a tie or conjunction) signifying an agreement on a certain act which has the object of creating legal consequences.[4] The term 'aqd has a broader meaning in Muslim law than contract in Western law: for it essentially stresses agreement, or meeting of minds, as the basic element in the 'aqd, regardless of the

[3] Ṭabarī, *op. cit.*, p. 15.

[4] Shaybānī, *al-Siyar al-Kabīr* with Sarakhsī's Commentary, Vol. IV, p. 60.

form or procedure. If consent is arrived at, by one party making a proposal ('ijāb) and acceptance (qabūl) by the other—the "meeting of the minds" is achieved, regardless of whether it is based on a strict mutuality of advantage or not—the contract is regarded as legally binding.[5]

The *Majalla* defines contract as follows:

> Contract is what the parties bind themselves and undertake to do with reference to a particular matter. It is composed of a combination of offer and acceptance.[6]

Thus in Islam, a treaty (as a form of 'aqd) originates from agreement and consent, not necessarily from the observance of any specific form or procedure. Once the provisions of the treaty are agreed upon, the treaty becomes binding on both parties. The writing as well as the signing and the dating (in certain cases the witnessing) of the treaty are not necessarily legal prerequisites; they are merely to indicate that an agreement has been reached as well as to record the actual terms of the treaty and its duration.[7]

Once the treaty is concluded Muslim authorities are strict in regard to the necessity of living up to its terms. The Qur'ān urges the Muslims "not to break oaths after making them,"[8] and if the non-Muslims do not break them, then "fulfill their agreement to the end of their term. . . ."[9] Thus the principle *pacta sunt servanda* is inherent in the conception of 'aqd and is recognized by all Muslim jurist-theologians. The imām is advised to honor the obligations he has undertaken on behalf

[5] See Abdur Rahim, *The Principles of Muhammadan Jurisprudence* (Madras, 1911) p. 282; Ṣubḥī al-Maḥmaṣānī, *al-Nazariyya al 'Āmma Li'l-Mūjibāt wa'l-'Uqūd* (Beirut, 1948), Vol. II, pp. 68 ff.

[6] *Al-Majalla,* Article 103. (Charles A. Hooper's translation in *Civil Law of Palestine and Transjordan* [Jerusalem, 1933], Vol. I, p. 31).

[7] Shaybānī, *op. cit.,* Vol. IV, pp. 60-1.

[8] Q. XVI, 93.

[9] Q. IX, 4.

of Islam, unless he fears an imminent attack from the enemy (in such a case he is obliged to send a notice for the termination of the treaty) or if the enemy has violated or repudiated the treaty.[10]

Before an analysis of the types and character of Muslim treaties is made, an examination of representative treaties—especially those of the Prophet Muḥammad—seems to be in order. It is not our purpose to provide an exhaustive history of every treaty; only a general background of some representative treaties (including their texts) will be given.

Prophet Muḥammad's First Treaty

While the Qur'ān laid down the principle *pacta sunt servanda,* it was Muḥammad's practice that established precedents on the basis of which treaties were concluded between Muslim and non-Muslim authorities. The Prophet Muḥammad made a variety of treaties in accordance with the political objectives and circumstances which dictated their conclusion. These treaties were regarded as models which his successors followed to the letter. Muḥammad's treaties varied from the conciliation treaty between the Aws and Khazraj tribes, to which the Jews of Madīna adhered and which constituted a charter for that city, to the treaty of Ḥudaybiya which established a temporary peace between the Muslims of Madīna and the polytheists of Makka. Muḥammad also issued constitutional charters to the Jews and Christians who were incorporated as subjects of the Muslim state.

Muḥammad's first treaty was that in which he sought to reconcile the tribes of Madīna after the hijra. The text is preserved in Ibn Hishām's *Sīra*[11] and in part in Wāqidī's

[10] See p. 220, below.

[11] Ibn Hishām, *Kitāb Sīrat Rasūl Allah,* ed. Ferdinand Wüstenfeld (Gottingen, 1858), Vol. I, pp. 341-4.

Maghāzī.[12] The first part of the treaty deals with the relations of the Madīna tribes; the latter with the alliance with the Jews. The date of the treaty is not reported by Ibn Hishām, but there is no doubt that it was signed between A.H. 1 and 2 (A.D. 623-24), as the Aws and Khazraj, together with their Jewish allies, faced the Makkans in the battle of Badr in A.H. 2 (A.D. 624).[13] The text of the treaty follows:

In the name of Allah, the Compassionate, the Merciful;

This is a document from Muḥammad, the Apostle of Allah to the believers and Muslims of Quraysh and Yathrib, and to all who followed them and fought [jāhada] with them. They constitute one 'umma [nation] in distinction from the rest of the people;

The émigrés of Quraysh unite together and pay ransom graciously for acquiring their relative-prisoners. The Banū 'Awf unite together as they were at first, and every division among them pays ransom for acquitting its relative-prisoners.

(This clause is repeated with the same phraseology concerning Banū Sā'ida, Banū Ḥarth, Banū Jusham, Banū al-Najār, Banū 'Amr Ibn 'Awf, Banū al-Nabīt, and Banū 'Aws.)

The believers should never leave any possibility to be followed graciously for paying ransom for their relative-prisoners.

[12] Wāqidī, *Kitāb al-Maghāzī*, ed. von Kremer (Calcutta, 1856), p. 177.

[13] M. Ḥamīdullah contends that the first part of the treaty was drawn up a few months after the arrival of the Prophet Muḥammad at Madīna, that is, in the first year of the hijra. The Jews were then invited to adhere and another treaty was drawn up concerning the relations of both the Aws and Khazraj with the Jews. The two texts were then amalgamated into one, as reported by Ibn Hishām (Muḥammad Ḥamīdullah, *Documents sur la Diplomatie à l'Epoque du Prophete et des Khalifes Orthodoxes* [Paris, 1935], p. 20). It is likely that the reconciliation between the Aws and Khazraj took place before the alliance with the Jews. Ibn Hishām reports two speeches given by the Prophet to this effect (see Ibn Hishām, *op. cit.*, Vol. I, pp. 340-1). But there is no evidence that a treaty was actually drawn up at that time. A verbal reconciliation was perhaps reached between the Aws and Khazraj, but was recorded only after the adherence of the Jews.

A believer should not ally himself with the mawla [slave] of another believer;

The pious believers shall combine together against any one who committed crimes unjustly or with oppression, even if he were the son of them [the believers];

A believer should not kill another believer, nor should he support an unbeliever against a believer;

The protection of Allah is one [and is equally] extended to the humblest of the believers. The believers are supported by each other;

The Jews who may follow us will have our support equally, without suppression, nor do we intend to combine [and turn] against them.

The believers make peace together. No believer should conclude peace, after a battle in the path of Allah, except with the others on the basis of equality and justice among the believers;

Warriors who fight on our side shall follow each other;

The believers shall co-operate with each other to avenge their blood in the path of Allah;

The pious believers follow the best and just path. Never shall a mushrik [polytheist] grant Quraysh goods or persons nor shall he prevent a believer [from an attack on Quraysh];

He who kills a believer is required to satisfy the walī [person responsible for and protector] of that believer. The believers shall combine against the killer and require him to fulfill that satisfaction;

No believer, who approves what is written in this document and believes in Allah and the Day of Judgment, shall help a criminal or give him refuge. Those who give him refuge and help him shall have the curse and anger of Allah in the Day of Resurrection. His indemnity is not to be accepted;

Anything which you may disagree upon is to be referred to Allah and to Muḥammad;

The Jews shall contribute to the expenditure of battle as long as they fight with the believers;

The Jews of Banū 'Awf form a nation with the believers. The Jews shall have their own religion, and the Muslims shall have their own religion; each with their mawālis [slaves] and persons, except those criminals and sinners who will do harm to themselves and to their families;

The Jews of Banū al-Najār, of Banū Ḥarth, of Banū Sā'ida, of Banū Jusham, of Banū 'Aws, and of Banū Tha'laba will have the same rights and obligations as those of Banū 'Awf, except the criminals and sinners who do harm to themselves and to their families;

Jafna, a family of Tha'laba, shall have the same rights and obligations as those of Tha'laba;

The Jews of Banū al-Shuṭayba shall have the same rights and obligations as those of Banū 'Awf;

The mawāli [slaves] of Tha'laba will be considered as Banū Tha'laba themselves;

The Biṭāna [adherents] of the Jews are considered as the Jews themselves;

No Jew is allowed to join [the Muslims in battle] without the authorization of Muḥammad;

Blood revenge is not prohibited. He who kills and his family are alone responsible to the one who has been done injustice by him. Allah will guarantee this agreement;

The Jews shall bear their own expenses and the Muslims shall bear their own expenses;

By their [co-operation] they will have victory over those who fight the allies of this agreement. They will get counsel and benevolence but never sins. No one shall prejudice his ally, for victory will be on the side of the oppressed;

The Jews shall contribute to the cost of battle with the believers as long as they fight;

The jawf [interior] of Yathrib will be sacred to the possessors of this document;

The neighbor shall be treated as ourselves, unmolested and innocently;

No protection is to be given [in the name of a family] except by the permission of that family;

Any dispute or quarrel between the parties to this agreement which may lead to an unfortunate result, shall be referred to Allah and to Muḥammad, the Apostle of Allah. Allah will guarantee the observance of this document;

Quraysh should not be helped, nor her supporters;

They [the Muslims and the Jews] will have victory over those who may attack Yathrib;

If they [the Jews] were invited to conclude peace, they must adhere to peace [with the Muslims];

If they were invited [by the Muslims] to the same, they will have the same obligations, save those who fight for religion;

Each shall have his share from his own side. . . .

The Jews of al-'Aws, their slaves and themselves, shall have the same rights and obligations, as stated in this agreement, with the best benevolence of the parties of the agreement. . . .

No one shall go against this agreement, except an oppressor or a sinner. Those who will go out [for fighting] are safeguarded; those who will live in Yathrib are protected, save an oppressor or a sinner. Allah and Muḥammad, the Apostle of Allah, will protect those who observe and guarantee this agreement.[14]

The treaty appears as a tripartite agreement between the muhājirūn or *émigrés* of Makka, the anṣār or adherents of Madīna, and the Jews. A careful examination of the text shows, however, that it was more than a treaty of alliance. The first part indeed indicates more than an attempt at reconciliation between the tribes; it is a pact for fusing all the rival elements of the Arab tribes in Madīna to "constitute one nation in distinction from the rest of the people." It is, in other words, a constitution for the Islamic state in its embryonic stage rather than a loose alliance of tribes. In this the Prophet Muḥammad had attempted to dissolve the narrow tribal loyalties within a new superstructure, by shifting their focus of attention to a new religion and state.

The second part of the treaty shows an alliance between the Arabian tribes, constituting one party, and the Jewish tribes as the other. Each Jewish tribe constituted a "nation with the believers"; but the Jewish tribes as a whole do not form a nation by themselves. Each Jewish tribe, however, will have its own religion, mawālis, and followers. The nature of this part of the treaty, therefore, shows that a kind of confederation was established between the Arab and Jewish tribes, with the state of Madīna taking the lead and the prominent position. This

[14] Ibn Hishām, *op. cit.,* Vol. I, pp. 341-4. A French translation is to be found in Ḥamīdullah, *op. cit.,* (Corpus), pp. 9-14; a German translation in J. Wellhausen, *Skizzen und Vorarbeiten* (Berlin, 1889), Vol. IV, pp. 67-73.

alliance made it possible to maintain cordial relations between the confederates as a whole in case one Jewish tribe was at war with the Muslims.[15]

The Ḥudaybiya Treaty

During the period from the battle of Badr to the signing of the treaty with Makka (A.D. 624-30) the position of the Prophet Muḥammad was firmly established in Madīna and he sought to bring the tribes around that city under Islam's authority. Starting his military success at the Battle of Badr, Muḥammad had become virtually, in the words of Ibn Hishām, "king of the Ḥijāz."[16] The defeat at Uḥud (A.D. 625) did not have lasting effect on him, as he attained another success at al-Khandaq (A.D. 627).

At this juncture the alliance with the Jews was abrogated. The reason, Arab chroniclers report, was the attempt of the Jews upon the Prophet's life.[17] Thus the Prophet, keeping his friendly relations with the rest of his Jewish confederates, marched against Banū Naḍīr and subjugated them. The quarrel with the Jews did not end with this event, as the rest of the Jews, especially the Banū Qurayza, who were sympathetic with their coreligionists, became also hostile to him. Their hostility ended at last their alliance with Madīna.

The Prophet Muḥammad crowned his successes by first con-

[15] This is precisely what happened when the Muslims, while they fought the Jews of Banū Naḍīr, kept peaceful relations with the rest of the Jews. For further examination of the treaty see, J. Wellhausen, *op. cit.*, Vol. IV, pp. 67-83; and M. Ḥamīdullah, *op. cit.*, pp. 19-22.

[16] Ibn Hishām, *op. cit.*, Vol. II, p. 763. "The victory of Badr," says Nicholson, "turned all eyes upon Muḥammad. However little the Arabs cared for his religion, they could not but respect the man who had humbled the lords of Mecca. He was now a power in the land." R. Nicholson, *A Literary History of the Arabs* (Cambridge 1930), pp. 174-5. The victory of Badr is celebrated in the Qur'ān in Sūra III, verses 119-20.

[17] Wāqidī, *op. cit.*, p. 358.

cluding a treaty of peace with Quraysh, his bitter enemy, and then his final capture of their city, Makka. Arab chroniclers report that the Prophet's motive for coming to terms with Quraysh was his desire to go on a pilgrimage to Makka.[18] While pilgrimage was an immediate reason for entering into treaty negotiations, the circumstances on both sides indicated that at least temporarily there was an equilibrium of power. The Quraysh was still too powerful for the authority at Madīna to subjugate, especially after the abrogation of the alliance with the Jews. The Makkans, on the other hand, were twice defeated at Badr and al-Khandaq while Muḥammad was cutting their trade relations with Syria and plundering their caravans with impunity. Both sides therefore were desirous of peace, at least for a short period. The events that led up to the signing of the peace treaty may be summed up as follows:

The Prophet, with a handful of his followers, proceeded to Makka with the intention of making a pilgrimage. The Quraysh not unnaturally suspected the Prophet's intention and were determined to resist his move. Finally Muḥammad sent 'Uthmān ibn 'Affān, his son-in-law and the future third caliph, to carry his peace message to the Quraysh. The Makkans accepted the offer and sent Suhayl ibn 'Amr to negotiate peace. This resulted in the signing of a peace treaty known as the Ḥudaybiya treaty. 'Alī ibn Abī Ṭālib, the Prophet's cousin and son-in-law and the future fourth caliph, acted as secretary. The text of the treaty follows:

In thy Name, O Allah![19]

This is what Muḥammad ibn 'Abd-Allah has agreed upon peacefully with Suhayl ibn 'Amr;[20]

[18] Ibn Hishām, Vol. II, p. 740; Wāqidī, p. 383.

[19] Muḥammad proposed to write "in the name of Allah, the Compassionate, the Merciful." Suhayl objected on the ground that he did not recognize such a statement. See ibn Hishām, Vol. II, p. 747.

[20] Muḥammad proposed to begin the preamble by saying: "This is what

They agreed peacefully to postpone war for a period of ten years. People shall be secured and guaranteed [from attack] by each other;

If anyone from Quraysh wishes to join Muḥammad without the authorization of his walī [protector] he should be sent back; if anyone of Muḥammad's followers wishes to join Quraysh, he will not be refused.

Unbecoming acts between each of us are prohibited; and there shall not be between us defection, nor treason;

Those [people] who want to join Muḥammad's alliance and his pact may do so; those who want to join Quraysh's alliance and its pact may do so.[21]

To assure the Makkans of his good intention, Muḥammad brought witnesses who swore to observe the treaty's provisions. Among the witnesses were Abū Bakr, 'Umar ibn al-Khaṭṭāb, and 'Abd al-Raḥmān ibn 'Awf. This treaty marked another success for Islam. For the aristocracy of Quraysh had at last recognized Muḥammad's authority in Madīna and, by inference, Islam as the official religion of that authority. This very fact enhanced Muḥammad's prestige in Makka after he had been scorned and persecuted before his migration to Madīna.

The Ḥudaybiya treaty established the precedent that Muslim authorities might come to terms with polytheists, provided it was only for a temporary period. While the jurists disagree as to the duration of this period, ranging from a maximum of ten years, the period provided in the text, to three or two, depending on the actual period it was in force, they all agree that a temporary peace with the enemy is not inconsistent with Islam's interests.

The treaty was in fact violated within a period of two years. The reason, as reported in the chronicles, was the attack of

---

Muḥammad, the Apostle of Allah. . . ." But Suhayl objected on the ground that he did not believe that Muḥammad was the Apostle of Allah, otherwise he would not have fought him. Ibn Hishām, Vol. II, p. 747; and Wāqidī, p. 387.

[21] For the text of the treaty see ibn Hishām, Vol. II, pp. 747-8; and Wāqidī, p. 387.

Quraysh on Muḥammad's adherents. This action was construed as violation of the clause "those who want to join Muḥammad's alliance and his pact may do so. . . ."[22] Negotiations were conducted to restore peace relations, but to no avail. Muḥammad, whose prestige and power had become predominant, disliked the attack on his adherents.[23] The Muslims, accordingly, decided to march on Makka, and they captured it in A.H. 8 (A.D. 630). The Quraysh, now weak and divided, offered no resistance, and Muḥammad entered the city without difficulty.[24] The capture of Makka ended the rivalry between the two city-states and established Islam's supremacy over the Ḥijāz. Muḥammad's mission looked to a wider horizon.

Dhimmī Pacts as Constitutional Charters

The Prophet Muḥammad concluded a set of treaties of a different character which should be distinguished from the foregoing. These comprise the agreements which he reached with the Scripturaries of Arabia in which a pledge of perpetual security for their lives, property, and freedom of religious practices was given as long as they remained loyal to their pacts. A study of the legal character of these pacts has been made elsewhere in this work.[25] In this chapter an examination of the form and procedure of these pacts will be made, indicating their relations with other treaties. For this purpose no better model could be given than the treaty which the Patriarch of

[22] Ibn Hishām, Vol. II, p. 803.

[23] For an evaluation of the prestige and power of Muḥammad, see Abū Sufyān's account to the Makkans which stated that Muḥammad was respected more than Caesar and Kisra. See Wāqidī, p. 405.

[24] This is the basis for differences among the jurists as to the taking of Makka. The Shāfi'ī jurists considered it by peace, and the Mīlikīs and the Ḥanafīs by force. See Māwardī, *Kitāb al-Aḥkām al-Sulṭāniyya*, ed. Enger (Bonn, 1853), p. 284.

[25] See chap. XVII.

Jerusalem signed with the Caliph 'Umar ibn al-Khaṭṭāb. Unlike the Ḥīra and Damascus treaties, the Patriarch of Jerusalem demanded that the Jerusalem treaty should be signed by the Caliph himself rather than by his representative. 'Umar agreed and came to Jerusalem to sign the treaty in A.H. 17 (A.D. 638). The text of the treaty follows:

In the name of Allah, the Compassionate, the Merciful;

This is what 'Abd-Allah 'Umar, Prince of the Believers, has guaranteed to the people of Iliā' [Jerusalem];

He guaranteed their lives, property, churches, and crosses. . . .

Their churches will not be dwelt in [by foreigners], nor will they be destroyed or ruined in any part. Nor will their crosses or property [be destroyed];

They will not be persecuted for their religion, nor will they be molested;

Jews shall not be allowed to live with them in Iliā';

The inhabitants of Iliā' shall pay the jizya as much as that of the inhabitants of Madā'in;

They shall require the Rūm [Byzantines] and the thieves to leave the city. If they leave, they shall be secured in their lives and property until they reach [their country]. Those [Byzantines] who prefer to stay, shall be given security and should accept the same obligations as those of the inhabitants of Iliā' concerning the jizya.

Those who prefer to go with the Rūm from among the inhabitants of Iliā' shall be secured in their lives and property, [provided] they leave their churches and crosses. . . .

Those who were in it [the city] from among the people of the land [farmers?], before the death of *so-and-so,* shall be allowed, if they wish, to stay in the city and shall have the same obligations as those of the inhabitants of Iliā' concerning the jizya. Those who prefer to leave with the Rūm, [may do so]; those who prefer to go to their people [their land], [may do so] until the time of their harvest;

This document is guaranteed by the assurance of Allah, of His Apostle, of the Caliphs, and of the believers, if [the inhabitants] paid their duties of the jizya;

Witnesses are: Khālid ibn al-Walīd, 'Amr ibn al-'Ās, 'Abd al-Raḥmān ibn 'Awf, and Mu'āwiya ibn Abī Sufyān. It was signed in 15 A.H.[26]

[26] The text is to be found in Ṭabarī, *Ta'rīkh* edited by de Goeje (Leiden, 1893), Series I, Vol. V, pp. 2405-6; cf. Balādhurī, *op. cit.,* pp. 138-ff.

Apart from the usual payment of the jizya established by precedent as the regular poll tax paid by Scripturaries, the other stipulations constitute a Bill of Rights for the dhimmīs, the new subjects of the Muslim state. This treaty, although negotiated and signed like others, is different in at least two important respects. First, it is designed to be a perpetual pact, for even if its terms were violated by a few, it remained binding upon the other party. Second, from the moment the treaty came into force, the Scripturaries became subjects of the caliph and their territory part of the dār al-Islam. It follows that the character of these treaties, originally signed between two separate communities, was inevitably changed when the Scripturary communities (the dhimmīs), although retaining certain measures of self-government, were merged within the Islamic nation. The jurists, it will be recalled have regarded the law governing the relations of the dhimmīs with Islam as part of the sharī'a and thus their treaties (referred to later as the Covenant of 'Umar)[27] assumed a constitutional character.

Muslim Treaties Under Muḥammad's Successors

Muḥammad's treaties were regarded as models which were followed by his successors to the letter. Neither in their legal character nor perhaps in their form have the caliphs' treaties differed from those of early Islam. As was expected, the aims and the circumstances naturally differed, thus producing a new type of treaty dominated by political and administrative purposes, in contrast to the early Islamic treaties, in which the religious aim was emphasized.

Under Umayyad rule both Mu'āwiya I and 'Abd al-Malik concluded treaties with the Byzantines in which they paid tribute in order to avoid attack while the Muslims were engaged in civil wars. Mu'āwiya, while he was not yet proclaimed a

[27] See p. 193, above.

caliph and was still busy in his struggle with the Caliph 'Alī, came to terms with the Byzantine emperor, Constans II, and signed on his own authority a treaty (A.D. 658) in which a tribute was paid to the emperor. The Caliph 'Abd al-Malik (A.H. 65-86, or A.D. 685-705) was also obliged to conclude peace treaties with the Byzantines while he was fighting the insurgents in Iraq. The jurists have differed as to the validity of the imām's action in paying a tribute to non-Muslim authories. Both al-Awzā'ī (died in A.H. 157, or A.D. 773) and Sufyān al-Thawrī (died A.H. 161, or A.D. 777), who lived under Umayyad rule, saw no harm in doing so in case of necessity;[28] but al-Shāfi'ī, who lived during the height of Muslim power, advised against it.[29] The Ḥanafī jurists advised against paying tribute unless it was absolutely necessary.[30] The majority of the jurists seem to advise against paying an annual tribute, although they saw no harm in paying it—under exceptional circumstances—for a short period. Only al-Lū'lū'ī, an extremist, went so far as to argue that the imām should go to war even if he felt weakness in Islam, rather than to pay tribute to the enemy, for agreement to pay tribute to the enemy would place the Muslims in the same status as those who pay the jizya, that is, a degraded position in the eyes of the enemy.[31]

Under 'Abbāsid rule the caliphs concluded treaties with the Byzantines for a variety of reasons. First, in order to stop frequent violations of the frontiers; for the 'Abbāsid-Byzantine boundaries, owing to the lack of a natural barrier, were crossed and re-crossed by one side or the other. This type of treaty,

[28] Ṭabarī, *op. cit.*, pp. 17-8.

[29] Shāfi'ī, *op. cit.*, Vol. IV, p. 110. Shāfi'ī agreed only to the paying of a tribute to the enemy in battle, in case the Muslim felt unable to repulse the enemy, but not in the form of an annual tribute. See Ṭabarī, *op. cit.*, p. 18-9.

[30] Abū Yūsuf, *Kitāb al-Kharāj*, p. 207; Ṭabarī, *op. cit.*, p. 19.

[31] Ṭabarī, p. 19-20.

concluded in the first period of the 'Abbāsid dynasty, forced the Byzantine emperors to pay annual tribute to Baghdad. Thus the Empress Irene (died A.D. 802) paid tribute to the Caliph Harūn al-Rashīd and avoided his periodical attack on the eastern borders of her empire. This peace lasted until the accession of the Emperor Nicephoros, who sent a scornful letter to Baghdad, demanding the return of the tribute that had been paid. Harūn, offended by Nicephoros' letter, took the field and forced him to pay a new tribute.[32] But when the power and prestige of the caliphs declined, the emperors of Constantinople stopped payment of tribute and even frequently crossed the borders of the empire. Such treaties were also concluded between Muslim authorities and the Crusader princes for the purpose of terminating local fighting, for facilitating travel for civilian purposes, or for pilgrimage. The last was the specific purpose for which the treaty between Ṣalāḥ al-Dīn (Saladin) and Richard Coeur de Lion was concluded in A.D. 1192.[33]

The other type of treaty which was concluded during the 'Abbāsid caliphate was the so-called fidā' (ransom) treaties. The purpose was to release prisoners of war by exchange or by paying a certain amount of money agreed upon. This system made it possible for the victor to collect a considerable amount of revenue for the state treasury. It made it possible, on the other hand, to save the lives of thousands of prisoners who would otherwise have suffered or perished.[34]

Chronicles make no mention of fidā' treaties during the Umayyad period, although prisoners were often released by

[32] Ṭabarī, *Ta'rīkh*, ed. de Goeje, Series III, Vol. II, p. 696.

[33] For the negotiation and terms of the treaty, see W. B. Stevenson, *The Crusaders in the East* (Cambridge, 1907), pp. 286-7.

[34] For details on the law of fidā', see Shaybānī, *op. cit.*, Vol. III, pp. 119, 307-39.

exchange on an individual basis. As a system organized by treaties, the fidā' treaty, Arab chronicles report, was made during the reign of Harūn al-Rashīd in A.H. 181. The Muslims who were released numbered about 3700 prisoners. Al-Mas'ūdī reports twelve treaties from the time of Harūn to his day.[35] The release of prisoners was made after special ceremonies in which receiving parties from both sides went out to celebrate the occasion.

To ensure the execution of the terms of treaties, hostages (rahā'in) were often given or exchanged. The system of hostages was common among the nations of antiquity and was practiced in ancient China and Rome.[36] Ancient practice was such that, if the treaty obligations were fulfilled, the hostages were returned unharmed to their country. If, however, the treaty was violated, the hostages were regarded as prisoners of war and sometimes were subjected to certain measures of hardships. The Muslims regarded hostages as inviolable and were treated with consideration and kindness. If the treaty were violated and war was declared, the Muslims sent back the hostages to their country; but if war was not declared the hostages were either kept at hand or sent back home.[37]

General Characteristics of Treaties

On the basis of the foregoing discussion of Muslim treaties, certain general observations might be summed up as follows:

First, Muslim treaties were, on the whole, brief and general,

[35] Ṭabarī, *Ta'rīkh,* ed. de Goeje, Series II, Vol. II, pp. 706-7; and Mas'ūdī, *al-Tanbīh wa'l-Ishrāf* (Cairo, 1938), pp. 160-6. For the release of Raymond III by ransom, see Stevenson, *op. cit.,* p. 213.

[36] See Coleman Phillipson, *International Law and Custom of Ancient Greece and Rome* (London, 1911), Vol. I, p. 398.

[37] Māwardī, *Kitāb al-Aḥkām al-Sulṭāniyya,* ed. Enger (Bonn, 1835), pp. 84-5. For the practice of taking hostages during the Crusade period, see W. B. Stevenson, p. 210.

and no attempt was made to supply details as to the applicability of their provisions. The phraseology was simple and even, at times, vague owing to the brevity of the text.

Second, the preamble of every treaty consisted of the so-called basmala (i.e., in the name of Allah, etc.) and the names of the representatives of the parties concerned, with their titles. Thus in the treaties which were concluded by Muḥammad, the title Apostle of Allah was always mentioned (except in the Ḥudaybiya treaty) and the title khalīfa or amīr al-mu'minīn, for Muḥammad's successors.

The treaty often ends by stating the names of the witnesses who were present at the time of drafting the text.

Third, the contents of the treaties varied with the purposes of making them, such as those which dealt with religious matters (especially the early Muslim treaties) and those which later caliphs concluded for political or economic purposes. The Muslim jurists, however, distinguished between the permanent and temporary treaties, depending on the parties with whom the Muslim authorities were negotiating, rather than on the content of the treaties. The treaties with the dhimmīs are known as perpetual, and those with dār al-ḥarb, in which the jihād is temporarily suspended, are known as temporary treaties.

Fourth, the duration of the treaties with non-Muslim authorities was specified by Muslim jurists. The Ḥanafī and Shāfi'ī schools held that a peace treaty with the enemy should not exceed a period of ten years. They based their argument on the precedent of the Ḥudaybiya treaty, which, it will be recalled, stipulated that the period of peace would last for ten years.[38] Certain jurists maintained that the Ḥudaybiya peace did not last ten years; they, accordingly, tolerated no peace

[38] Abū Yūsuf, *Kitāb al-Kharāj*, pp. 207-8; Shaybānī, *op. cit.*, Vol. IV, pp. 60-1; Shāfi'ī, *op. cit.*, Vol. IV, pp. 109-10; Māwardī, *op. cit.*, p. 84.

treaty for a period exceeding three or four years.[39] A number of treaties which were concluded during the Crusade period were specified to last for ten years and ten or eleven months, but not for twelve months.[40]

The treaties with the dhimmīs were treated differently. Not only were they regarded as perpetual but also as instruments between two unequal parties; for in almost all of them the terms were in the nature of pledges or guarantees given by the Muslims to the dhimmīs rather than between equals. Thus the dhimmī treaties, it will be recalled, were in the form of constitutional guarantees from the moment the dhimmī communities ceased to be separate entities.

Finally, Muslim authorities tended to regard their contractual understandings as religious obligations which should be strictly observed. While the jurists were not inclined to advise the Muslims to make peace treaties with non-Muslims, they insisted that once a treaty was concluded, its terms should be observed to the end of its duration.

Termination of Treaties

By their very nature treaties must be of temporary duration, for in Muslim legal theory the normal relations between Muslim and non-Muslim territories are not peaceful, but warlike. Since in theory the jihād could not possibly be suspended more than ten years, treaties must necessarily be terminated by the end of that period, even though the duration is not specified in its terms. But the jurists advise the imām to specify the

[39] See Ibn Rushd (al-Ḥafīd), *Bidāyat al-Mujtahid* (Istanbul, A.H. 1333), Vol. I, pp. 313-4. Other jurists, like the Ḥanbalī jurist al-Ḥajjawī, advised the imām to conclude a peace treaty for more than ten years if the Muslims were weak and unable to resume the war with the enemy. See Sharaf al-Dīn al-Ḥajjawī, *al-Iqnā'* (Cairo, n.d.), Vol. I, p. 40. Cf. Ibn Qudāma, *al-Mughnī,* Vol. VIII, p. 460.

[40] See W. B. Stevenson, *op. cit.,* pp. 331, 345, 348.

period of duration in order to indicate clearly the temporary character of treaties.[41]

The imām is also advised not to conclude treaties inconsistent with Islam's interest. For if he concluded a treaty in which, for instance, he agreed to surrender arms and armaments to the enemy, the treaty is regarded as fāsid (irregular) and should either be revised, in order to regularize it, or declared terminated.[42]

If the imām entered into treaty arrangements which provided terms he was incapable of fulfilling, the treaty was regarded as void (bāṭil).[43] Even if the treaty were regular, but the imām found that its terms were harmful to Islam he was permitted to declare its termination, provided an adequate prior notification (nabdh) was sent to the other party informing them of Muslim intention to terminate the treaty.[44]

Before termination by the end of its duration, the treaty might be declared terminated by mutual consent; the imām, however, should never agree to a treaty in which only one of the two parties was allowed to terminate the treaty, even if he were the one given the right. Mutual consent must be the underlying principle of termination in the same way as it is the underlying principle for signing a treaty.[45]

Treaties with the dhimmīs, however, are by their very nature perpetual in character and could not be terminated. Even if a few dhimmīs violate their contractual obligations, the treaty remained in force regarding the others. This is not only because the treaties with the dhimmīs were essentially pledges of

[41] Ibn Qudāma, *al-Mughnī* with Rashīd Riḍa's Commentary (Cairo, A.H. 1367), Vol. III, pp. 459-60.

[42] *Ibid.*, p. 466.

[43] Shaybānī, *al-Siyar al-Kabīr* with Sarakhsī's Commentary, Vol. IV, p. 66.

[44] Shaybānī, Vol. III, p. 261; and Ibn Qudāma, Vol. VIII, p. 463.

[45] Ibn Qudāma, Vol. VIII, pp. 461-2.

security given by Muslim authorities to the Scripturary communities who agreed to live under Muslim rule, but also because those treaties took the form of constitutional guarantees once the dhimmīs were merged within Islam. Thus, if a dhimmī failed to observe his duties he was ordinarily punished, although in theory he had the right to renounce his obligations and leave for the dār al-ḥarb.

"And when prayer is ended, then disperse abroad in the land and go in quest of the bounties of Allah: and, that it may be well with you, oft remember Allah." Qur'ān LXII, 10.

CHAPTER XIX

COMMERCIAL RELATIONS

Islam and Commerce

Islam is a system of religion which stresses both worldly and heavenly values; the believer is encouraged to seek worldly life as if he is to live forever, and salvation as if he is to die tomorrow. While the law does not discourage believers who devote their lives completely to heavenly pursuits, indulgence in worldly affairs at the expense of the heavenly is not permitted. Commerce (tijāra) is one of the professions which, if practiced within the bounds of the law, might secure worldly recompense without compromising religious duties.[1]

[1] Q. XXIV, 37: "Men whom neither merchandize nor selling divert from the remembrance of Allah and steadfastness in prayer and giving alms, who fear a day when hearts and eyes shall be upset. . . ." See also Ghazzālī, *Kitāb Iḥyā' 'Ulūm al-Dīn* (Cairo, A.H. 1334), Vol. II, pp. 56-8. Cf. Ibn Khaldūn, *al-Muqaddima,* ed. Quatremère (Paris, 1858), Vol. II, p. 304, 305.

The environment in which Islam had arisen was renowned as a commercial center and Muḥammad's early experiences as a merchant were reflected in divine legislation. Not only is commerce recommended in the Qur'ān to those who seek Allah's bounties, but also commercial terms and concepts are used to express religious ideas.[2] Throughout Islamic history, commerce was highly esteemed and the merchants contributed to the wealth and prosperity of society at the height of Muslim power. Although few were the merchants who could influence public policy, there were men in business, like the jurist Abū Ḥanīfa, whose influence surpassed many in high authority. The process of exchanging commodities among nations, honored by the Arabs before Islam, persisted throughout the centuries as one of the most significant professions in Muslim society.

Although the jurists have agreed as to the need for trade among the various peoples and countries of dār al-Islam, they do not all approve, however, of international trade, namely, the exchange of commodities between dār al-Islam and dār al-ḥarb. Thus the Mālikī jurists advise Muslims to avoid trade with dār al-ḥarb, whether by land or by sea.[3] Mālik permits non-Muslims to enter dār al-Islam and trade with Muslims but does not approve of Muslims going to dār al-ḥarb for this purpose. The reason is that Mālik does not approve of Muslims living in a country "where people do not respect their ancestors or associate gods with the Compassionate by worshipping idols."[4] The other schools of law permit trade with non-Mus-

[2] See, e.g., Q. VI, 153; XVII, 37. See also Charles C. Torrey, *The Commercial-Theological Terms in the Koran* (Leyden, 1892).

[3] Saḥnūn, *al-Mudawwana al-Kubra* (Cairo, A.H. 1323), Vol. X, p. 102; and Ibn Rushd, *al-Muqaddimāt al-Mumahhidāt* (Cairo, A.H. 1325), Vol. II, p. 285.

[4] Ibn Rushd, *op. cit.*, Vol. II, p. 287. The Ẓāhirī jurist Ibn Ḥazm supports Mālik in advising against Muslims going over to dār al-ḥarb and cites a

lims, whether within or without dār al-Islam, but they impose certain limitations with regard both to the movement of persons and commodities.

Non-Muslim Trade with Dār al-Islam

Muslim authorities have shown considerable tolerance by throwing open the doors of dār al-Islam to non-Muslims for trade purposes. Non-Muslim merchants were as a rule granted amān for four months, subject to renewal if their business transactions were not completed during the interim.[5] If the merchant desired to stay for a minimum of one year and agreed to pay the jizya in the capacity of a dhimmī, his request was ordinarily granted. As a musta'min,[6] he could with perfect freedom move within dār al-Islam but not visit the ḥaram, the sacred places of the Ḥijāz.[7]

The jurists, however, have formulated certain limitations upon the free exchange of commodities which they advised the imām to enforce upon foreign merchants. The general principle implied is that dār al-Islam, being at war with dār al-ḥarb, should not permit the export of war materiel which might strengthen dār al-ḥarb against dār al-Islam. All the jurists agree that weapons and war implements are contraband the sale of which is absolutely prohibited; but many of them are of the opinion that horses, mules, and slaves are so useful in war that their sale must also be prohibited.[8] Mālik goes so far as to ad-

---

ḥadīth ascribed to the Prophet Muḥammad to this effect. See Ibn Ḥazm, *al-Maḥallī* (Cairo, A.H. 1347), Vol. VII, p. 349.

5 Ṭabarī, *Kitāb al-Jihād*, ed. Schacht, (Leiden, 1933), p. 36.

6 See p. 163, above.

7 Māwardī, *Kitāb al-Aḥkām al-Sulṭāniyya*, ed. Enger (Bonn, 1853), p. 291-2; Ibn Qudāma, *al-Mughnī*, ed. Rashīd Riḍa (Cairo, A.H. 1367) Vol. VIII, p. 531.

8 Shaybānī, *Kitāb al-Āthār* (Lucknow, n.d.), p. 135.

vise against the export of certain foodstuffs and the sale of the Qur'ān.[9] If the foreign merchant buys certain prohibited goods, the sale is not regarded as void, but the merchant has to resell the goods before departing from dār al-Islam. Abū Yūsuf advises the imām to set up guarding centers (masāliḥ) on the frontiers of dār al-Islam to inspect foreign merchants and prevent the export of contraband.[10] Foreign merchants are, of course, not allowed to sell prohibited goods such as pork and wine. In practice, however, these rules were not so rigidly enforced as is required by the sharī'a and the freedom of the export of commodities from dār al-Islam was almost as complete as the flow of commodities from dār al-ḥarb.

Foreign merchants were required to pay a duty of 10 per cent ('ushr) on all the goods they sold in dār al-Islam which exceeded 200 dirhams.[11] This rate could be lowered by the imām, if he wanted to encourage foreign trade, or raised, if he were in need of further revenue. But such a duty should not be collected more than once a year.[12] If the country of the foreign merchant does not impose a duty of Muslim merchants, the imām is advised to reciprocate by enforcing free trade.[13] The dhimmīs, although subjects of the imām, pay a similar tax if they trade in the Ḥijāz, but they are exempt from duties elsewhere.

[9] Saḥnūn, *op. cit.*, Vol. X, p. 102, 107; Ibn Rushd, *op. cit.*, Vol. II, pp. 287-8.

[10] Abū Yūsuf, *Kitāb al-Kharāj* (Cairo, A.H. 1352), p. 188, 190; Ibn Rushd, Vol. II, p. 287.

[11] Abū Yūsuf, pp. 132-3.

[12] Abū Yūsuf, p. 135; Ghazzālī, *Kitāb al-Wajīz* (Cairo, A.H. 1317), Vol. II, p. 201.

[13] Shaybānī, *al-Siyar al-Kabīr*, with Sarakhsī's Commentary (Hyderabad, A.H. 1335), Vol. IV, p. 67; Ibn Qudāma, *op. cit.*, Vol. VIII, p. 521.

Muslim Trade with Dār al-Ḥarb

Muslim jurists show less tolerance with regard to Muslim merchants who trade with dār al-ḥarb than in permitting non-Muslim merchants to trade with dār al-Islam. The Mālikī and Ẓāhirī jurists are averse to the idea of Muslims going to dār al-ḥarb and being exposed to the worship of idolatry or subjected to its law.[14] Mālik advises the imām to inspect travelers on the frontiers of dār al-Islam and to prevent the merchant Muslims from going to dār al-ḥarb.[15] Ibn Ḥazm held that the imām should permit entry to dār al-ḥarb only for those who go over for purposes of jihād or for carrying messages to chiefs of state.[16]

The majority of jurists, however, were more tolerant and some of them, especially the Ḥanafī jurists, went so far as to overcome certain obstacles by casuistry (al-ḥiyal al-shar'iyya).[17] Muslim publicists have written extant treaties and have expatiated on the kinds of commodities imported as well as on the wealth and other advantages accrued to Islam by the exchange of commodities with foreign countries.[18]

As in the case of trade within dār al-Islam, the Muslim is not permitted to trade in such prohibited goods as pork and wine, or in the practice of riba (usury), and he is advised to abstain from trade in animals and plants which are filthy and harmful. Some jurists advise, likewise, against trade in goods for

14 Saḥnūn, *op. cit.*, Vol. X, p. 102; Ibn Ḥazm, *al-Maḥallī*, Vol. VII, p. 349.

15 Ibn Rushd, *op. cit.*, Vol. II, p. 287.

16 Ibn Ḥazm, *op. cit.*, Vol. VII, p. 349.

17 See Shaybānī, *Kitāb al-Makhārij fi'l Ḥiyal*, ed. J. Schacht (Leipzig, 1930) Khaṣṣāf, *Kitāb al-Ḥiyal* (Cairo, A.H. 1314).

18 Jāḥiz, "Kitāb al-Tabaṣṣur bi'l-Tijāra," ed. 'Abd al-Wahhāb al-Ṣamādiḥī, *Majallat al-Majma' al-'Ilmī al-'Arabī*, Vol. XII, (1932), pp. 326-51; Dimashqī, *al-Ishāra ila Maḥāsin al-Tijāra* (Cairo, A.H. 1318), a German translation of this book is by H. Ritter, *Ein Arabisches Handbuch der Handelswissenschaft* (Berlin, 1920).

amusement, such as ivory, images, and musical instruments.[19] Neither should he enter into business transactions with merchants who are minors, insane, or blind, or with slaves. The reason is that minors and the insane lack the legal competence for sale, and the slaves are themselves the property of their masters. The blind is unable to examine the property—a prerequisite for sale—unless another person undertakes to do it on his behalf.

The Muslim merchant is not allowed to carry contraband with him to dār al-ḥarb, for the same reason that the non-Muslim merchant is not permitted to carry it home with him. Nor should the Muslim carry sabī (women and children as spoils) or iron or any material which could be used for war purposes.[20] If, however, the Muslim merchant carried with him slaves and weapons for his own protection, with the understanding that these would be brought back upon his return, they were permitted to cross the frontiers of Islam.[21]

During his visit to dār al-ḥarb, whether he entered by amān or not, the Muslim merchant should observe his own law in addition to the law of the country of his sojourn, and he is required to follow the same rules as those imposed on the Muslim musta'min while he is in non-Muslim lands.[22] If he commits crimes against other Muslims, he is also liable for punishment upon his return to dār al-Islam. He may pay certain duties to foreign governments while he is in dār al-ḥarb, but no such duties are imposed upon him after his return, save those ordinarily required from other Muslims in proportion to his income, including the money he earned from dār al-ḥarb.

[19] Ghazzālī, *Kitāb Iḥyā' 'Ulūm al-Dīn* (Cairo, A.H. 1334), Vol. II, pp. 59-60.

[20] Shaybāni, *op. cit.,* Vol. III, pp. 177-8, 273-4.

[21] *Ibid.,* p. 275-6.

[22] See p. 171 ff., above.

Significance of Foreign Trade

Contrary to the contention of the jurists, who feared that the believers' traveling in dār al-ḥarb might compromise their belief, commerce with non-Muslims greatly influenced the expansion of Islam along trade routes across Central Asia, India, Southeast Asia, as well as East and Equatorial Africa. The Islamic world expanded by commercial and cultural contacts far beyond the political frontiers established by military conquest. While commercial relations between the Levant and Europe were interrupted after the rise of Islam (probably owing to the refusal of Christendom to trade with Islam rather than to Islam's deliberate policy of cutting off such relations with Europe—as Henri Pirenne maintained),[23] Muslim trade found outlets in other directions which greatly increased the wealth and prosperity of Islam.[24] It was not until the Crusades that commercial intercourse between the Levant and Europe was resumed, to be interrupted again at the opening of the fifteenth century, as a result of the discovery of new routes to India and the Far East round the Cape of Good Hope. Direct commercial relations between Europe and the Levant were not revived until the opening of the nineteenth century which assumed a new phase in the relationship between Islam and Christendom.[25]

Muslim trade with foreign countries, whether by land or sea, contributed to the development and diffusion of certain com-

[23] Henri Pirenne, *Mohammed and Charlemagne* (New York, 1929). For criticism of Pirenne's theses, see Daniel C. Dennett, "Pirenne and Muhammad," *Speculum,* Vol. XXIII (1948), pp. 165-190.

[24] S. A. Ḥuzayyin, *Arabia and the Far East* (Cairo, 1942); Badr al-Dīn al-Ṣinī, *al-'Alāqāt Bayn al-'Arab wa'l-Ṣīn* (Cairo, 1950); Ṣāliḥ Aḥmad al-'Alī, *alTanzīmāt al-Ijtimā'iyya wa'l-Iqtiṣādiyya fi'l-Baṣra fi'l-Qarn al-Awwal al-Hijrī* (Baghdad, 1953), Chap. 11; A.A. Dūrī, *Ta'rīkh al-'Iraq al-Iqtiṣādī fi'l-Qarn al-Rābi' al-Hijrī* (Baghdad, 1948), chap. 4.

[25] See Chap. XXIII, below.

mercial techniques and practices throughout the world. Not only did they bring from East Asia new goods and commodities, which were later introduced into Europe, but also adopted from China the practice of issuing paper money and passed it on to other nations. Further, the Muslims contributed to the development of the techniques of international banking. Checks were widely used and letters of credit and bills of exchange were popularized by Muslim bankers. Muslim merchants from certain commercial centers, such as Baṣra, were found in North Africa as well as in East Asia, which indicates the extent to which one important commercial city could with freedom exchange goods from one extreme part of the then known world to the other.[26]

[26] For a survey of Muslim commercial relations, especially since the period of the Crusades, see W. Heyd, *Histoire du Commerce du Levant* (Leipzig, 1885-6), 2 vols. See also Archibald R. Lewis, *Naval Power and Trade in the Mediterranean, A.D. 500-1100* (Princeton, 1951). Chap. 5; Adam Mez., *op. cit.*, Chap. 26.

"O ye who believe! Obey Allah and obey the Apostle, and those among you invested with authority; and if aught ye differ about anything, refer it to Allah and the Apostle, if ye believe in Allah and in the last day. This is the best and fairest way of settlement." Qur'ān IV, 62.

CHAPTER XX

ARBITRATION

Arbitration Before Islam

In the broad sense of settling disputes between parties in accordance with commonly accepted rules and usages arbitration is an old institution which goes back to antiquity. The main objective was to settle disputes by peaceful means; but the institution of arbitration was more in the nature of conciliation, by trying to bring the disputing parties into agreement on a settlement through compromise, not necessarily on the basis of the determination of which of the parties was right. This procedure is so old that in a treaty concluded in the fourth millenium B.C. (*circa* 3100) between Eannatum, ruler of the Mesopotamian city-state of Lagash, and the people of Umma, another Mesopotamian city-state, an arbitration clause was included for the settlement of a long-standing boundary dispute.[1] Other cases of arbitration have been reported in the ancient Near East, but in Greece this institution was much more developed. It occurred in disputes among city-states in such matters as boundaries and rivers as well as individual conflicts. The oracle at Delphi often acted as arbiter, and its decisions were almost invariably accepted. A third state also acted as an arbitrator who, on the basis of the investigation of an appointed committee, gave its arbitral decision.[2]

In pre-Islamic Arabia the tribal chief and the kāhin (soothsayer) acted as arbiters in inter-tribal disputes. The chiefs of the tribe of Tamīm were reputed for their success as arbiters among rival tribes. Persons of high reputation often acted as arbiters, especially during the annual fairs, such as that of 'Ukāz, or during the months of truce (ashhur al-ḥarām) in which war was prohibited.[3] Such persons also acted as mediators to end wars among tribes that had lasted for a long time. A case in point is the war between the 'Abs and the Dhubyān tribes which was settled, according to Arab chronicles, by the mediation of al-Ḥārith ibn 'Awf and Khārija.[4] Muḥammad,

[1] M. Rostovtseff, "International Relations in the Ancient World," in G. A. Walsh, *History and Nature of International Relations* (London, 1922), pp. 31, 40.

[2] Coleman Phillipson, *The International Law and Custom of Ancient Greece and Rome* (London, 1911), Vol. II, p. 133.

[3] See M. Ḥamīdullah, "Administration of Justice in Early Islam," *Islamic Culture*, Vol. IX (1937), pp. 163-71.

[4] According to traditional reports al-Ḥārith wanted to marry the daughter of Aws ibn Ḥāritha. The wife of Aws was from the 'Abs tribe. Thus when al-Ḥārith proposed to marry Aws's daughter, the latter replied: "What a light heart you have to wed women while the Arabs are slaying one another!" Al-Ḥārith inquired: "What should I do?" The daughter replied: "Go forth to your kindred, and make peace between them. Then return to your wife, and you will not miss what you desire." Al-Ḥārith said: "By Allah? What a noble and wise woman!" Thus al-Ḥārith with his friend Khārija acted as mediators and arbiters. Though the story is a

before his prophethood, himself acted as an arbitrator (ḥakam). The dispute among the Arab chiefs about lifting the Black Stone was a case which was settled by arbitration (taḥkīm).[5] A more important case was the dispute between the Aws and Khazraj tribes of Madīna, in which Muḥammad acted as a mediator, in accordance with Arab tradition, and ended their historic enmity.[6]

Islam and Arbitration

Islam recognized the Arab system of arbitration, whether it aimed at conciliating two Muslim rival parties or settling a dispute between them, since it fitted well the aim and spirit of Islam which sought peace and harmony among its followers. In matters which lead to no compromise with the Islamic creed, arbitration was also permitted between Muslim and non-Muslim communities. The Qur'ān and the practice of the Prophet Muḥammad support this position.[7] The arbitration between Muḥammad and Banū Qurayza, a Jewish tribe, in which both parties agreed to submit their dispute to a person chosen by

---

poetical one, it reveals the practice of arbitration. The story is also told by the poet Zuhayr who, in a long poem, eulogized al-Ḥārith for terminating the war between 'Abs and Dhubyān. See Abū'l Faraj al-Isbahānī, *al-Aghānī* (Cairo, A.H. 1285), Vol. IX, pp. 149-50. For a discussion on the role of women in the conciliation and the settlement of disputes among the Arab tribes, see Ilse Lichtenstadter, *Women in the Aiyām al-'Arab* (London, 1935).

[5] In rebuilding the Ka'ba shrine, the Arab chiefs could not agree on who would have the honor of lifting the Black Stone. Muḥammad, who was reputed for his good character, acted as an arbiter. Muḥammad made a satisfactory decision by putting the Black Stone in a mantle himself and then asking all the chiefs to participate in lifting it up; and then he himself put it in its place in the wall.

[6] See p. 205, above.

[7] Q. IV, 62.

them, is a case in point.[8] On the basis of this precedent, al-Shaybānī advises the imām that the Muslims may agree to submit to a third party a dispute on matters connected with the termination of fighting or of a particular battle.[9] As in the case of a judge, the arbiter must be a sane and just believer whose reputation is beyond reproach. His award must be accepted by both parties, provided he is chosen freely by them. If he had acted as an arbiter without their prior agreement, or if he made a decision regarding a dispute in which his parents, wife, or children were involved, his award was not binding.[10]

Arbitration Between 'Alī and Mu'āwiya

Probably the most notable case of arbitration to be found in Muslim annals was that which 'Alī, the fourth caliph (A.D. 656-661), and Mu'āwiya, governor of Syria, created to end civil war. Although its character was political rather than legal, the way the case was formally handled reflected the nature and procedure of arbitration as it was then understood.

The appeal to arbitration was requested by Mu'āwiya who, acting under the advice of the astute 'Amr ibn al-'Ās (who sensed the probable defeat of his forces), ordered his warriors to have the Qur'ān raised on their lances. This meant that Mu'āwiya demanded the end of the struggle by an appeal to the Qur'ān as the arbiter between himself and 'Alī. Although 'Alī was aware of the trickery in this procedure, he could not turn down an appeal to the Qur'ān, a plea which found support among his followers. Each of the two parties agreed to appoint an arbi-

[8] Ibn Hishām, *Kitāb al-Sīra,* ed. Wüstenfeld (Göttingen, 1859), Vol. II, pp. 688-9.

[9] Shaybānī, *al-Siyar al-Kabīr* with Sarakhsī's Commentary (Hyderabad, A.H. 1335). Vol. I, pp. 363-4.

[10] Marghinānī, *al-Hidāya* (Cairo, 1936), Vol. III, pp. 79-80; and Ḥamīdullah, *Muslim Conduct of State* (Lahore, 1945), pp. 141-4.

trator (ḥakam) who was given full powers to make a decision, provided it was based on the Qur'ān and sunna. Mu'āwiya appointed 'Amr ibn al-'Ās, and 'Alī, on the insistence of his followers, appointed Abū Mūsa al-Ash'arī. The two arbitrators were secured in their lives, property, and the lives of their families and were required to give their award within a period of one year.[11]

The two arbitrators met at Adhruḥ (A.H. 38, or A.D. 659) and began their discussion on the basis of a treaty, already agreed upon by both parties. The Ḥudaybiya treaty was looked upon as a model for drawing up the draft of the arbitration treaty. This precedent helped to deprive 'Alī of his official title as a caliph and to place him on the same footing as Mu'āwiya, his governor of Syria. The text of the treaty follows:

> In the name of Allah, the Compassionate, the Merciful;
>
> This is what is agreed upon for arbitration, between 'Alī ibn Abī Ṭālib and Mu'āwiya ibn Sufyān. 'Ali represents the people of Kūfa and their followers of the believers and Muslims; and Mu'āwiya represents al-Shām [Syria] and their followers of the believers and Muslims;
>
> We appeal to the arbitration of Allah and His Book; and that there is no other basis than this . . . and that the two arbitrators Abū Mūsa al-Ash'arī and 'Amr ibn al-'Ās will act on the basis of Allah's Book . . . and if nothing is to be found in Allah's Book, then the justiciable sunna will be the basis. . . .[12]

The text of the treaty is obviously brief and vague. It is silent about the object of arbitration and the specific issues to be discussed. The only point mentioned is that the Qur'ān and sunna were to be the basis of arbitration. The brevity and vagueness gave 'Amr an excellent opportunity to ignore the original issue,

[11] 'Alī realized that 'Amr was too clever for Abū Mūsa and tried unsuccessfully to appoint another arbitrator. See Ṭabarī, *Ta'rīkh,* ed. de Goeje (Leiden, 1879), Series I, Vol. VI, p. 3334.

[12] Ṭabarī, p. 3336.

and he shifted the discussion by putting to Abū Mūsa the following question:

"Abū Mūsa, don't you agree [with me] that 'Uthmān [the late caliph] was assassinated unjustly?" Abū Mūsa replied in the affirmative.

'Amr then added: "Don't you agree that Mu'āwiya and his relatives are ['Uthmān's] heirs?" Abū Mūsa agreed to this.

'Amr then said that Allah has said: ". . . whosoever shall be slain unjustly, to his heirs we have given authority; he shall not exceed the limits in slaying, and surely he is assisted." (Q. XVII, 35). "Why therefore," said 'Amr, "is not Mu'āwiya the heir of 'Uthmān?" "But," 'Amr continued, "if you fear that the people will complain that Mu'āwiya will rule without qualifications, then you may reply that Mu'āwiya is the heir of 'Uthmān [who was assassinated] unjustly . . . and that he is artful in politics and administration, and that he is the brother of Umm Ḥubayba, the wife of the Prophet, and he was a companion of the Prophet. . . ."

Abū Mūsa replied: "O 'Amr, be fearful of Allah. . . . 'Alī ibn Abī Ṭālib is more distinguished in Quraysh. . . ."[13]

The discussion, touching very little on the ways and means of ending the civil war, was confined to determining who was the best fitted to be a caliph. Abū Mūsa was inclined to nominate 'Abd-Allah ibn 'Umar (son of the second caliph) while 'Amr supported Mu'āwiya. Finally 'Amr addressed the following question to Abū Mūsa: "What is your opinion?"

Abū Mūsa replied: "My opinion is to depose these two men and to leave the matter for popular election (shūra) to the Muslims who will choose for themselves whom they like."

'Amr said: "My opinion is as yours."[14]

The two arbitrators, having apparently reached an agree-

[13] *Ibid.*, pp. 3355-8.

[14] *Ibid.*, pp. 3358.

ment, proceeded to announce officially their decision to the public.[15] 'Amr politely asked Abū Mūsa, on the basis of seniority, to give the decision first while he would follow to confirm it. Abū Mūsa praised Allah and said:

> O people! We have examined the matter of this nation and could not find a better solution . . . than to depose [both] 'Alī and Mu'āwiya, so that this nation will take the matter and intrust for rulership whom it would like. I have [decided] to depose [both] 'Alī and Mu'āwiya . . . and you may choose whom you consider is qualified.[16]

'Amr, succeeding Abū Mūsa, made, after he praised Allah the following statement:

> You have listened to this man [Abū Mūsa] who had [decided] to depose his companion. I have [also decided] to depose his companion as he deposed him, [but] I confirm my companion Mu'āwiya, as he is the heir of 'Uthmān . . . and the best qualified for this position. . . .[17]

The disagreement in the announcement of the decision naturally gave 'Alī ample reason to reject it. He condemned the arbitrators on the ground that they had

> . . . left the rules of the Qur'ān behind them . . . and that each one had followed his own opinion without [taking into consideration] a standard. Their decision [therefore] has no ground of evidence or precedent; and [moreover] they have disagreed on their decision. . . .[18]

'Amr has been attacked by Arab chroniclers for having tricked Abū Mūsa, but the question seems to be not so much of trickery and deceit as of 'Amr's ability to influence Abū Mūsa to tackle a question which was not the subject of dispute.

[15] Mas'ūdī departs from other chroniclers and asserts that no public statements were made; that Abū Mūsa and 'Amr agreed only on deposing 'Alī and Mu'āwiya; and that this deposition was stated in a written document. See Mas'ūdī, *Murūj al-Dhahab* (Cairo, A.H. 1346), Vol. II, p. 27.

[16] Ṭabarī, pp. 3358-9.

[17] *Ibid.*, p. 3359.

[18] *Ibid.*, p. 3368.

Abū Mūsa's mistake therefore lies in his failure to distinguish between the specific issue on which they were called upon to pronounce judgment, namely the termination of fighting between 'Alī and Mu'āwiya, and another which was beyond their competence.[19]

Significance of Arbitration

There has been a tendency among writers to exaggerate the significance of arbitration, whether in classical or Islamic times, as a means of settling disputes.[20] Not only was arbitration in Arabia limited to inter-tribal feuds but also after the rise of Islam it was rarely resorted to. Because of the difficulty of separating the legal from political issues, as in the case of the Adhruḥ arbitration, the caliphs as well as provincial governors, resorted to diplomacy and war rather than to litigation by arbitration. In purely technical matters, such as the payment of blood-money in inter-tribal feuds, and even in disputes among individuals or local rulers, arbitration tended to serve certain limited purposes and was enforced by tribal public opinion and the coercive authority of rulers.

[19] Cf. H. Lammens, "Adhruḥ," *Encyclopedia of Islam,* Vol. I, pp. 135-6.

[20] Cf. Najīb al-Armanāzī, *al-Shar' al-Dawlī fi'l Islām* (Damascus, 1930), pp. 91, 95; Nussbaum, *A Concise History of the Law of Nations* (New York, 1947), pp. 14-15.

"Ibn Mas'ūd said: 'The emissaries of Musaylima, the liar prophet, came to Muḥammad, who inquired: "Do you believe that I am the Apostle of Allah?" The emissaries replied: "We believe that Musaylima is the Apostle of Allah!" Whereupon Muḥammad remarked, "If I were in the habit of executing emissaries, I would have ordered you killed."' Ibn Mas'ūd continued that the tradition since then was set that emissaries should not be executed." a ḥadīth.

CHAPTER XXI

DIPLOMACY

Muslim Conception of Diplomacy

Although the practice of diplomacy for the maintenance of peaceful intercourse among nations was known from antiquity, its adoption by Islam was not essentially for peaceful purposes as long as the state of war was regarded as the normal relation between Islam and other nations. In early Islam, diplomacy was resorted to as an auxiliary to or as a substitute for war: it served either as a herald to deliver the message of Islam before fighting began or as a means to exchange prisoners of war after the termination of fighting. Certain peaceful purposes, such as the exchange of gifts or the negotiation of ransom treaties, were not resorted to until the 'Abbāsid period. Even then, emissaries were dispatched in connection with a definite event or crisis and were almost always suspected as spies. Thus diplomacy was understood in the broad sense of statecraft—not as an instrument to facilitate intercourse among nations—and had the character of being inherently Machiavellian.

The right of legation was a device to secure temporary representation of the head of state in the courts of foreign monarchs to achieve certain specific objectives. The emissaries, once they had delivered their messages, returned to their chiefs to report whether they had succeeded or failed in their mission. Although often received with ceremonies and lavish entertainment, the emissaries were rarely looked upon as other than official spies; they were, accordingly, carefully watched and denied access to information or contact with civilians.

Emissaries

The diplomatic agent was called by Muslim publicists either a rasūl (plural, rusul) or safīr (plural, sufarā'). The term rasūl is derived from irsāl, which literally means sending and includes the dispatch of an agent charged with a specific mission.[1] Thus the term rasūl may mean either a prophet or an emissary. The term safīr is derived from safar which means, in addition to the functions of rasūl, conciliation and peaceful settlement.[2] In practice, however, the two terms were often used interchangeably, although later text-writers restricted the use of safīr for diplomatic agents and reserved the religious meaning of apostle for rasūl.[3]

Muslim emissaries, representing caliphs and sultans, were ordinarily chosen from among confidants who were reputed for their knowledge, adroitness, and dependability. They were also chosen for their external physical appearance and charm

[1] Jurjānī, *Kitāb al-Ta'rīfāt,* ed. Flügel (Leipzic, 1845), p. 115; and Ibn al-Farrā', *Kitāb Rusul al-Mulūk,* ed. Ṣalaḥ al-Dīn al-Munajjid (Cairo, 1947), pp. 7, 107-8.

[2] Qalqashandī, *Ṣubḥ al-A'sha* (Cairo, 1915), Vol. VI, p. 15.

[3] Ibn al-Farrā', p. 2-6.

no less than their ability, courage, and presence of mind. They were instructed to abstain from drinking, if they were in the habit of drinking, and to keep away from women—too tempting for secrecy.[4] Not infrequently the caliphs and sultans, unable to find a single person with the necessary qualifications, sent a mission of two or three emissaries, one of them was a man of the sword, the other a man of learning, and the third a scribe who could act as a secretary.[5]

The emissaries were supplied with official letters and were instructed to address them to the heads of state of the receiving countries. These letters served either as letters of credence, empowering the emissary to deliver an oral message, or contained general statements on the purpose of the mission, indicating that the secret information was to be delivered orally by the emissary.

From the time of the Prophet Muḥammad, emissaries were sent abroad for religious or political purposes. According to Muslim chronicles, the Prophet Muḥammad sent emissaries to Byzantium, Egypt, Persia, and Ethiopia, inviting them to adopt Islam. The phraseology of the traditional reports of these letters is almost the same, with slight variations. The text of one of them, sent to the Byzantine emperor, is as follows:

> In the name of Allah, the Compassionate, the Merciful.
>
> From Muḥammad, the Apostle of Allah, to Heraclius, grand chief of the Rūm [Byzantines].
>
> Peace be on those who follow the Truth. [It is my duty to] call you to Islam, in the name of Allah. Be a Muslim, and you will be safe; for Allah will compensate you double the merits. And you, People of the Book, will find the same words [of God] among us. Let us worship no other god than

[4] Ibn al-Farrā', pp. 20-1, 22, 25, 29.

[5] Al-Ḥasan ibn 'Abd-Allah, *Athār al-Uwal fī Tartīb al-Duwal* (Cairo, A.H. 1295), p. 93.

Allah nor adopt other gods besides him. If you believe, then say: "We are Muslims," if not, you will be responsible for the sins of your people. . . .[6]

According to the traditions, the emperor of Ethiopia and the Muqawqas of Egypt accepted the invitation; the Byzantine emperor replied that his nation was not of the opinion of adopting Islam; and the king of Persia tore up the letter and dismissed the emissaries. When Muḥammad learned the news about the action of the Persian king, he remarked: "His kingdom will be torn!"[7] The character of this diplomatic intercourse was essentially religious.

Diplomatic intercourse during the early caliphate (the Orthodox and Umayyad periods) was chiefly with the Byzantines for the purpose of signing peace treaties or paying tribute. The Umayyad caliphs, especially in the reign of Mu'āwiya I and 'Abd al-Malik, negotiated peace treaties and paid annual tribute in order to avoid Byzantine attack at a time when they were fully involved in civil wars. Arab chronicles hardly mention these events and no records are preserved about the negotiation or the texts of these treaties.[8]

The 'Abbāsid caliphs entered into more important diplomatic relations than their Umayyad predecessors. Owing to the almost annual campaigns sent to the Byzantine borders, there was need to negotiate treaties for the exchange of prisoners of war or the payments of ransom.[9] Emissaries were also frequently sent to contemporary rulers, Muslims and non-Muslims, for various political, commercial or social purposes. The

[6] Ya'qūbī, *Ta'rīkh,* ed. M. Th. Houtsma (Leiden, 1883), Vol. II, pp. 83-4; Ṣubḥ al-A'sha, Vol. VI, pp. 376-7.

[7] *Ibid.,* p. 83; Bukhārī, *Kitāb al-Jāmi' al-Ṣaḥīḥ* ed. Krehl (Leiden, 1864), Vol. II, p. 232.

[8] Some references to diplomatic intercourse of this period are made in Ibn al-Farrā', *op. cit.,* Chap. 21.

[9] For ransom treaties, see p. 217, above.

Fāṭimid and Mamlūk rulers continued this practice and their emissaries reached Europe as well as central and East Asia.[10]

Reception of Emissaries

Foreign emissaries can enter dār al-Islam without amān, for the moment they declare themselves as emissaries they are allowed to proceed to the capital, and they are often accompanied by an official who acted as a guide. The right to enter dār al-Islam without amān is inherent in the diplomatic immunity which they enjoy during their temporary mission, provided they observe their duties and abstain from prohibited acts such as spying or buying weapons for the purpose of taking them to dār al-ḥarb.[11] Although this immunity was not strictly observed, especially at times of ill-feeling between ruling monarchs, both Muslim and non-Muslim rulers found it mutually advantageous to observe the rule of diplomatic immunity.[12]

The emissaries were ordinarily received with ceremonies surpassing those accorded to many of the official visitors from the highest Muslim dignitaries, especially during the late 'Abbāsid period. This reflected the need for a display of grandeur at the time of decline of Muslim power. The emissaries were met by representatives of the caliph (or sultan) and received in the capitals of Islam (Baghdad, Cairo, Cordova, etc.) with great pomp. They entered the capital in a procession, marching through streets lined with soldiers and decorations, and resided as guests in houses reserved for such occasions where they were

[10] For texts of letters sent by Muslim rulers, see Qalqashandī, *op. cit.*, Vol. VI, pp. 382, 421, 443, 457-63.

[11] Abū Yūsuf, *Kitāb al-Kharāj*, pp. 188, 189; Shaybānī, *al-Siyar al-Kabīr* with Sarakhsī's Commentary, Vol. IV, pp. 66-7.

[12] For texts of agreements on diplomatic immunity, see Ṣalāḥ al-Dīn al-Munajjid, "al-Rusul wa'l-Sufarā' 'ind al-'Arab" in *Kitāb Rusul al-Mulūk*, pp. 139-40.

lavishly entertained.[13] Muslim chroniclers give detailed descriptions of the visits of several Byzantine emissaries to Baghdad. Most profusely described is that which took place in A.H. 305 (A.D. 918), during the reign of Al-Muqtadir, in which the Byzantine emissary was shown all the wonders and richness and lavishness which the caliph and his able vizir, Ibn al-Furāt, desired to display to the representative of their Byzantine rival ruler.[14] A similar case is the reception of the Fāṭimid emissary (A.D. 890) by the Caliph al-Ṭā'i' and the Buwayhid prince 'Aḍud al-Dawla—the actual ruler—who was impressed by the pomp and reverential awe shown to the caliph by 'Aḍud al-Dawla.[15] The caliphs of Cordova and the Mamluks of Egypt granted similar privileges to foreign emissaries.

During their sojourn the emissaries were not only lavishly entertained but also shown the magnificent palaces and other places of interest and showered with gifts and robes of honor reflecting the hospitality of the host state and the excellences of its refined crafts. These gifts were naturally exchanged by both sides as part of the diplomatic ceremonies.

When the emissaries had accomplished their mission they requested leave and they were often accorded ceremonies similar to those at their reception. If, however, the mission proved to be a failure, they were dismissed with obvious coolness, and in certain circumstances, if hostilities began when the emissaries were still on Muslim soil, they were either insulted or imprisoned or even killed.

13 Al-Ḥasan ibn 'Abd-Allah, *op. cit.*, pp. 94-6.

14 'Arīb ibn Sa'd, *Ṣilat Ta'rīkh al-Ṭabarī*, ed. M. J. de Goeje (Leiden 1897), pp. 64-5; Ibn Miskawayh, *Tajārib al-Umam*, ed. D. S. Margoliouth (Oxford, 1921), Vol. V, pp. 53-54; al-Khaṭṭīb al-Baghdādī, *Ta'rīkh Baghdād* (Cairo, 1931), Vol. I, pp. 102-5.

15 Quṭb al-Dīn al-Nabrawālī, *Kitāb al-I'lām li A'lām Bayt Allah al-Ḥarām*, Wüstenfeld (Leipzig, 1857), pp. 168-9.

Functions of Diplomatic Missions

Since diplomatic missions were not exchanged on a permanent basis they ordinarily accomplished certain specific functions when they were dispatched. These functions varied in accordance with the need and circumstances of the Muslim ruler. In early Islam the functions were, in the first place, to invite the enemy to adopt Islam. Such an invitation served also as a notification of hostilities or declaration of war, in case the enemy refused to adopt Islam. In the second place, the emissaries negotiated for peace in case the enemy was willing to come to terms with Islam.

To these functions were added others of a different character when the Islamic empire was stabilized, especially under 'Abbāsid rule. Emissaries were exchanged between Islam and Christendom not only for signing truces and peace treaties, but also for the exchange of gifts and prisoners of war and for conciliating differences or facilitating trade. They were also instructed to inquire into the internal state of affairs of the host state. Spying, in other words, was a function of diplomatic agents whom both the sending and receiving states were keen to exploit to their advantage and alert against being exploited.

Among Muslim rulers and *de facto* independent provincial governors emissaries were dispatched, in addition to carrying official messages, for purposes of conveying messages of congratulations and condolences or for negotiating marriages among ruling families. Messages of good will were often exchanged among Muslim and non-Muslim rulers in order to avoid conflict or to facilitate travel and the exchange of goods.

During the 'Abbāsid period when hostilities with the Byzantines broke out almost every year, emissaries were sent for the exchange of prisoners of war or for the payment of ransom for the release of prisoners.[16] Further, alliances were negotiated

[16] See pp. 216-17, above.

for the purpose of rallying one state to another against a common enemy. One of the most famous cases in Western tradition is the exchange of emissaries between Charlemagne and Harūn al-Rashīd, in which the former, in addition to the exchange of valuable gifts, sought to establish an alliance with the 'Abbāsids against Byzantium. The significance of this embassy in the international relations of the ninth century of the Christian era calls for a more detailed statement.

Muslim Diplomacy and World Politics

In the period when the Muslim empire was stabilized under 'Abbāsid rule, there were four big powers in the world. In the East there were the 'Abbāsid and Byzantine empires which, inheriting the long Roman-Persian rivalry, were encroaching on each other's frontiers, and peace treaties were frequently violated. In Europe there were the Frankish empire and the Umayyads of Spain who were almost in constant state of hostilities, beginning with the defeat of 'Abd al-Raḥmān by Charles Martel at the battle of Tours (A.D. 732).

The rivalry between the two Eastern powers, on the one hand, and the two Western powers on the other, continued for a long time and led to the opening of significant diplomatic intercourse. Pippin III (the Short) tried to effect reconciliation with the Byzantines; he actually sent a mission to Constantinople in A.D. 757, and the emperor responded by sending a return mission. But the policy of the Papacy at this time was to prevent any alliance between the Franks and the Byzantines.[17] The 'Abbāsids, likewise, tried unsuccessfully to bring Spain under their control. Thus the rivalry continued between the two Muslim states, on the one hand, and the two Christian

[17] The Pope was against the Byzantines on account of the question of image worship.

states, on the other. This state of affairs tended to induce the Frankish rulers and the 'Abbāsid caliphs to develop cordial relations with each other. It also tended to develop friendly relations between Cordova and Constantinople.

The story of the diplomatic intercourse between Frankish and 'Abbāsid rulers is to be found only in the Latin sources, while the contemporary Muslim chronicles are completely silent about it.[18] The silence of the Muslim sources led several scholars to deny that actual diplomatic intercourse had taken place between Aachen and Baghdad, at least in the form reported by Western chronicles.[19]

According to Western sources the initiative to begin the diplomatic intercourse between the Franks and the 'Abbāsids was made in A.D. 765 by Pippin, who sent the first of a series of diplomatic missions to al-Manṣūr, the second 'Abbāsid caliph, then at war with the Byzantine emperor. After three years the mission returned, accompanied by an embassy from the caliph and gifts. Pippin honorably received the Muslim emissaries and subsequently permitted them to return to Marseilles.

Charlemagne, the son of Pippin, dispatched several missions to the East. Two missions (in A.D. 797 and 802) were sent to the court of Harūn al-Rashīd, and one (A.D. 799) to the Patriarch of Jerusalem. In 797, two Franks and a Jewish inter-

[18] The first Latin source which discussed the exchange of diplomatic agents between the Franks and the 'Abbāsids is the *Annales Regni Francorum,* which Einhard, secretary of Charlemagne, used with additional material in his *Vita Karoli Magni* (6th, ed., Hanover, 1911). While Einhard is not regarded as completely reliable in his details, he was in a position to know the facts. For a critical study of this question, see L. Halphen, *Etudes critiques sur l'histoire de Charlemagne* (Paris, 1921).

[19] For a discussion of this controversy see M. Khadduri, *The Diplomatic Relations between Harūn al-Rashīd and Charlemagne* (Baghdad, 1939) (In Arabic).

preter were sent; the two Franks died in the East, and the interpreter returned with an elephant after four years.[20] In 802 Charlemagne sent a second mission to Baghdad. It is alleged that his mission attained "what was requested to be done," and Charlemagne was granted the "sacred and salutary place he assigned to his power." Buckler maintains that this diplomatic intercourse resulted in the "transaction of the nature of a transfer to Charles of some form of authority over Jerusalem."[21] Buckler then defines the status of Charlemagne as a wāli of Jerusalem under the 'Abbāsid Caliph. He argues that such an office, in accordance with al-Māwardī's work on the ordinances of the caliphate, may devolve on a non-Muslim.[22]

In 799, the Patriarch of Jerusalem sent a mission to Charlemagne and the latter sent a return mission with alms and offerings. In 800 another mission was sent from the Patriarch carrying to Charlemagne, by way of a blessing, the keys of the Holy Sepulchre and of the place of Calvary, together with a banner.

If the traditional reports of the Latin sources are to be accepted, we are inclined to think that the purpose of the diplomatic relations was merely the desire to establish friendly relations among two great monarchs. Both Charlemagne and Harūn, as the then greatest rulers of Christendom and Islam, might have sought a close friendly relationship for the enhancement of their prestige no less than a combination against Constantinople and Cordova. Palestine was too valuable a prize to

[20] For the story of the elephant, see F. W. Buckler, *Harunu'l Rashid and Charles the Great* (Cambridge, Mass., 1931), app. 3.

[21] Buckler, p. 29.

[22] Buckler, pp. 34-5. Bréhier maintains that Charlemagne attained a protectorate over Palestine. See Louis Bréhier, "Charlemagne et la Palestine," *Revue Historique,* Vol. CLVII (1928), pp. 277-91.

be given to Charlemagne, as events proved during the subsequent two centuries. When the Crusaders made an attempt to take Palestine, at a time when Muslim power had declined, they were obstinately resisted.

As to the purpose of the correspondence of the Patriarch with Charlemagne it seems that it was strictly religious rather than political. For the Patriarch, as the head of the Christian community in Palestine, could not enter into a political bargaining without the knowledge or the authorization of the caliph. It would seem that in view of the cordial relations that might have been established between Charlemagne and Harūn al-Rashīd, it is likely that the Patriarch tried to take advantage of this situation by establishing relations with a Western Christian monarch, seeking to enhance the prestige of the church in the East morally and materially. The keys and the banners sent by the Patriarch to Charlemagne were symbolic gifts rather than an act of surrendering any political privileges which were beyond the powers of the Patriarch.[23]

Importance of Diplomacy

Like the amān, making possible the movement of persons from one region to another that is normally at war with the other, diplomacy served as a means by virtue of which official contact was made possible between Muslim and non-Muslim authorities. The jihād, as just war, required certain formalities, such as the necessity of invitation to Islam before fighting should begin, and these could be fulfilled only through diplomatic channels. Moreover, the sharī'a permitted Muslim authorities to make peace with the enemy (for a period not

[23] See Einar Joranson, "The Alleged Frankish Protectorate in Palestine," *American Historical Review,* Vol. XXXII (1927), p. 245; and Steven Runciman, "Charlemagne and Palestine," *English Historical Review,* Vol. I (1935), p. 610.

exceeding ten years), and this could be achieved only after the emissaries of Muslim and non-Muslims had met to negotiate. Thus diplomacy, supplementing the war objectives of Islam, was regarded as an integral part of the law of the jihād.

When the jihād entered into the passive stage and peaceful relations between Islam and other nations developed, diplomacy gained increasing significance, especially in matters of peaceful character, such as facilitating trade relations, exchanging gifts, and fulfilling other social purposes.

At a time when the means of communication among nations had not yet sufficiently developed, the dispatch of emissaries served not only to exchange information among nations, but also to facilitate contacts for economic and cultural purposes. The emissaries, in addition to their diplomatic functions, often carried back with them commodities, books, and rarities from distant countries which served to acquaint their people with information about nations which they hardly ever heard about. In an age when such travelers as Ibn Jubayr (A.D. 1145-1217) and Ibn Baṭṭūṭa (A.D. 1304-1377), who covered a wide range of the then known world, made reputations by the information they gathered during their long odysseys; the emissaries who saw no less strange lands than these travelers (such as Charlemagne's emissaries) must have reported to their masters and the palace entourages the wonders they encountered during their long journeys. Thus, diplomatic intercourse perhaps served as a means for social and cultural development no less than for other purposes.

"'Umayr ibn Sa'd once came to 'Umar ibn al-Khaṭṭāb and said: 'There lies between us and the Byzantines a city called 'Arabsūs, whose people disclose to our enemy our secrets, but do not disclose to us our enemy's.' Thereupon 'Umar replied: 'When you go there, propose to give them for every ewe they possess, two; for every cow, two; and for everything, two. If they agree to this, give that to them, expel them, and destroy their city. But if they refuse then notify them to repudiate our agreement, and give them one year at the expiration of which you may destroy the city.'" Balādhurī, Futūḥ al-Buldān, 156-7.

CHAPTER XXII

NEUTRALITY

Islam and Neutrality

The state which regards its normal relations with the entire world as permanently hostile and permits short intervals of peace only when regulated by treaties obviously has no place left for the country which chooses to be on good terms with that state and also with its enemies. If neutrality is taken to mean the attitude of a state which voluntarily desires to keep out of war by not taking sides, no such a status is recognized in Muslim legal theory. For Islam must *ipso jure* be at war with any state which refuses to come to terms with it either by submitting to Muslim rule or by accepting a temporary peace arrangement. The world, it will be recalled, was sharply divided under Muslim law into two divisions: the dār al-Islām, comprising Muslim territory and those lands which submitted to Muslim rule, and the dār al-ḥarb, comprising the rest of the world. While some jurists recognized a third division of the world, called dār al-'ahd, or dār al-ṣulḥ, comprising countries in treaty relations with Islam, most of them considered this division as part either of the dār al-Islām or dār al-ḥarb.[1] No jurist, however, would approve of a country being allowed to choose without Islam's consent an intermediary status between dār al-Islām and dār al-ḥarb.

If in principle the concept of neutrality has no place in the Muslim jural order, the law, however, was not enforced without regard to certain exceptional cases for doctrinal no less than for practical considerations. Islam voluntarily refrained from attacking certain territories which were regarded, whether in deference to their benevolent attitude toward the Prophet Muḥammad and his companions or because of their inaccessibility, as immune from the jihād. Such territories, constituting a separate division of the world, may be called—following the pattern of dividing the world into dārs—dār al-ḥiyād or the world of neutrality.

The world of neutrality, however, is not a self-constituting division of the world, for under the legal system which regards all countries as inherently inimical save those which have obtained security by Islam's consent, only those states which Islam agreed to spare from the jihād might be regarded as neutral. Strictly speaking, such states were not neutral, in the sense of the modern law of nations, which recognizes the right of a state to declare her neutrality toward two or more belligerent powers; these states were neutralized states, that is, their neutrality was guaranteed by the powers, including the belligerent power or powers themselves. Neutralization, therefore, not neutrality, may be said to have been permissible in Muslim legal theory, and practice, perhaps, supplied more precedents than the opinions of text-writers.

[1] See pp. 144-5, above.

The Status of Ethiopia

Ethiopia enjoyed a unique position in the eyes of the Muslims and may be regarded as the classic example of a non-Muslim state which Islam voluntarily declared to be immune from the jihād. In formulating their opinions, Muslim publicists were primarily guided by the traditional reports about Islam's early relations with Ethiopia as well as by the fact that Ethiopia remained for centuries untouched by Muslim forces. A discussion of the nature of Ethiopia's position in Muslim law calls for a little historical background.

Before Islam, Ethiopia had invaded the Yaman and re-established Christianity; it had also attacked Makka in the very year, according to tradition, in which Muḥammad was born (A.D. 570).[2] These military expeditions were not the only form of contact between Arabia and Ethiopia, for there were trade relations and cultural influences, the impact of which was reflected in the presence of an Abyssinian colony in Makka and the infiltration of Abyssinian words into the Arabic language.[3]

When Islam emerged in a hostile environment it was therefore not unnatural for Muḥammad to look to Ethiopia as a potential supporter as she had already opposed paganism in Arabia. Some of Muḥammad's followers were of Abyssinian origin, the most famous of whom was Bilāl, Muḥammad's favorite mu'azzin (one who calls to prayer). The history of Muḥammad's relations with Ethiopia, although mixed with legend, put this country in a favorable light vis-a-vis Islam. All the Muslim chronicles report, although they are confused as to details, that some of Muḥammad's early followers, in order to escape persecution, sought refuge in Ethiopia. This is often

[2] See Sir Ernest A. Wallis Budge, *A History of Ethiopia* (London, 1928), Vol. I, pp. 260-9.

[3] See Richard Bell, *The Origin of Islam in Its Christian Environment* (London, 1926), pp. 28-32.

referred to as the first Ethiopian hijra, which took place in A.D. 615.[4] According to the traditional report the chiefs of Quraysh, rulers of Makka, sent a deputation to the Najāshī, the Ethiopian King,[5] to demand the return of the refugees. The Najāshī summoned the refugees to inquire about their dispute with Quraysh and Ja'far ibn Abī Ṭālib, their chief, replied in words which were often repeated by other Muslim representatives on other occasions,[6] as follows:

> O King we were a nation in the days of ignorance (jāhiliyya) worshipping idols, eating carrion, committing shameful acts, killing our next of kin, violating our obligations towards our neighbors, the strong among us eating the weak. This continued until Allah sent us an Apostle from us, whose ancestry, honesty, trustworthiness and chastity are known to us. He summoned us to Allah to believe in His oneness, to worship Him and abandon stones and idols which we and our forefathers had worshipped instead. He ordered us to speak the truth, to be faithful, to observe our obligations to our next of kin and neighbors, to refrain from forbidden acts and bloodshed, from committing shameful acts and telling the false, from dispossessing orphans and slandering virtuous women. He ordered us to worship Allah and associate no other with Him, to pray, give alms and fast. . . . So we believed in him and followed what was brought to him from Allah. We, therefore, worshipped Allah alone, associating no one with Him, abandoning what was forbidden to us and doing what was allowed to us. This resulted in the enmity of our people who persecuted us and tried to abjure us in our religion and go back to idolatry.[7]

Ja'far's discourse with the Najāshī, supported by quotations from the Qur'ān (XIX, 16-34), resulted in the Najāshī's de-

[4] For a traditional account of these events, see Ibn Hishām, *Kitāb al-Sīra,* ed. Wüstenfeld (Göttingen, 1858), Vol. I, pp. 208-21. Cf. W. Montgomery Watt, *Muhammad at Mecca* (Oxford, 1953), pp. 112-7.

[5] The name of the Ethiopian king, according to Budge, was 'Armaḥ (Budge, *op. cit.,)* p. 270.

[6] See pp. 99-100, above.

[7] Ibn Hishām, *Kitāb al-Sīra,* ed. Wüstenfeld (Göttingen, 1858), Vol. I, pp. 219-20. Translation adapted from J. S. Trimingham, *Islam in Ethiopia* (London, 1952) p. 45.

cision to protect the Muslims without even listening to the demands of the Quraysh deputation. It is reported that one or two more emigrations were to follow before Islam was firmly established.

Another incident which made the Muslims well disposed toward Ethiopia was the favorable reply of the Najāshī to Muḥammad's letter of invitation to accept Islam. In the eighth year of the hijra Muḥammad had sent a letter, as he did to other rulers, to the Najāshī, in which he said:

In the name of Allah, the Merciful, the Compassionate. From Muḥammad, the Apostle of Allah, to the Najāshī, King of Abyssinia. Peace be on you. Glory be to Allah, the only One, the Holy One, the peaceful and faithful protector. I testify that 'Īsa [Jesus], son of Mary, is the spirit and word of Allah, and that He sent them down into Mary, the blessed and immaculate Virgin, and she conceived. He created 'Īsa of his own spirit and made him to live by His breath, even as he did Adam. I now summon thee to worship Allah who is without partner and who rules the heavens and earth. Accept my mission, follow me, and become one of my disciples, for I am the Apostle of Allah. . . . Set aside the pride of thy sovereignty. I call upon thee and thy hosts to accept the worship of the supreme Being. My mission is over. I have preached, and may heaven grant that my counsel may be of benefit to those who hear. Peace shall be with the man who shall walk in the light of the true belief.[8]

According to the Muslim chronicles the Najāshī laid the letter on his head as a mark of respect, and accepted Muḥammad's mission. He replied, with gifts sent to Muḥammad, as follows:

In the name of Allah, the Merciful, the Compassionate. To Muḥammad, the Apostle of Allah, peace be on you. May Allah shelter thee under His compassion, and give thee blessings in abundance. There is no god but Allah, who has brought me to Islam. Thy letter I have read. What thou hast said about Jesus is the right belief, for He hath said nothing more than that. I testify my belief in the King of heaven and of earth. Thine

[8] Ṭabarī, *Ta'rīkh*, ed. de Goeje (Leiden, 1885), Series I, Vol. III, p. 1569. Translation adapted from Budge, *op. cit.*, Vol. I, pp. 271-2.

advice I have pondered over deeply. . . . I testify that thou art the Apostle of Allah, and I have sworn this in the presence of Ja'far, and have acknowledged Islam before him. I attach myself to the worship of the Lord of the worlds, O Prophet. I send my son as my envoy to thee, but if thou dost command it, I will go myself and do homage to the holiness of thy mission. I testify that thy words are true.[9]

"When we remember the ardent and fanatical character of Abyssinian Christianity," says Budge, "it must come as a surprise that 'Armaḥ and his bishops accepted Islam."[10] As Muḥammad only stressed in his letter to the Najāshī his views about Christ, making no claim to political domination, the Najāshī saw no reason why he should reject this offer. Sir Ernest Budge adds that there was another good reason for the Najāshī's submission, and that was political in character. The Najāshī must have heard about Muḥammad's exploits in Arabia and was desirous to spare his people from Muslim attack. His apparent submission to Islam should not necessarily result in the infiltration of Muslims into his country, for the geographical situation of Ethiopia and its physical character were not very attractive to Muslims. In the glosses on Suyūṭī's commentary on a ḥadīth in which Muḥammad warned against an attack on Ethiopia, Abū al-Ḥasan Muḥammad ibn 'Abd al-Hādī said that the reason for Muḥammad's warning against an attack on Ethiopia was "Ethiopia's roughness and the mountains and rugged valleys and seas that lie between it and the Muslims."[11] It was perhaps on account of the physical character no less than for the Najāshī's submission that Ethiopia assumed a special position in the eyes of Muḥammad and his followers. Thus Ethiopia was spared an attack in early Islam and for several centuries it remained undisturbed by

[9] Ṭabarī, *op. cit.*, p. 1570-1; Budge, 272.

[10] Budge, p. 273.

[11] Nasā'ī, *Sunan*, with Suyūṭī's Commentary and Abū al-Ḥasan's glosses (Cairo, A.H. 1312), Vol. II, p. 65 (margin).

Muslim forces. Islam penetrated later peacefully, especially during the eighteenth and nineteenth century, when Muslims controlled its commercial relations with the Red Sea countries, but not by the force of arms.[12]

In formulating their legal opinion on the status of Ethiopia the jurist-theologians were, perhaps, guided more by the ḥadīths and athārs, although apocryphal, on the benevolent attitude which Ethiopia had taken toward the early Muslims than by any other considerations. The Prophet Muḥammad is reported to have made several favorable remarks about the honesty, courage, and straightforwardness of the Abyssinians. Most important, of course, is the oft-quoted ḥadīth in which Muḥammad warned the Muslims: "Leave the Abyssinians in peace, so long as they do not take the offensive."[13] While Mālik was not sure as to the genuineness of this ḥadīth, he advised abiding by it, adding that the Muslims had habitually refrained from attacking Ethiopia.[14] 'Aṭā' ibn Abī Rabāḥ, in supporting this stand, argued that the Qur'ānic verses about the Christians (Q. VI, 85-6), which put them in favorable light in the eyes of the Muslims, were specific references to the Abyssinians with whom Muḥammad's early followers were associated.[15]

[12] The Ottoman Empire was probably the first Muslim power to launch an attack on Ethiopia and occupy certain parts of its territory in the sixteenth century. For an account of this war, see 'Arab Faqīh, *Futūḥ al-Ḥabasha,* ed. Rene Basset (Paris, 1898).

[13] Abū Dā'ūd, *Sunan* (Cairo, 1935), Vol. IV, pp. 112, 114; Nasā'ī, *op. cit.,* Vol. II p. 64-5. It is also reported that when the Najāshī died, Muḥammad ordered his followers to pray for him.

[14] Ibn Rushd (al-Ḥafīd), *Bidāyat al-Mujtahid* (Istanbul, A.H. 1333), Vol. I, p. 308.

[15] Muḥammad al-Ḥafnī al-Qanā'ī, *al-Jawāhir al-Ḥisān . . . fī al-Ḥibshān* (Cairo, A.H. 1320), p. 44; and Muḥammad ibn 'Abd al-Bāqī al-Bukhārī, *Al-Ṭīraz al-Manqūsh fī Maḥāsin al-Ḥubūsh* (MS, Dār al-Kutub al-Miṣriyya),

Traditions were supported by practice. Owing to the fact that from the very beginning of Muslim expansion, at a time when an offensive was launched on all Islam's neighbors except Ethiopia, precedent had been established that Ethiopia became immune from the jihād.[16] This is precisely what Mālik meant, in giving his legal opinion about Ethiopia, that Muslim authorities had habitually refrained from attacking Ethiopia.

In Muslim legal theory, the country which is excluded from the jihād must belong either to dār al-Islām or dār al-'ahd (the latter being either part of, or in alliance with, dār al-Islām).[17] It might be argued that the Najāshī's acceptance of Muḥammad's invitation to Islam was construed as a symbolic act that his country had become a part of dār al-Islām; but since Islamic law was not enforced in Ethiopian territory—a criterion which determines whether a territory is dār al-Islām or not—it could not be regarded as part of dār al-Islām, even though its ruler had accepted, or rather recognized, Muḥammad as the Apostle of Allah.

If Ethiopia is neither dār al-Islām nor dār al-ḥarb, it must therefore belong to the intermediary territory which may be called dār al-ḥiyād, or the world of neutrality. Since it is a territory which Islam had voluntarily declared to be outside the bounds of its area of expansion; it formed, accordingly, a neutralized territory which Islam was under legal obligation to refrain from attacking as long as it reciprocally refrained from attacking Muslim territory.

---

cited in 'Abd al-Majīd 'Abdīn, *Bayn al-Ḥabasha Wa'l-'Arab* (Cairo, n.d.), pp. 86-7.

[16] Caetani gives the account of a naval expedition which Caliph 'Umar had sent to Ethiopia, but which failed (Caetani, *Annali dell' Islam,* Vol. IV, pp. 219, 366-7). This is not a reliable story and Trimingham contends that the naval expedition was probably directed against piratical lairs on the Red Sea coast (Trimingham, *op. cit.,* p. 46).

[17] See pp. 144-5, above.

Nubia

After an unsuccessful attempt to annex her, Nubia, unlike Ethiopia, forced Islam to respect her independence and establish reciprocal trade relations with her. After the occupation of Egypt by 'Amr ibn al-'Āṣ, the encounters between Muslims and Nubians taught both the lesson that they could come to terms with each other and refrain from attacking the territory of one another. Thereupon, the new governor of Egypt, 'Abd-Allah ibn Abī Sarḥ, concluded a treaty (A.D. 652) by virtue of which the Nubians were to pay an annual tribute (baqṭ) of 360 slaves with a *quid pro quo* of wheat, barley, horses, and clothing. The text of the treaty follows:

This is the treaty granted by the Commander 'Abd-Allah ibn Sa'd ibn Abī Sarḥ to the Chief of Nubia and to all the people of his territory, a covenant binding upon the people of Nubia, great and small, from the frontier of Aswān to that of 'Alwa.

'Abd-Allah ibn Sa'd ensures security and peace among them and the neighboring Muslims in Egypt, together with other Muslims and dhimmīs.

You people of the Nubian race shall be secure under the safeguard of Allah and His Apostle, Muḥammad the Prophet. We shall neither attack you, nor wage war against you, nor make raids upon you so long as you observe the conditions between us and you. You may enter our land as travellers, not as settlers. We may enter your land as travellers not settlers. It is your duty to protect those Muslims or their allies who put in your land or travel there until they depart. You shall restore to Muslim territory every run-away slave of the Muslims who will have fled to you. You must not take possession of him, nor prevent or thwart a Muslim who comes to take him and must help him until he goes. You shall take care of the mosque which the Muslims have built in the square of your city and not prevent any from praying there. You shall keep it swept and illuminate it and respect it.

Every year you shall pay three hundred and sixty head of slaves to the Chief of the Muslims. They shall be of the medium type of slaves of your land, free from bodily defects, both male and female, neither extremely old men or old women, nor children under age. These you shall hand over to the Governor of Aswān.

No Muslim shall be obliged to repel an enemy who attacks you or defend you against him from the frontier of 'Alwa to that of Aswān. If you give refuge to a slave of a Muslim, or kill a Muslim or ally, or attempt to ruin the mosque which the Muslims have built in your city, or withhold any of the three hundred and sixty head of slaves, then this peace and security shall be cancelled and we and you shall return to hostility until Allah judges between us, for He is the best of all judges.

Upon these conditions we are bound by the covenant of Allah and His pledge and that of His Apostle the Prophet Muḥammad; and you stand pledged to us by those you hold most holy in your faith, by the Messiah, the Apostles and all those you venerate in your religion and community. Allah be the witness between us and you.

Written by 'Umar ibn Shuraḥbīl in Ramaḍan, A.H. 31 (A.D. April-May, 652).[18]

The tribute, known as the baqṭ,[19] was not in the form of jizya, for neither had the Nubians become dhimmīs nor was the annual payment a sign of submission. It was rather a reciprocal trade agreement; for at the time of its payment, following the signing of the treaty, the Nubians handed over forty additional slaves and other presents (especially rare animals such as elephants, giraffes, and leopards), and the Muslims paid wheat, barley, wine, horses, and other materials.

The reciprocal character of the treaty is shown not only in its economic clauses, but also in the legal and political terms. Both Muslims and Nubians were to permit travelers in each other's territory, to respect the apostles and the religious practices in each other's land (e.g. the mosque for Muslims in Nubia), and both parties were to refrain from attacking each other. The treaty, with no specified duration, obviously could not last more than ten years; but since the payment of the

[18] Maqrīzī, *Khiṭāṭ,* Vol. I, pp. 323-4. Translation adapted from J. S. Trimingham, *Islam in the Sudan* (London, 1949), pp. 61-2.

[19] Becker suggests that the term baqṭ is derived from *pactum* (C. H. Becker, "Baḳṭ," *Encyclopaedia of Islam,* Vol. I, pp. 608-9). Cf. Trimingham, *op. cit.,* page 62.

baqṭ was annual, the two parties must have tacitly or overtly renewed the treaty from time to time. In practice it lasted for over six hundred years, until Fāṭimid rule in Egypt.

Before its annexation, the position of Nubia in treaty relations with Islam, presents another problem of status under Muslim law. It differs from the case of Ethiopia in two important points. First, Islam did not regard Nubia as immune from the jihād for all time as was Ethiopia, but was not subject to attack for the duration of the treaty. Her exclusion from dār al-ḥarb was therefore temporary, depending on the willingness of both parties to observe their treaty obligations. Once the treaty was violated, or once one of the two parties decided to terminate it by sending a notice to this effect (nabdh), Nubia would immediately revert to dār al-ḥarb. Second, Islam did not exclude Nubia voluntarily from dār al-ḥarb but was forced —at least at the initial stages—to make peace arrangements which proved in practice to be of mutual interest. It follows therefore that in theory Islam took the view that Nubia was temporarily outside the bounds of the jihād, although the period of exclusion lasted for six centuries.

During the period of exclusion, however, Nubia's position was neither in dār al-Islām, for Islamic law was not in force in the territory, nor in dār al-ḥarb. It may be argued that Nubia was dār al-'ahd, as it was in treaty relations with Islam; but since the nature of the treaty is such that it did not pay tribute to Islam for the maintenance of peace (as in other tributary relations) but paid rather on a reciprocal basis, it follows that its position resembles in some respects that of Ethiopia, defined by the terms of the treaty which gave her a special status in Muslim law. This status, agreed upon by both parties to last for the duration of the treaty, is a qualified status of neutralization.

Cyprus

Cyprus (*Qubrus*) presents still another situation whose treaty relations with Islam put her in a special position in the Muslim legal system.

Cyprus was a Byzantine tributary island when it was attacked by Mu'āwiya I in A.D. 648. Since an annexation of Cyprus would involve the Muslims in another war with the Byzantines, with whom the Muslims were already in rivalry over the control of the Mediterranean, a treaty was concluded by which Cyprus was made a buffer state. The treaty provided that 7,200 dinārs were to be paid annually to the Muslims. A similar tribute, already agreed upon with the Byzantines, was to remain obligatory on the Cypriots. Cyprus undertook to take no part in war between the Muslims and their enemies but did inform the Muslims regarding the movement of their enemies, the Byzantines. "Thus when the Muslims were engaged in a naval expedition," says al-Balādhurī, "they would not harm the Cypriots nor were the Cypriots under obligation to support them or any one against them."[20]

In A.D. 654, Mu'āwiya attacked Cyprus again, for Cyprian ships were offered as an aid to the Byzantines in an expedition on the sea. Although the Cypriots violated their treaty, Mu'āwiya confirmed them in the terms previously made, and sent to the island 12,000 men and erected a mosque. Further, Mu'āwiya erected a city on the island and transplanted from Ba'labakk (Baalbek) a few men and a garrison that remained until Yazīd, Mu'āwiya's son, sent them back and ordered the city destroyed.[21] The status of Cyprus remained substantially the same as under the treaty of 648.

[20] Balādhurī, *Futūḥ al-Buldān*, ed. de Goeje (Leiden 1866), pp. 152-3; and Hitti's translation, *Origins of the Islamic State* (New York, 1916), pp. 235-6.

[21] *Ibid.*, p. 153; Hitti, p. 236.

Under the Caliph 'Abd al-Malik (A.D. 685-705) the influence of the Muslims was considerably reduced as a result of a naval engagement in which the Caliph, following the signing of a treaty in A.D. 689, agreed to pay an annual tribute to Constantinople, the revenues of Cyprus were to be divided, and Cyprus itself to occupy a neutral position between the two contending empires.[22]

The position of Cyprus was extremely precarious, ranging from a dependent status under Byzantine or Muslim rule, to complete independence, when the two rival powers agreed to respect Cyprus' independence, each satisfied with half of the annual tribute.

Under 'Abbāsid rule the situation became more favorable to the Byzantines owing to the reduction of Islam's sea power in the eastern Mediterranean, their rivalry with the Umayyads in Spain and the rise of rival Aghlabid and Fāṭimid dynasties in Africa. In order to win the Cypriots to the Muslim side, Caliph Abū Ja'far al-Manṣūr (A.D. 754-775) reduced the annual tribute, which was several times increased under the Umayyads, to the original amount under the treaty of 648. This hardly improved the situation, as the sympathies of the Cypriots were with the Byzantines.[23]

During the governorship of 'Abd al-Malik ibn Ṣāliḥ ibn 'Abbās (died A.D. 812) an opposition party in Cyprus raised a rebellion, probably under Byzantine instigation, to free Cyprus of the tribute. The governor, desirous of suppressing the rebellion and annexing the island, sought a legal opinion to justify the cancellation of the treaty with Cyprus. He addressed

[22] See Sir George Hill, *A History of Cyprus* (Cambridge, 1940), Vol. I, pp. 286-7 and Archibald R. Lewis, *Naval Power and Trade in the Mediterranean, 500-1100* (Princeton, 1951), pp. 62-3.

[23] Balādhurī, pp. 155-6; and R. Hartmann, "Cyprus," *Encyclopaedia of Islam*, Vol. I, pp. 882-4.

a question to leading jurists of his time for an opinion; the responses were not all in the affirmative. Some of them, discussing the legal status of Cyprus, are of particular interest to our discussion and therefore deserve to be quoted in full.

Mālik ibn Anas (died, A.D. 795), the founder of the Mālikī School of law, answered as follows:

Our peace with the Cypriots is of old standing and has been carefully observed by their governors, because they considered the terms a humiliation and belittlement to the Cypriots, and a source of strength to the Muslims, in view of the tax paid to them and the chance they had of attacking their enemy. Yet I know of no governor who broke their terms or expelled them from the city. I, therefore, consider it best to hesitate in breaking their covenant and notifying them of the termination of the treaty until the evidence [of disloyalty] is well established against them, for Allah says: "Fulfill for them then your covenant until the time agreed upon with them."[24] If, after that, they do not behave properly and abandon their deceit, and thou art convinced of their perfidy, then thou mayest attack them. In that case, the attack would be justified and would be crowned with success; and they would suffer humiliation and disgrace, by Allah's will."[25]

Mūsa ibn A'yun gave his opinion as follows:

Similar cases occurred in the past, but in each case the governors would grant a period of respite; and so far as I know, none of the early men ever broke a covenant with the Cypriots or any other people. It may be that the common people and the mass among the Cypriots had no hand in what their leaders did. I, therefore, consider it best to abide by the covenant, and fulfill the conditions thereof, in spite of what they have done. I have heard al-Awzā'ī say regarding the case of some, who, after making terms with the Muslims conveyed information about their secret things and pointed them out to the unbelievers: "If they are dhimmīs, they have thereby violated their covenant and forfeited their claim on security, making it right for the governor to kill or crucify them, if he so desires; but if they had been taken by capitulation and are not entitled to the Muslim's

[24] Q. IX, 4.

[25] Balādhurī, pp. 155-6; Hitti, pp. 239-40.

security, then the governor would repudiate their treaty, for Allah loveth not the machinations of deceivers."[26]

Ismā'il ibn 'Ayyāsh gave his opinion as follows:

> The people of Cyprus are humiliated and oppressed and they are subjugated, together with their wives, by the Byzantines. It is therefore proper for us to defend and protect them. In the covenant of the people of Taflīs, Ḥabīb ibn Maslama wrote: "In case something should arise to divert the attention of the Muslims from you and some enemy should subjugate you, that would not be a violation of your covenant, so long as ye keep loyal to the Muslims." I, therefore, consider it best that they be left on their covenant and the security promised them, especially because when al-Walīd ibn Yazīd expelled them to Syria, the Muslims considered the act outrageous, and the canonists disapproved of it; so much so that when Yazid ibn al-Walīd ibn 'Abd al-Malik came to power, he restored them to Cyprus, which act was approved of by the Muslims and considered just.[27]

Other jurists, such as al-Layth ibn Sa'd, Sufyān ibn 'Uyayna, Yaḥya ibn Ḥamza, Abū Isḥāq al-Fazarī, and Makhlad ibn al-Ḥusayn gave answers to the effect that since the people of Cyprus had violated their treaty obligations the Muslims could repudiate the treaty and punish them.[28]

In the answers of the jurists who advised against the repudiation of the Cyprus treaty there are several points worth examining which have bearing on the legal status of Cyprus. First, Cyprus was not a tributary state to Islam alone, but to Byzantium also; hence its conduct regarding the discharge of its obligations to Islam depended on Byzantine machinations. If Cyprus failed to live up to the terms of the treaty under Byzantine pressure, as ibn 'Ayyāsh pointed out, the treaty would not be regarded as violated from the Muslim side. This viewpoint regards Cyprus, even when it fails to live up to its obligation

[26] Balādhurī, p. 156; Hitti, p. 240.
[27] Balādhurī, p. 156; Hitti, p. 241.
[28] Balādhurī, pp. 155, 156, 157, 158.

to Islam, as immune from attack by Islam, because of its joint obligations to the Byzantines and the Muslims. In terms of international politics Cyprus was a buffer state whose status was respected because of the rivalry of its neighbors.

Second, although Cyprus paid a tribute to Islam, its inhabitants were not regarded as dhimmīs, as Mūsa ibn A'yun stated, and therefore their action in conveying information to Islam's enemies—thus violating their neutral attitude—would be a cause of repudiating the treaty by the Muslims. In the case of the dhimmīs, their disclosure of information to the enemy would make them liable, as subjects of the imām, to punishment rather than the repudiation of their pacts.

Although in treaty relations with Islam, Cyprus was not regarded as part of dār al-Islām, as neither were her inhabitants dhimmīs nor was Islamic law enforced in its territory; nor was it dār al-ḥarb, for the Muslims as well as the Byzantines promised to refrain from attacking her. Further, it was not out of regard for her benevolent attitude to Islam, as in the case of Ethiopia, nor because of her resistance to Muslim power, as in the case of Nubia, that Islam excluded Cyprus from the jihād area; Cyprus happened to be located in a sea which was the scene of indecisive struggles for supremacy between Muslim and Byzantine sea power. When a territory happened to fall between two great rival powers, its neutrality was likely to be respected. Thus, Cyprus, by agreement of the two great Mediterranean powers, was declared a neutralized state whose status, under Muslim law, would fall in the category of the world of neutrality.

Conclusion

There is a ḥadīth to the effect that the last people whom the Muslims should attack would be the Turks, owing to the toughness of this race and the physical nature of their country.[29] Whether this tradition is apocryphal or not, it well expresses the attitude of Islam towards non-Muslim countries, namely, that sooner or later the jihād must be enforced on all people, regardless of their racial character or the physical nature of their country. Perhaps with the exception of Ethiopia, no land or people have ever been declared immune from the jihād in the authoritative sources of Islamic law. Nubia, Cyprus and, perhaps, the Turks were, strictly speaking, never permanently excluded from the jihād; they were rather set aside as neutral territories so long as they observed the terms of their treaties. But since by the very nature of the law the treaty must expire some time—however often the ten-years' period was renewed—the time must come in theory when the challenge of war must be met.

The law of neutrality, not unlike the law of peace, was designed to serve a temporary purpose, that is, until the entire world would become Islamic. Later, however, the jihād entered into a passive period, the law of both peace and neutrality will continue as long as Muslims and non-Muslims live together in this world. In the case of neutrality, the law, although still valid regarding Ethiopia, is no longer applicable to Cyprus, Nubia, and the Turks—the latter two have been absorbed by Islam and the former (after annexation by the Ottomans in A.D. 1570, a period lasting for more than three centuries) reverted to Christian rule in 1878. But there is no reason why the law of neutrality could not be revived if circumstances which permitted its applicability should reappear.

29 Bukhārī, *Kitāb al-Jāmi' al-Ṣaḥīḥ,* ed. Krehl (Leiden, 1864), Vol. III, p. 230; and Nasā'ī, *Sunan,* Vol. I, p. 65. Abū Dā'ūd reports this ḥadīth as part of the one of Ethiopia, that is, the Muslims should not attack the Turks, owing to the toughness of this people (Abū Dā'ūd, *Sunan,* Vol. IV, p. 112). For a discussion of the strength and toughness of the Turks, see al-Jāḥiz, "Risāla ila al-Fatḥ ibn Khāqān fī Manāqib al-Turk," *Thalāth Rasā'il,* ed. Van Vloten, (Leiden, 1903), pp. 1-56.

"It is an accepted fact that the terms of the law vary with the change of time." The Majalla, Article 39.

CHAPTER XXIII

EPILOGUE

Impact of the West on Muslim Concepts of the Law of Nations

It may not be out of place to supplement our study of the classical system of the law of nations with a brief discussion on the changes that took place after the decline and fall of the medieval caliphate. These changes, which made possible Islam's intimate contact with Christendom, as well as its integration into the larger world community, may well prove to be the most significant landmark in its development since the formative period. Although in the past, Islamic law had been exposed to foreign influences, it had on the whole preserved its basic character. The greatest challenge to this law in modern times has come from the West, under the impact of which it is bound to change. The attempt to change Islamic law, despite its notorious rigidity, is worthy of a close study. An adequate treatment of this subject will obviously require a separate volume. It is proposed to study in this chapter only the fundamental changes and the forces operating to transform the Muslim law of nations from a medieval to a modern system.

Changes in the Character of Dār al-Islām

Although the authority of the Caliph of Baghdad had been challenged by *de facto* independent rulers and at times defied by two rival caliphs in Spain and Egypt, the legal unity of dār al-Islām was in theory maintained, since the provincial independent rulers recognized the overlordship of the 'Abbāsid caliph while the caliphs of Spain and Egypt received only limited allegiance within their territories. The position of the *de facto* independent rulers in Islamdom was not unlike that of the kings in medieval Christendom who were independent within their own realms, but in theory derived their authority from the emperor (or the Pope). The rival authority of Byzantium resembled that of the caliphate of Fāṭimid Egypt or Umayyad Spain; for, though Byzantium rejected the overlordship of the Western Empire, it did not challenge the theoretical unity of Christendom.

The fall of Baghdad in A.D. 1258 marked a significant change in the character of dār al-Islām. Henceforward that symbol of legal unity not only ceased to exist (although a puppet 'Abbāsid caliph, whom none but his Mamlūk lords recognized resided in Cairo), but the highest authority charged with the enforcement of the sharī'a disappeared as well. The Mongol invaders, despite their care not to interfere in matters religious, governed Muslim territories as alien rulers in accordance with their own principles of government and public law. Even when Ghāzān Maḥmūd (A.D. 1295-1304) adopted Islam, he and his successors continued to issue decrees in accordance with Mongol law in addition to Islamic law. He established a precedent that the later Saljūk and Ottoman sultans continued, whereby a new ruling institution was set up side by side with the sharī'a in that part of dār al-Islām under their control.

The disappearance of the 'Abbāsid caliphate was followed by the rise of an increasing number of petty states and secular rulers who, after an intense rivalry for power for more than two centuries, in their turn disappeared for the most part, allowing dār al-Islām to break up into major political divisions. At the opening of the sixteenth century, the Ottoman sultans, after they had firmly established their rule in Europe, turned to the east to extend their domination over rival Muslim rulers. Their expansion eastward was halted by the rise of a new dynasty in Persia, established by Shāh Ismā'īl Ṣafawī (1500-25), who proclaimed shī'ism as the official religion in that country. Not only had the enforcement of Shī'ī law and doctrine in Persia accentuated local differences within Islam which had already become shaped, but also led to the virtual break-up of dār al-Islām into three main divisions: the Ottoman state (comprising their dominions in Europe and western Asia), Persia under the Ṣafawī regime, and Central Asia and India under the Mughal rule.[1] This split of dār al-Islam marked the beginning of a change in the conception of the Muslim state (accentuated later by the Western concept of nationality) from universal to national.[2]

The disintegration of dār al-Islām into separate political units carried with it serious consequences, including the shrink-

[1] For a discussion of this schism in the Muslim world of the sixteenth century, see A. J. Toynbee, *A Study of History* (London, 1934), Vol. I, pp. 346-402.

[2] E. G. Browne goes so far as to argue that the establishment of shī'ism in Persia under the Ṣafawī dynasty marked the beginning of the national stage in that country (Browne, *A Literary History of Persia* (Cambridge, 1930), Vol. IV, pp. 3, 12 ff.).

ing of Muslim territory and the penetration of Western influence into Muslim lands. Although it is true that Ottoman expansion extended the frontiers of Islam into Christian lands, Islam had to withdraw from portions of territory already under its control. Spain was completely restored to Christian rule at the close of the fifteenth century, and Portuguese activities in the Indian Ocean, after the discovery of the African Cape route to India, delivered a death blow to Muslim trade via the Red Sea. The Portuguese followed up their victories by the occupation of certain trade centers in East Africa and the Persian Gulf which brought Muslim territory under their control. France and Great Britain followed in the footsteps of the Portuguese, and their activities in the Indian Ocean during the seventeenth and eighteenth centuries placed under their control additional Muslim territories. Great Britain, eventually replacing French rule, dominated all the Muslim lands lying to the east of Persia (leaving Central Asia for future Russian annexation) and extended their influence (by direct or indirect rule) into the Persian Gulf, the southern shores of Arabia, and East Africa. During the latter years of the nineteenth and the early years of the twentieth century, Great Britain owing to the continuing weakness and then the final break-up of the Ottoman Empire, extended her control over additional Muslim territory. France, forced to withdraw from the Indian Ocean during the eighteenth century, extended her control over North Africa during the nineteenth century.

Recognition of Christendom by Islam Under Ottoman Rule

The establishment of the Ottoman Empire gave a fresh impetus for the development of the Muslim law of nations. Not only did the Ottoman sultan adopt the relatively liberal Ḥanafī school as official, but he also followed an old Turkish practice of issuing decrees, having the force of law, based on custom and precedent. These decrees were often compiled in statute books known as qānūn-namé, which supplied valuable additions to the sharī'a. Although the qānūns could not in theory supersede the sharī'a, the latter in practice was modified by the former so as to accommodate itself to the new circumstances of the Empire. This significant change in the making of legislation afforded the sultans possibilities for developing new principles and rules for the conduct of foreign relations.

In their relations with Christendom, the Ottoman sultans followed a liberal policy for the purpose of reviving commerce with the West at a time when the discovery of the new route to India via the African Cape was threatening the commerce of the eastern Mediterranean.[3] The Mamlūks of Egypt and Muḥammad the Conqueror had already granted such liberal terms to Western merchants that the Treaty of 1535 which gave expression to the general principles governing Western trade and the treatment of foreigners in Ottoman (Muslim) land was merely giving a sanction to the practice that already existed.[4]

This treaty provided a few innovations in Islam's relations with Christendom. The preamble treated the King of France and his representatives as equals with Sultan Sulaymān and his representatives. Article 1 provided for the establishment of a "valid and sure peace" (*bonne et sure paix*) between the Sultan and the King, "during their lives," and granted reciprocal rights to the subjects of each monarch in the territory of the

[3] It has been held that the Turks discouraged trade with the West, see, A. H. Lybyer, "The Ottoman Turks and the Routes of Oriental Trade," *English Historical Review,* Vol. XXX (1915), pp. 577-88.

[4] For the text of the treaty, see Baron I. de Testa, *Recueil des Traités de la Porte Ottomane* (Paris, 1864), Vol. I, pp. 15-21; and G. Noradounghian, *Recueil d'acts internationaux de l'empire Ottoman* (Paris, 1897), Vol. I, pp. 83-7. For an English translation, see Nasim Sousa, *The Capitulatory Regime in Turkey* (Baltimore, 1933), pp. 314-20.

other. The French were to enjoy exemption rights from the poll tax, the right to practice their religion, and the right of trial in their own consulates by their own law. The King of France was also given the right to

> send to Constantinople or Pera or other places of this Empire a bailiff—just as at present he has a consul at Alexandria. The said bailiff and consul shall be received and maintained in proper authority so that each one of them may in his locality, and without being hindered by any judge, qāḍī, soubashī, or other, according to his faith and law, hear, judge, and determine all causes, suits and differences, both civil and criminal, which might arise between merchants and other subjects of the King (of France). . . . The qāḍī or other officers of the Grand Signior may not try any difference between the merchants and subjects of the King, even if the said merchants should request it, and if perchance the said qāḍīs should hear a case their judgment shall be null and void. (Article 2).

The Muslim law of nations, it will be recalled, permitted peace to be established with the enemy for a period not exceeding ten years. The Ottoman practice modified this rule by extending this period to the lifetime of the sultan who made the treaty. The Treaty of 1535, in addition, treated the contracting parties on the basis of equality and mutuality of interests. This might be regarded, as many writers have maintained, as a special privilege given to the King of France before other Christian princes were accorded similar status. Article 15, however, stated that such a privilege would be granted to other monarchs. The text of the article reads:

> The King of France has proposed that His Holiness the Pope, the King of England, his brother and perpetual ally, and the King of Scotland should be entitled to adhere to this treaty of peace if they please, on condition that when desirous of doing so they shall within eight months from date send their ratifications to the Grand Signior and obtain his.

Although the above mentioned monarchs failed to adhere to the treaty (England preferred to sign a separate treaty with the

Sultan in 1580), the Sultan sought to establish a principle which would apply to other Christian princes as well.

Another principle of Islamic law which the treaty of 1535 modified was to grant non-Muslims (if residing in dār al-Islām more than a year) exemption from the poll tax. (The non-Muslim subjects of the Sultan continued to pay this tax until it was abolished in 1839.) With respect to the right granted to Frenchmen of being tried by their own consulates, the treaty at first gave expression to the classical principle of the personality of the law; but the modification of this principle in subsequent treaties (especially that of 1740), by which all law suits involving foreigners and Muslims were to be handled by foreign consulates, greatly modified the classical principle that Islamic law must be applied in such cases.

The Treaty of 1535, concluded at a time when the modern law of nations was at the beginning of its development, might have provided an excellent opportunity to reconcile Christian and Muslim law in the conduct of foreign relations. But historical development after the sixteenth century, as will be indicated below, produced different trends in Christendom and Islamdom which separated the systems of laws governing the two worlds.

Christendom's Attitude Toward the Ottoman Empire

The Treaty of 1535 might have appeared as the favorable moment for initiating a peaceful method for reconciling the conflicting interests of Christendom and Islamdom. The commercial provisions of the treaty were attractive to Western merchants, but the political motives which brought the treaty to life had nothing to do with peaceful commercial relations. Francis was in dire need of support against his Christian rival, Charles V, and Sulaymān, after his unsuccessful attack on Vienna (1529), sought to divide the combination against him by creating dissension among Christian princes. The fact that the treaty was left open for adherence by other Christian monarchs could hardly have brought reconciliation between Islam and Christendom. Nor were the religious principles underlying the treaty conducive to reconciling Christian with Islamic law or to integrating Islamdom into the Western Christian order. The legal justification for granting favorable terms to a Christian monarch was based not on the principle of equality and reciprocity, but on the principle of the personality of the law which permitted the subjects of a non-Muslim state to enjoy certain privileges when they resided in Muslim territory.

Nor was Europe at the time of the Reformation in the mood to tolerate a non-Christian power's participation in the religious issues that dominated its life. The Ottoman Empire, as a Muslim state, was regarded as a foreign element in the Christian body politic. Certain Christian princes looked upon the Treaty of 1535 as a violation of the law of Christianity, even though the medieval conception of a Christian universal state, headed by the Emperor and regulated by Christian canon law, was breaking down.[5]

The European jurists and publicists, who advocated a new law of nations based on the principles of territorial sovereignty and equality of nations, hardly changed their attitude toward the Ottoman sultans. The traditional viewpoint of Christendom seemed to take it for granted that the Ottoman Empire lay outside the pale of the newly developing law of nations. Albericus Gentilis (1552-1608), who did not favor religious wars and criticized Spain for making war on the Indians, made an exception with respect to the Turks.[6] He criticized Francis I

[5] See D. J. Hill, *A History of Diplomacy in the International Development of Europe* (New York, 1906), Vol. II, pp. 435, 439-40.

[6] Gentilis, *De Jure Belli* (1588), Lib. I, C. 12. See also T. A. Walker, *A History of the Law of Nations* (Cambridge, 1899), Vol. I, pp. 254, 271-2.

for making an alliance with the Turks. An alliance between Christian and infidel princes, he stated, could not possibly be tolerated. Even Grotius, who emphasized the law of nature as the basis of the modern law of nations, advocated discriminatory treatment against non-Christian states. He was prepared to tolerate the signing of treaties with enemies of the Christian religion—arguing that it was permissible by the law of nature—but advocated that all Christian princes should make common cause against the advance of the enemies of the faith.[7] Thus in its formative period, the modern law of nations developed principles to govern the relations among Christian nations alone, namely, those who enjoyed the benefits of Christian civilization. It follows that the rights which that law would protect were only the rights of "civilized" powers.[8]

No less concerned with the problem of Turkey in Europe were those utopian writers who sought to establish peace in Christendom. During the seventeenth and eighteenth centuries several schemes were laid down for reconciling the conflicting interests of Christian monarchs in order that peace might be established. Most of these schemes, like that of Dubois in medieval times, had the common theme that an appeal be made to the Christian princes to compose their differences and unite against the Turks. Thus W. Penn considered the subjection of the Turks as a prerequisite for the general pacifications of Europe.[9] Leibnitz advised Louis XIV to occupy Egypt instead of attacking Holland. Emeric Crucé and Abbé de Saint-Pierre, however, in their schemes for a general union of

[7] Grotius, *De Jure Belli ac Pacis* (1625), Lib. II, c. 20. See also Walker *op. cit.*, Vol. I, pp. 300, 306-7.

[8] See Edward P. Cheyney, "International Law under Queen Elizabeth," *English Historical Review*, Vol. XX (1905), p. 660.

[9] W. Penn, *Essay on the Present and Future Peace of Europe* (London, 1693).

states, thought that the Turks might be included. St. Pierre contended that such a union would not necessarily lead to conciliation of the various religions, but it would help to establish peace between states with different religions.[10] Most elaborate of the schemes for establishing peace in Christendom at the expense of the Turks was that of Cardinal Alberoni, Prime Minister of Spain, who published a book at Lausanne (1753) entitled *Testament Politique du Cardinal Jule Alberoni,* in which he sought the setting up of a general diet, composed of the representatives of European princes, for discussing all matters of common concern to Christendom. But before such a plan for perpetual peace could ever become a reality, Cardinal Alberoni thought that the Turks must be expelled from Europe by a combination of Christian forces. He published a brochure in German and English entitled *Cardinal Alberoni's Scheme for Reducing the Turkish Empire to the Obedience of Christian Princes* (London, 1736).[11] In his general scheme of peace Alberoni stated:

> It would seem to be for the absolute interest of the whole of Christian Europe that the attention of the emperors of Germany should be directed solely to the defense of their territory against the power of the Ottoman Empire, and to seek to extend their dominions in that direction only. . . . They would have the means to induce the Princes of the Empire to combine all their forces for the purpose of conquering Turkish territory by rewarding these Princes with some of the domains belonging to the

[10] Abbé de Saint-Pierre, *Projet pour rendre la paix perpetuelle en Europe* (Utrecht, 1713). For a comprehensive treatment of these plans, see S. J. Hemleben, *Plans for World Peace through Six Centuries* (Chicago, 1943).

[11] The original, apparently lost, has been preserved in an Italian translation. For an English rendering of the Italian manuscript, see Theodore Henckels, "Cardinal Alberoni's Scheme For Reducing the Turkish Empire to the Obedience of Christian Princes," *American Journal of International Law,* Vol. VII (1913), pp. 83-107.

House of Austria, in Germany, as they were making progress toward the Orient. . . .

It would seem that, through the execution of this system, all the old sources of quarrels between the Houses of Austria and Bourbon might be removed. Nothing would prevent them from acting concertedly in order to drive the infidels out of Christendom, to settle all differences pending between their neighbors, to render justice to whom it is due and to establish commerce on a footing of equality which encouraged industry and honesty among all nations. Thus, enjoying peaceful possession of their legitimate states the Christians will then think of relieving their subjects harassed by wars or by apprehensions of wars which follow conditions of uncertainty and jealousy. They will have a beautiful field within which to exercise their power and their prowess against the infidels, and to set their conscience at peace for the shedding of Christian blood for which the indecision of their pretensions has been responsible in the course of the latter centuries.[12]

It would be a tempting conclusion to make that neither Islam nor Christendom had yet been prepared to meet on a common ground and adapt their religious principles for the purpose of developing a law of nations based on equality and reciprocity of interests. The mistrust and, perhaps, the lack of mutual respect, were not conducive to an understanding between Islam and Christendom. Their conduct of foreign relations tended to be Machiavellian and coercive. The European representatives at the Ottoman Porte often resorted to bribery and intrigue in order to achieve their ends, while the Ottoman viziers frightened and misused European envoys to extract disclosure of their instructions.[13] In the circumstances the relations between Christendom and Islamdom showed no ap-

[12] For a full statement of this system see *ibid.*, pp. 62-66.

[13] See C. T. Forster and F. H. B. Daniell, *The Life and Letters of Ogier Ghiselin de Busbecq* (London, 1881), Vol. I, pp. 176-177. See also the experience of Sir John Finch, Queen Elizabeth's Ambassador to Turkey, as recorded in the study of his life in G. F. Abbott, *Under the Turk in Constantinople* (London, 1920).

preciable improvement over that established between Sulaymān and Francis I. The factors governing their relationship depended less on law than on the relative strength or weakness of either side.

The Ottoman Empire and the Modern Law of Nations

In the latter portion of the seventeenth century, the development of the modern law of nations along secular lines, based on the principle *cuius regio, eius religio,* received additional impetus. The Reformation had shattered the conception of the universal state, and the state system that emerged was maintained by a balance of power and regulated by the law of nations. The Ottoman Empire, for reasons already given, remained outside the Family of Nations, a fact which helped to shape the development of international relations during the greatest portion of the two centuries that followed. Had the Ottoman Empire been integrated into the European system of law, the law of nations might have been universal in shape at an earlier period.

The growing strength of Europe and the secularization of its legal and political systems was matched by a steady decline in Ottoman power. The Sultans were quick to adopt Western weapons and military skills, but they were not prepared to adopt the new political and legal concepts which would have transformed Islamdom into a modern state. The encounters between the European states and Islam proved a disaster for Islam after the latter portion of the eighteenth century. Its defeats came as a surprise to the European powers who had attained their military and diplomatic victories with relative ease. This was well reflected in the unfavorable revision of the Treaty of 1535 in 1740, granting France the right of protection over the Christian nationals of the Sultan and the similar rights given to Russia in the Treaty of Küchük Qaynarja in

1774. The reason is that the disintegration of the Muslim society had gone too far to deal on a par with the European powers. The Europeans, on their part, when they dealt with the Muslim world, were astonished to find that Islamic civilization was so "inferior" and so different from their own, yet not appreciating the differences in the cultural values and the relative state of decadence. They preferred to attain immediate advantages rather than to deal with Islam on a basis of equality and mutual interests. The European powers found it more expedient to leave behind them the rules and practices of the modern law of nations and to resort to force, whenever diplomacy failed them. As a result, neither were the European powers prepared to regard Muslim countries as falling under the operation of the law of nations nor would Islam recognize Christian rule when its territory fell into European hands. The European powers, in their dealings with backward areas such as the Muslim world, treated them as savage communities to whom the principles of the law of war did not apply. Conquest of Muslim territory, like conversion to Christianity, was considered meritorious.[14]

At the opening of the nineteenth century, when the rivalry among European powers over Ottoman dominions threatened the peace of Europe, it was deemed necessary to invite the Ottoman sultan to join the community of European nations for the purpose of maintaining the integrity of his empire by affording him the benefits of the law of nations. When such an invitation was suggested at the Congress of Vienna (1814-15), Russia objected on the grounds that Turkey was barbarous. "Barbarous as it is," retorted Castlereagh to Tsar Alexander,

[14] See Q. Wright, "The Bombardment of Damascus," *American Journal of International Law,* Vol. XX (1926), p. 266; *Mandates under the League of Nations* (Chicago, 1930), pp. 7-8; and *Legal Problems in the Far Eastern Conflict* (New York, 1941), pp. 18-29.

"Turkey forms in the system of Europe a necessary evil." But Russia, seeking a free hand in the Sultan's dominions, insisted that Turkey be kept out of the community of European nations.

Nor were the jurists agreed as to whether Turkey had become a subject under the law of nations despite the fact that she had established for a long while diplomatic intercourse with Europe. The jurists were divided as to Turkey's ability to meet her obligations in accordance with European standards. In *The Hurtige Hane,* Sir William Scott argued that the law of nations should not be applied to nations outside Europe "in its full rigour"; for, as he went on to say,

> . . . it would be extremely hard on persons residing in the kingdom of Morocco, if they should be held bound by all the rules of the law of nations, as it is practised among European states. On many accounts undoubtedly they are not to be strictly considered on the same footing as European merchants; they may, on some points of the law of nations, be entitled a very relaxed application of the principles, established by long usage, between the states of Europe, holding an intimate and constant intercourse with each other.[15]

In *The Madonna del Burso,* Sir William Scott reiterated the same view in more general terms:

> The inhabitants of those countries (Ottoman Empire) are not professors of exactly the same law of nations with ourselves: In consideration of the peculiarities of their situation and character, the Court has repeatedly expressed a disposition, not to hold them bound to the utmost rigour of that system of public law, on which European states have so long acted, in their intercourse with one another.[16]

[15] *The Hurtige Hane,* High Court of Admiralty, 1801, 3 C. Rob. 324. See J. B. Scott and W. H. E. Jaeger, *Cases on International Law* (St. Paul, Minnesota, 1937), pp. 62-4.

[16] *The Madonna del Burso,* High Court of the Admiralty, 1802, 4 C. Rob. 169. See Scott and Jaeger, *op. cit.,* pp. 65-6. In *The Fortuna,* 2 C. Rob. 92 (1803), Sir William Scott said: "Considering this case as merely

Even after the Ottoman Empire had been admitted to the Concert of Europe in 1856, some jurists, such as Lorimer, continued to regard her out of the operation of the law of nations. Writing in 1883, Lorimer divided humanity into "three concentric zones or spheres—that of civilized humanity, that of barbarous humanity, and that of savage humanity," entitled respectively to "plenary political recognition, partial political recognition, and natural or mere human recognition."[17] To the second category belong the non-European countries which were not European dependencies. As stated by Lorimer:

> The sphere of partial political recognition extends to Turkey in Europe and in Asia, and to the old historical states of Asia which have not become European dependencies—viz., to Persia and the other separate states of Central Asia, to China, Siam, and Japan.

To these territories, continued Lorimer, the jurist

> . . . is not bound to apply the positive law of nations . . . but he is bound to ascertain the points at which, and the directions in which, barbarians or savages come within the scope of partial recognition.[18]

Analyzing the juridical bases for refusing recognition, Lorimer distinguished non-age, imbecility, criminality, as well as religious differences among nations. "The Turks as a race," he said, "are probably incapable of the political development which would render their adoption of constitutional govern-

---

between the British captors and Algerian claimants, I do not, at the same time, mean to apply to such claimants the exact rigour of the law of nations as understood and practised amongst the civilized states of Europe; it would be to try them by a law not familiar to any law or practice of theirs. . . ." See also *The Kinders Kinder,* High Court of Admiralty, 1799. 2 C. Rob. 88; and *The Helena,* High Court of Admiralty, 1801. 4 C. Rob. 3.

[17] James Lorimer, *Institutes of the Law of Nations* (Edinburgh, 1883), Vol. I, p. 101.

[18] *Ibid.,* p. 102.

ment possible."[19] But to religious differences he attached greater weight:

So long as Islam endures, the reconciliation of its adherents, even with Jews and Christians, and still more with the rest of mankind, must continue to be an insoluble problem. . . . For an indefinite future, however reluctantly, we must confine our political recognition to the professors of those religions which, by conscious or unconscious processes, have been reasoned out from the facts of nature, and which preach the doctrine of "live and let live."[20]

Other jurists, such as T. E. Holland and W. E. Hall, emphasized differences in the degree of civilization, not religion, as a bar to full recognition, and this, they held, would be merely a transitional stage until non-European states would become members of the Family of Nations.[21]

Another school of thought held that since the Ottoman Empire had maintained diplomatic intercourse with European powers for many centuries and concluded treaties with them, the general body of the law of nations was accordingly considered applicable.[22] However, there is no clear evidence to indicate that during the first half of the nineteenth century Turkey and other Muslim countries had enjoyed the full advantages of the law of nations. Writing in 1845, Wheaton was perhaps reflecting this state of affairs when he said:

In respect to the mutual intercourse between the Christian and Mohammedan Powers, the former have been sometimes content to take the law

[19] *Ibid.*, p. 123.

[20] *Ibid.*, p. 124. In another work Lorimer rejects the ethical basis of Islam as suitable for a political system (J. Lorimer, *Studies National and International* (Edinburgh, 1890), pp. 132-47.)

[21] See T. E. Holland, *Lectures on International Law,* ed. Walker and Walker, (London, 1933), p. 38; W. E. Hall, *International Law,* ed. Higgins (eighth ed., Oxford, 1924), pp. 48-9.

[22] See A. H. Smith, *Great Britain and the Law of Nations* (London, 1932), Vol. I, pp. 16, 17.

from the Mohammedan, and in others to modify the International Law of Christianity in its relation to them. Instances of the first may be found in the ransom of prisoners, the rights of ambassadors, and many others where the milder usages established among Christian nations have not yet been adopted by the Mohammedan Powers. On some others they are considered as entitled to a very relaxed application of the peculiar principles established by long usage among the states of Europe in constant intercourse with one another.[23]

Toward the end of the first half of the nineteenth century the European Powers seemed to have come to the conclusion that Turkey's exclusion from the full advantages of the law of nations had become inconsistent with the trend of an expanding Family of Nations. As a member of the European community of nations, Turkey was fully entitled to a law that had first developed among European nations. Her exclusion from the Concert of Europe in 1815 had perhaps postponed her participation in the operation of the law of nations; but her admission to the Concert in 1856 must have fully entitled her (subject to foreign capitulatory rights which were not abolished until 1924) to the full advantages of that law. The European powers have slowly come to this conclusion and this may well be illustrated by another citation from Wheaton, writing shortly before the formal admission of Turkey to the Concert of Europe, in which he stated:

Recent intercourse between the Christian nations of Europe and the Mohammedan and pagan nations of Asia and Africa indicates a disposition on the part of the latter to renounce their particular international usages and adopt those of Christendom. The rights of legation have been recognized by, and reciprocally extended to, Turkey, Persia, Egypt and the States of Barbary. The independence and integrity of the Ottoman Empire have been long regarded as forming essential elements in the European balance of power, and, as such, have recently become the objects of conventional stipulations between the Christian States of Europe and that

[23] Henry Wheaton, *History of the Modern Law of Nations* (New York, 1845), p. 555.

Empire, which may be considered as bringing it within the pale of the public law of the former.[24]

Western jurists have been confused as to the meaning of article 7 of the Treaty of Paris (1856) providing for the admission of Turkey to the "Public law and Concert of Europe." Most of them have construed the clause as one admitting Turkey to the advantages of the law of nations. Few have argued that it merely meant her admission to the European community of nations and that it had no bearing on the subject of her participation in the operation of the law of nations.[25] The Ottoman Empire was recognized only by slow stages as a subject of the law of nations, but the action taken by the European powers at Paris removed any doubt as to the possibility of remaining out of the bounds of that law.

Integration of Islam into the Family of Nations

Although the European bar to admitting the Ottoman Empire to the community of nations had at last been removed, the problem of adapting Islam to European legal concepts remained to be resolved. For a long while the Ottoman Sultan had been advised by Western sympathizers, as well as by Muslim liberals, to put his house in order, so as to gather strength to maintain his position among the powers and to discharge his duties as the head of a modern state; but the Sultan, who was willing to adopt the new weapons and military skills of the West, was not prepared to adopt Western concepts which would comprise or materially change Muslim law and institutions. Faced with a threat from within—provincial uprisings, local claims for independence, and the insistence of lib-

[24] Henry Wheaton, *Elements of the Law of Nations* (New York, 1846), chap. 1, sec. 13.

[25] See Hugh M. Wood, "The Treaty of Paris and Turkey's Status in International Law," *American Journal of International Law*, Vol. XXXVII, (1943), pp. 262-74.

erals for reform—the Sultan could afford as little to please the conservatives as to reject the pleadings of Western sympathizers to strengthen his Empire against the Russian threat. This constructive approach to strengthening the Ottoman Empire by modernizing it along Western constitutional lines is collectively known as the Tanzimāt, or Reform Movement. For it became quite obvious to the Sultan and his leading statesmen that the Empire had either to change or to collapse.

In the conduct of foreign relations, the Sultan had already compromised certain traditional Islamic rules in order to conform to Western practice. Although permanent diplomatic missions had been in vogue in Europe since early modern times, only friendly powers were admitted to the Sultan's capital in the sixteenth century. In the eighteenth century the Sultan approved of this practice on a reciprocal basis. After 1792 the Sultan himself established permanent missions in Paris, London, Vienna, and Berlin.

The Sultan, following Western practice, permitted freedom of navigation through the Straits, first to Russia (in the Treaty of Küchük Qaynarja, 1774),[26] and then to other powers. This permission was at first limited to certain merchant vessels but was later made more liberal until it came to be, as a rule, enjoyed by all powers from the time it was first granted to Austria in 1784, England in 1799, France in 1802, and Prussia in 1806.[27] The Ancient Rule of the Ottoman House, which closed the Straits to all warships of foreign powers, remained effective until the Sultan was forced by diplomatic pressure to modify it during the nineteenth century.[28]

[26] Article 2.

[27] See Erik Brüel, *International Straits* (London and Copenhagen, 1947), Vol. II, pp. 272-6.

[28] For a comprehensive study of the status of the Straits, see J. T. Shotwell and Francis Deák, *Turkey at the Straits* (New York, 1940).

A far more radical change, carried out under pressure by the Western powers, was in improving the position of the Christian subjects (the ra'āyā, a term replacing the classical dhimmīs) by granting France (1740), Russia (1774), and other powers the right to "protect" the ra'āyā by making representations to the Porte regarding their conditions. The implementation of these commitments was embodied in the Tanzimāt decrees, beginning with the promulgation of the khaṭṭī-sharīf Gulkhané of November 3, 1839, and followed by other enactments until they were finally incorporated in an elaborate constitutional document issued by Sultan 'Abd al-Ḥamīd II on December 23, 1876. These constitutional instruments covered a variety of legal reforms, but neither the Tanzimāt enactments nor the short-lived Midḥat Constitution of 1876 were destined to materialize, owing to the strong resistance of traditional Islam to Western concepts of law and justice.[29]

The failure to reform the Ottoman Empire by merely adopting Western enactments prompted many a Muslim thinker, who became impatient with the Sultan's despotism enforced in the name of Islam, to seek a change in the character of the Muslim state. The new generation, during the latter part of the Ḥamīdian period (1876-1909), had been influenced by Western constitutionalism and nationalism and hoped that the adoption of these Western concepts might create a strong Ottoman state. The liberals argued that religion as the basis for a modern state was no longer adequate and suggested its

[29] For a more detailed account on the Tanzimāt, see E. Engelhardt, *La Turquie et le Tanzimat* (Paris, 1882-4), 2 vols.; F. E. Bailey, *British Policy and the Turkish Reform Movement* (Cambridge, Mass., 1942); A. J. Toynbee, *A Study of History* (London, 1954), Vol. VIII, pp. 239-57; R. D. Davison, "Turkish Attitudes Concerning Christian-Muslim Equality in the Nineteenth Century," *American Historical Review*, Vol. LIX (1954), pp. 844-64.

replacement by nationalism. The movement, beginning as a secret society, finally succeeded in forcing 'Abd al-Ḥamīd to restore the short-lived Constitution of 1876. The deposition of Sultan 'Abd al-Ḥamīd in 1909 ended the era of Pan-Islamism. The new regime of the Young Turks, professing nationalism as the basis of the state, entrusted authority to the hands of a responsible cabinet and provided that laws were to be enacted by Parliament. This regime also provided that no discrimination was to be permitted on the basis of religion, and all subjects were declared free and equal before the law.

The change in the character of the state from Islamic to national marked a significant landmark in the development of Islamic law. For nationalism, a product of Western thought, brought with it the secular conception of government and introduced the doctrine that the nation is the source of authority. Consequently, the sharī'a ceased to be the sole authoritative source for the conduct of the state. But no attempt was made at this stage to separate the religious from the secular powers, nor in fact was serious thought ever given to reconciling Islam with the new concepts of law and authority.

The change in the character of the state from a religious to national wrought havoc in the Ottoman Empire; for nationalism, in so composite a society as dār al-Islām (under Ottoman rule) proved to be not a unifying but a disintegrating factor. Thus nationalism speeded the break-up of an already disintegrating dār al-Islām. The successor states, still under the spell of nationalism, made further strides toward parting company with Islam as the basis of their legal structure. The degree of their emancipation varied from a complete break with the sharī'a, as in the case of Turkey, to its maintenance almost intact, as in the Arabian Peninsula. The Fertile Crescent and Egypt, paying lip service to Islam as the official religion of the state, followed a *via media* and proceeded to set up national regimes and follow Western rules and practices in the conduct of foreign relations. These states have now fully accepted their absorption by the Family of Nations as subjects of the modern law of nations.

The Secularization of Law and State

Although Western concepts of law and authority had been gradually adopted before the First World War, no efforts were made to repeal Muslim law or to abolish Muslim institutions. The First World War, resulting in the dissolution of the Ottoman Empire, brought matters to a head. Nationalism had triumphed in Turkey and most of the successor states, and the Muslim world was faced with the question of the caliphate—perhaps the very basic issue as to whether the Muslims would accept or reject the secularization of authority.

The Kemalist Reformists tried at the outset to separate the spiritual from the temporal authority, entrusting the temporal power to the Grand National Assembly and leaving the spiritual in the hands of the caliph. In a statement issued by the Grand National Assembly, published in a booklet in 1923, entitled *The Caliphate and the Sovereignty of the Nation,*[30] it was argued that the true caliphate had disappeared since the passing of the Orthodox Caliphate and that the Umayyads had transformed it into temporal rulership. The action of the Grand National Assembly was therefore no new innovation, as the position of the caliph had for centuries been devoid of the real caliphial character. Further, this separation of the temporal from the spiritual powers, the apologia of the Grand National Assembly went on to say, was in accordance with a Muḥammadan tradition, as stated by Nasafī, to the effect that

[30] For circulation in the Arab World, it was translated and published in Cairo by 'Abd al-Ghanī Sanī Beg under the title *al-Khilāfa wa Sulṭat al-Umma* (Cairo, 1924).

the Prophet himself stated that the caliphate was to last, after his death, for but thirty years and that henceforth it would become a temporal rulership.[31] There was therefore, for the new Turkey, no legal ground for the maintenance of the traditional caliphate.[32] The conservative elements, not satisfied with this interpretation, launched a trenchant attack on the Kemalist Reformists, although the Caliph himself made a statement to the effect that he would not interfere in political affairs. This prompted the Grand National Assembly to take the drastic step of declaring the caliphate abolished (1924) and with it the sharī'a disestablished. Thus Turkey became a secular state.[33]

The debate as to the validity of Turkey's unilateral abolition of the caliphate was taken up by other Muslim nations in order to decide whether they should confirm the Turkish action or appoint a new caliph. A caliphate conference was held in Cairo in May, 1926, and a resolution was passed declaring the caliphate a necessity in Islam, but failed to give effect to this decision.[34] Two other Islamic conferences were held in Makka (1926) and Jerusalem (1931), but both failed to discuss

[31] See Nasafī's *Creed* and Taftāzānī's *Commentary,* trans. E. E. Elder (New York, 1950), p. 141.

[32] This action had its precedents in the eighteenth century Ottoman practice, when the sultans found it convenient to put forward certain claims, in dealing with Christian Powers, to the effect that their spiritual authority, as caliphs, should continue over Muslims dwelling outside their dominions. The first precedent in which such a claim was put forward was in the Treaty of Küchük Qaynarja, in 1774, in order to perpetuate their spiritual authority over the lost territories of the Crimea and Kuban. See Sir Thomas Arnold, *The Caliphate* (Oxford, 1924), pp. 164-5.

[33] For the steps leading up to the abolition of the caliphate, see A. J. Toynbee, *Survey of International Affairs, 1925* (London, 1927), Vol. I, pp. 25-67.

[34] See A. J. Toynbee, *op. cit.,* pp. 81-90.

the question of the caliphate,[35] an indication that it probably had become obsolete, although it by no means should be regarded as a dead issue.

The abolition of the caliphate raised the question as to whether the Islamic state should not be secularized. Perhaps the most significant study published on this subject was a book entitled, *Islam and the Principles of Government,* by Shaykh 'Alī 'Abd al-Rāziq, one of the 'ulama of the Azhar University and judge of a sharī'a court.[36] In support of a secular state and the abolition of the caliphate, Rāziq argued that Islam was not designed by the Prophet Muḥammad as a political institution, although the Prophet himself found it necessary to exercise political and military functions (which were distinct from his primary religious functions as a Prophet), but like Christianity, as a system of religion for the regulation of the spiritual life of the Muslims. He rejected the view that the caliphate had its bases in the Qur'ān, ḥadīth and ijmā', and argued that the history of this institution indicates that it was a controversial issue, by no means settled in the authoritative sources of Islam. Thus, he saw no reason why the caliphate should be tied to religion and could not be abolished, as indeed it had been instituted, by temporal action. The significance of Rāziq's theory of law lay in entrusting to the hands of the head of the state the power to conduct its foreign relations in accordance with the rules of the modern law of nations, relieved of the limitations of the sharī'a. This interpretation gave validity not only to the action of the Kemalist regime in Turkey but also justified the conduct of foreign relations of the very state which enforced the act of the disciplinary

[35] A. J. Toynbee, *op. cit.,* pp. 311-19; and H. A. R. Gibb, "The Islamic Congress at Jerusalem in December 1931," in A. J. Toynbee, *Survey of International Affairs, 1934* (London, 1935), pp. 99-109.

[36] See 'Alī 'Abd al-Rāziq, *Al-Islām wa Uṣūl al-Ḥukm* (Cairo, 1925).

council that rejected his theory. Rāziq's theory was officially repudiated by the 'ulama, and his name was dropped from their ranks, though no constructive criticism was then offered by them.

At the time of the Rāziq controversy a young Egyptian was studying law in Paris. He chose as the subject of his dissertation, the theme of which is indicated in its title, *The Caliphate: Its Development Toward an Oriental League of Nations*.[37] Dr. Sanhūrī rejected Rāziq's theory that political authority was not an integral part of Islam, but he saw no reason why Muslim public law could not develop to fit modern conditions of life. He therefore suggested that the caliphate, which had undergone many changes in the past, was still capable of further change and might develop into an Oriental league of nations. Although Sanhūrī disagreed with Rāziq on the question of dissociating the temporal power from Islam, he seems to have been reconciled, at least in the external relations of Islam, to the secular viewpoint, that is, the full participation of the Muslim states in the international community in accordance with the modern law of nations.[38]

The secular approach to foreign affairs has been accepted by almost all Muslim states whether completely secularized in their internal legal structure, as in the case of Turkey, or still recognizing the sharī'a as their basic law, as in the Arabian Peninsula. Their active participation in international conferences, in the League of Nations, and the United Nations and its agencies demonstrate that the dār al-Islām has at last reconciled itself to a peaceful coexistence with dār al-ḥārb. The great satisfaction shown throughout the Muslim world when two Muslim jurists were elected to the benches of the Inter-

[37] A. Sanhoury, *Le Califat: son évolution vers une Société des Nations Orientale* (Paris, 1926).

[38] *Ibid.*, p. 577 ff.

national Court of Justice and the eager desire of Muslims to serve on several international commissions bear witness to the fact that Islam has not only accepted secular standards in its external relations but also its integration into the larger international community. Even the Muslim jurist-theologians, who objected to the internal secularization of the state, have accepted marked departures from the traditional Muslim law governing Islam's foreign relations. Almost all of them, who often have invoked the jihād against Western encroachment on Islam, repudiated any claim that the jihād is offensive in character.[39] Some of them have gone so far as to argue that the law governing Islam's relations with other nations, as originally expounded by the Prophet Muḥammad, was based on the principle of the peaceful—not the hostile—relations among nations and that its humane rules and practices have anticipated—in certain instances surpassed—the rules and practices of the modern law of nations.[40]

Conclusion

Although the secularization of law and authority, despite the opposition of conservative elements, continued with ever increasing celerity, a few moderate thinkers paused to take stock of the enormous changes that had taken place during their lifetime. It is not an unhealthy sign to look back at one's

[39] For the view of Shaykh Rashīd Riḍa (d.1935) on the jihād, see his *al-Khilāfa* (Cairo, A.H. 1341), pp. 29-30; for a translation of this book, see H. Laoust, *Le Califat* (Beyrouth, 1938), pp. 50-1. For an earlier exposition of Rashīd Riḍa's views on the jihād, see W. R. W. Gardner, "Jihād", *Moslem World*, Vol. II (1912), pp. 347-57.

[40] See 'Abd al-Wahhāb Khallāf, *al-Siyāsa al-Shar'iyya* (Cairo, A.H. 1350), pp. 61-100; Sayyid Quṭb, *al-'Adāla al-Ijtimā'iyya* (Cairo, 1945), pp. 92, 94-5, English translation by John B. Hardie entitled *Social Justice in Islam,* by Sayed Kotb (Washington, 1953), p. 91, 93-4; M. Ḥamīdullah, *Muslim Conduct of State* (3rd. ed., Lahore, 1954).

own achievements, whether to iron out certain mental doubts or to gather momentum for further strides. Some modernists took a critical attitude towards the adoption of Western concepts and practices without regard to traditions and existing conditions, and their views gained support in certain quarters because the results achieved under the impact of the West did not measure up to expectations. Some critics began to evaluate the impact of Westernization and could see that Western concepts, transplanted into a new social milieu, were not likely to achieve results similar to those achieved in the West. In the field of international politics, these critics could point to the penetration of Western influence in Muslim lands and the decline of Islam's prestige in the world. They regretted that the dār al-Islām, by becoming national and Balkanized, failed to show sufficient solidarity in order to regain power in diplomatic councils.

Thinking along these lines has taken place recently, both in the national and international planes, as to the possible contribution of Islam to the modern world generally and the Muslim world in particular. This trend has been called neo-Panislamism, and, since the creation of Pakistan, in 1947, has become a notable movement. In domestic affairs, it is reflected in the recognition of the sharī'a as a primary source of legislation in the Syrian Constitution of 1950 (reiterated in the revised version of 1953), and in the new civil codes of Syria, Egypt, and Iraq, in the preparation of which Dr. Sanhūrī took a leading part. On November 2, 1953, the Constituent Assembly of Pakistan declared that country to be an Islamic Republic. Even Turkey has relaxed certain measures against religious activities, thus giving impetus for Islamic revival. In the international sphere, there has been a revival in holding Islamic conferences (such as those in Pakistan and Arabia), the exchanges of visits among Muslim statesmen, and the formation of certain regional pacts and alliances—all of these are signs indicative of a desire to co-operate as a Muslim bloc within the international community.

The Muslim states, however, are quite aware that at the present it is not possible to revive the traditional religious approach to foreign affairs, nor is it in their interests to do so, as the circumstances permitting the association of religion in the relations among nations have radically changed. Not only has the jihād become an obsolete weapon, although it was invoked simultaneously with the declaration of secular wars (ḥarb) on more than one occasion (perhaps for popular consumption), but also since Islam had in the past exhausted its power, and its initiative had passed to other great powers, it became permissible—even necessary, according to the sharī'a—that Islam look after its interests in accordance with the changed circumstances of life. If certain religious groups have insisted on a more active role for the sharī'a in the domestic affairs of Islam, their interest on the international plane has been primarily to demonstrate that the sharī'a can contribute to the development of the modern law of nations for the mutual benefit of Islamic and Christian nations.

The tendency to introduce a religious element in politics, on the international no less than on the domestic plane, can be very dangerous indeed. For religion—perhaps any form of ideology—would gravely disturb the operation of a system of law which is in the main the product of custom and convention rather than the crystallization of abstract doctrines. If the modern law of nations has become world-wide, in contrast to the medieval Christian and Islamic laws of nations, it was because the European powers had repudiated the association of religion with foreign affairs since the Peace of Westphalia and have accepted secular sources for its development in accordance with the growing needs of the Family of Nations. Thus

Islam has at last accepted, after a long period of tension and friction with Christendom, its integration into a world order which, though originating in western Europe, now tends to encompass the entire world.[41]

[41] The present writer has drawn freely from his paper "From Religious to National Law," in R. H. Anshen (ed.), *World-Center: Mid East* (New York, 1955). See also, Quincy Wright, "International Law and Ideologies," *American Journal of International Law,* Vol. 48 (1954), pp. 616-26.

GLOSSARY OF TERMS

'Abd: slave.

'Adl: justice.

Ahl al-ḥall wa al-'aqd: "those who loose and bind," i.e., those entrusted with the power of making a decision.

'Ajam: Persian, foreigner.

Ahl al-Kitāb: People of the Book. See *Scripturary.*

'Ālam: world.

Allah: God.

Amān: safe-conduct. One who is given amān is musta'min (pl. musta' minūn).

Amīr: prince, commander.

Amīr al-baḥr: admiral.

Amīr al-mu'minīn: commander of the believers.

'Anwatan: things acquired by force.

'Aqd: contract.

Ashhur al-ḥarām: sacred months (i.e., Shawwāl, Dhu'l-Qi'da, Dhu'l-Ḥijja, and Muḥarram).

Asīr (pl. *asra*): prisoner of war.

Baghī: dissension.

Baḥr: sea.

Baqṭ: the tribute paid by Nubia to Islam.

Bay'a: homage or allegiance to the caliph.

Caliph (*khalīfa*): successor to the Prophet Muḥammad, chief of state.

Dakhāla: asylum.

Dār al-'ahd: territory in treaty relation with Islam.

Dār al-ḥarb: enemy territory.

Dār al-Islām: Muslim territory.

Dār al-ṣulḥ: territory at peace with Islam. See *Dār al-'ahd.*

Dawla: regime, state (modern usage).

Dhimmīs: non-Muslim subjects of the caliph. See *Ahl al-Kitāb* and *Scripturary.*

Faqīh (pl. *fuqahā):* jurist.

Farḍ: obligation, duty.

Farḍ 'ayn: individual obligation.

Farḍ al-kifāya: collective obligation.

Fatwa: legal opinion.

Fay': booty.

Fidā': ransom.

Fiqh: jurisprudence.

Fitna: rebellion, civil war.

Ghanīma: spoil of war.

Ghayba: absence of the imām.

Ḥabasha: Ethiopia.

Ḥadīth: tradition.

Ḥajj: pilgrimage.

Ḥakam: arbitrator.

Ḥarām: prohibited.

Ḥarb: war.

Ḥarbī: foreigner, one who belongs to dār al-ḥarb.

Ḥarrāqa: fire-ship.

Hijra: migration of the Prophet Muḥammad to Madīna in A.D. 622; beginning of the Muslim Era.

Ḥiyād: neutrality.

Ḥiyal: casuistry.

Ḥukm: command, legal effect.

'Ibād-Allah: God's subjects.

'Īd: feast.

Iḥrāz: acquisition.

Ijmā': consensus.

Ijtihād: independent reasoning. One who exercises ijtihād is a mujtahid (pl. mujtahidūn).

Imām: leader of the people. See *Caliph.*

Islām: literally "submission" to the will of Allah; the followers of the Prophet Muḥammad who accepted Islam as their religion.

Istiḥsān: equity, juristic preference.

Jāhiliyya: "Days of Ignorance," or the pre-Islamic era.

Jā'iz: permitted.

Jamā'ā: community.

Jāsūs (pl. *jawāsīs*): spy.

Jihād: holy war, *bellum justum.*

Jihādist (mujāhid): one who takes part in the jihād. See *Jihād.*

Jizya: poll tax.

Jund (pl. *ajwād*): army, regiment.

Kāfir (pl. *kuffār*): infidel.

Kāhin: soothsayer.

Kharāj: land tax.

Khuṭba: Friday sermon.

Kitāb: book.

Kufr: unbelief.

Madhhab: school of law.

Mahdī: messiah.

Mujtahid: see *Ijtihād.*

Makrūh: objectionable.

Mandūb: recommended.

Mawāt: waste-land.

Mulk: authority, sovereignty.

Muqātila: warriors.

Muqāwqas: governor (or the Patriarch) of Egypt.

Murtadd: see *Ridda.*

Murtaziqa: mercenary army.

Muslim: see *Islām.*

Musta'min: see *Amān.*

Mutaṭawwi'ya: volunteers.

Mu'tazila: "Rationalists," or those who recognized reason as a means to interpret the creed and law in addition to revelations.

Nabī: Prophet.

Nafal: see *Tanfīl.*

Najāshī: king of Ethiopia.

Qāḍī: judge.

Qānūn: regulation, statute.

Qānūn-namé: statute-book.

Qawm: people, group.

Qiyās: analogy.

Qubrus: Cyprus.

Qur'ān: Muslim Scripture.

Quraysh: the tribe to which the Prophet Muḥammad belonged.

Ra'iyya (pl. *ra'āya*)*:* non-Muslim subjects of the sultan of Turkey.

Ramaḍān: month of fasting.

Rasūl (pl. *rusul*)*:* apostle, emissary.

Ra'y: opinion.

Ribāṭ: safeguarding the frontiers of dār al-Islām.

Ridda: session or apostasy. One who apostatizes is called murtadd (pl. murtaddūn)

Rumḥ: lance.

Sabī: women and children taken as spoil.

Safīr: ambassador.

Ṣaḥīḥ: authentic.

Sayyid: chief of a tribe in pre-Islamic Arabia; a descendant of the family of the Prophet Muḥammad; in recent usage it is equated with Mr.

Scripturary: one who belongs to the tolerated religions, who have a Scripture (Book).

Sharī'a: sacred law.

Shaykh: tribal chief.

Shī'a: partisans of 'Alī, the fourth caliph, who formed a heterodox sect in Islam.

Shirk: polytheism. A polytheist is mushrik (pl. mushrikūn).

Siyar: originally used as an account of battles, it was later applied to that branch of the sharī'a dealing with the conduct of state.

Ṣulḥ: peace.

Sulṭān: temporal ruler.

Sunna: custom, Muḥammadan tradition.

Sunnī: Orthodox Muslim.

Tafsīr: commentary on the Qur'ān.

Taḥkīm: arbitration. See *Ḥakam.*

Taqlīd: "imitation," conformism: following the canons of a recognized school of law.

Tanfīl: supererogation. Nafal is the amount given in tanfīl.

Tanzimāt: Ottoman Reform movement.

Tha'r: vendetta.

Tijāra: commerce.

Umma: people, nation (all Muslims, regardless of race or class).

'Ushr: tithe.

Uṣūl: "roots," or sources of the sharī'a.

Walāya: allegiance to a shī'ī imām.

BIBLIOGRAPHY

It is not the purpose of this bibliography to reproduce the works cited in the footnotes of the foregoing pages of this book, but rather to supply the original sources and the fundamental modern studies that have direct bearing on the subject of war and peace in Islam. Almost exhaustive bibliographies of classical works may be found in Ḥajjī Khalīfa's *Kashf al-Zanūn,* ed. G. Flügel (London, 1845) and Ibn al-Nadīm's *Kitāb al-Fihrist,* ed. G. Flügel (Leipzig, 1871). For modern critical studies of the law of Islam, the reader may be referred to D. Santillana's *Instituzioni di diritto musulmano malichita* (Rome, 1926-38); J. Schacht's *Origins of Muhammadan Jurisprudence* (Oxford, 1950); Louis Milliot's *Introduction du droit musulman* (Paris, 1953); and M. Khadduri and H. J. Liebesny (eds.), *Law in the Middle East* (Washington, 1955). Mention must also be made of the various articles of the *Encyclopedia of*

Islam (both the old and new editions) that have bearing on the subject of this study.

PRIMARY SOURCES

Abū Da'ūd, Sulaymān ibn al-Ash'ath al-Sijistānī. *Sunan.* 4 vols. Cairo, 1935.

Abū Ya'la, Muḥammad al-Ḥusayn al-Farrā'. *Kitāb al-Aḥkām al-Sulṭāniyya,* ed. M. Ḥamīd al-Fiqqī. Cairo, 1938.

Abū Yūsuf, Ya'qūb ibn Ibrāhim al-Anṣārī. *Kitāb al-Kharāj.* Cairo, A.H. 1352.

———. *Kitāb al-Radd 'Ala Siyar al-Awzā'ī,* ed. Abū al-Wafā al-Afghānī. Cairo, A.H. 1357.

Baghdādī, Abū Manṣūr 'Abd al-Qāhir ibn Ṭāhir. *Kitāb Uṣūl al-Dīn.* Vol. I. Istanbūl, 1928.

———. *Kitāb al-Farq Bayn al-Firaq,* ed. M. Zāhid ibn al-Ḥasan al-Kawtharī. Cairo, 1948. English translation by Kate C. Seelye. (New York, 1920), Part I; and A. S. Halkin (Tel-Aviv, 1935), Part II.

———. *Mukhtaṣar al-Farq Bayn al-Firaq,* by 'Abd al-Razzāq ibn Ruzq-Allah al-Ras'anī, ed. Philip K. Hitti. Cairo, 1924.

Balādhurī, Abū al-'Abbās Aḥmad ibn Yaḥya ibn Jābir. *Kitāb Futūḥ al-Buldān,* ed. M. J. de Goeje. Leiden, 1866. English translation, *The Origins of the Islamic State,* by Philip K. Hitti. New York, 1916.

———. *Ansāb al-Ashrāf,* ed. S. D. F. Goitein and Max Schloessinger. Vols. IV, B and V. Jerusalem, 1936-38.

Bukhārī, Abū 'Abd-Allah Muḥammad ibn Ismā'īl. *Kitāb al-Jāmi' al-Ṣaḥīḥ,* ed. M. Ludolf Krehl. 4 vols. Leiden, 1862-1908.

Dārimī, Abū Muḥammad 'Abd-Allah ibn 'Abd al-Raḥmān ibn Faḍl ibn Bahrām. *Sunan.* 2 vols. Damascus, A.H. 1349.

Ibn 'Abd-Allah, 'Abd al-Raḥmān. *Kitāb al-Minhāj al-Maslūk fī Siyāsat al-Mulūk.* Cairo, A.H. 1326.

Ibn 'Abd-Allah, al-Ḥasan. *Āthār al-Uwal fī Tartīb al-Duwal.* Cairo, A.H. 1395.

Ibn 'Abd al-Ḥakam, Abū al-Qāsim 'Abd al-Raḥman ibn 'Abd-Allah. *Kitāb Futūḥ Miṣr,* ed. Charles C. Torrey. New Haven, 1922.

Ibn Abī al-Rabī', Shihāb al-Dīn Aḥmad ibn Muḥammad. *Sulūk al-Mamālik fī Tadbīr al-Mamālik.* Cairo, A.H. 1329.

Ibn Ādam, Yaḥya. *Kitāb al-Kharāj.* Cairo, A.H. 1347.

Ibn Anas, Mālik. *Al-Muwaṭṭa',* with Suyūṭī's Commentary. 2 vols. Cairo, 1939.

Ibn al-Athīr, 'Izz al-Dīn. *Kitāb al-Kāmil fī al-Ta'rīkh*, ed. C. J. Torenberg. 14 vols. Leiden, 1851-76.

Ibn al-Farrā', Abū 'Alī al-Ḥusayn ibn Muḥammad. *Kitāb Rusul al-Mulūk*, ed. Ṣalah al-Dīn al-Munajjid. Cairo, 1947.

Ibn Ḥazm, Abū Muḥammad 'Alī ibn Aḥmad. *Kitāb al-Faṣl fī al-Milal wa al-Ahwā' wa al-Niḥal*. 5 vols. Cairo, A.H. 1321.

Ibn Hishām, Abū Muḥammad 'Abd al-Malik. *Kitāb Sīrat Sayyiduna Muḥammad*, ed. Ferdinand Wüstenfeld. 2 vols. Göttingen, 1858-60.

Ibn Hudhayl, Abū al-Ḥasan 'Alī ibn 'Abd al-Raḥman. *Tuḥfat al-Anfus wa Shi'ār Sukkān al-Andalus*, ed. Louis Merçais. Paris, 1936.

Ibn Jamā'a, Badr al-Dīn. *Taḥrīr al-Aḥkām fī Tadbīr Ahl al-Islām*, ed. H. Koefler. *Islamica*, Vol. VI (1934), pp. 352-95.

Ibn Khaldūn, 'Abd al-Raḥmān. *Al-Muqaddima*, ed. Quatremère. 3 vols. Paris, 1858.

Ibn Qudāma, Abū Muḥammad 'Abd-Allah ibn Aḥmad ibn Muḥammad. *Kitāb al-Mughnī*, ed. M. Rashīd Riḍa. 9 vols. Cairo, A.H. 1367.

Ibn al-Qayyim al-Jawziyya, Shams al-Dīn Abū 'Abd-Allah Muḥammad ibn 'Alī Bakr. *I'lām al-Muwaqqi'īn*. 4 vols. Cairo, n.d.

Ibn Qutayba, Abū Muḥammad 'Abd-Allah ibn Muslim. *Kitāb 'Uyūn al-Akhbār*. Cairo, 1925.

Ibn Sa'd, Muḥammad. *Kitāb al-Ṭabaqāt al-Kabīr*, ed. E. Mittwoch and E. Sachau. 9 vols. Leiden, 1905-1940.

Ibn Sallām, Abū 'Ubayd al-Qāsim. *Kitāb al-Amwāl*, ed. M. Ḥamīd al-Fiqqī. Cairo, A.H. 1353.

Ibn Taymiyya, Taqī al-Dīn ibn 'Abd al-Salām. *Kitāb al-Siyāsa al-Shar'iyya fī Iṣlāḥ al-Rā'ī wa al-Ra'iyya*. Cairo, A.H. 1322. French translation, *Le traité de droit public d'ibn Taimīya*, by Henri Laoust. Beyrouth, 1948.

Ibn Zayyān, Abū Ḥamū Mūsa ibn Yūsuf. *Kitāb Wāsiṭat al-Sulūk fī Siyāsat al-Mulūk*. Tunis, A.H. 1279.

Khaṭīb al-Baghdādī, Abū Bakr Aḥmad ibn 'Alī. *Ta'rīkh Baghdād*. 14 vols. Cairo, 1931.

Māwardī, Abū al-Ḥasan 'Alī ibn Muḥammad ibn Ḥabīb. *Kitāb al-Aḥkām al-Sulṭāniyya*, ed. M. Enger. Bonn, 1853.

Muslim, Abū al-Ḥusayn Muslim ibn al-Ḥajjāj, *Ṣaḥīḥ*, with Nawawi's Commentary, 18 vols. Cairo, 1929-30.

Nabrawālī, Quṭb al-Dīn. *Kitāb al-I'lām li A'lām Bayt Allah al-Ḥarām*, ed. Wüstenfeld. Leipzig, 1857.

Nasafī, Najm al-Dīn. *Creed of Islam*, with Taftāzānī's Commentary, trans. E. E. Elder. New York, 1950.

Nu'mān, Qāḍī Abū Ḥanīfa. *Da'ā'im al-Islām,* ed. Āṣif ibn 'Alī Aṣghar Fayḍī [A. A. A. Fyzee]. Vol. I. Cairo, 1951.

Qalqashandī, Abū al-'Abbās Aḥmad. *Kitāb Ṣubḥ al-A'sha.* 14 vols. Cairo, 1914-19.

Qur'ān. Although several renderings of the *Qur'ān* are available in the English language, there is as yet no fully adequate translation. Not infrequently a modified rendering based on one or two of the following translations have been used for the purposes of this book:

J. M. Rodwell, *The Koran* (Everyman's Library).

E. H. Palmer, *Qur'ān* (World's Classics)

Richard Bell, *The Qur'ān* (Edinburgh, 1937-39), 2 vols.

Saḥnūn, ibn Sa'īd al-Tanūkhī. *Al-Mudawwana al-Kubra.* 16 vols. Cairo, A.H. 1323.

Sarakhsī, Shams al-Dīn. *Kitāb al-Mabsūṭ.* 30 vols. Cairo, A.H. 1324.

Shāfi'ī, Abū 'Abd-Allah Muḥammad Idrīs. *Kitāb al-Umm.* 7 vols. Cairo, A.H. 1321-25.

Shahrastānī, Abū al-Fatḥ Muḥammad ibn 'Abd al-Karīm. *Kitāb al-Milal wa al-Niḥal,* ed. Cureton. London, 1846.

Shawkānī, Muḥammad ibn 'Alī ibn Muḥammad. *Nayl al-Awṭār.* 8 vols. 2nd. ed. Cairo, 1952.

Shaybānī, Muḥammad ibn al-Ḥasan. *Kitāb al-Siyar al-Kabīr,* with Sarakhsī's Commentary. 4 vols. Hyderabad, A.H. 1335.

Subkī, Tāj al-Dīn Abū Naṣr 'Abd al-Wahhāb ibn Taqī al-Dīn. *Ṭabaqāt al-Shāfi'iyya al-Kubra.* 6 vols. Cairo, A.H. 1324.

Ṭabarī, Abū Ja'far Muḥammad ibn Jarīr. *Ta'rīkh al-Rusul wa al-Mulūk,* ed. M. J. de Goeje. 15 vols. Leiden, 1879-1901.

———. *Kitāb al-Jihād wa Kitāb al-Jizya wa Aḥkām al-Muḥāribīn min Kitāb Ikhtilāf al-Fuqahā',* ed. J. Schacht. Leiden, 1933.

———. *Jāmi' al-Bayān fī Tafsīr al-Qur'ān.* 30 vols. Cairo, A.H. 1321.

Ṭarṭūshī, Abū Bakr Muḥammad ibn Muḥammad ibn al-Walīd. *Kitāb Sirāj al-Mulūk.* Cairo, A.H. 1319.

Tirmidhī, Muḥammad ibn 'Īsa. *Sunan.* Cairo, 1931.

Wāqidī, Abū 'Abd-Allah Muḥammad ibn 'Umar. *Kitāb al-Maghāzī,* ed. Alfred von Kremer. Calcutta, 1856.

Ya'qūbī, Aḥmad ibn Abū Ya'qūb. *Ta'rīkh,* ed. M. Th. Houtsma. 2 vols. Leiden, 1883.

SECONDARY WORKS

'Abd al-Rāziq, 'Alī. *Al-Islām wa Uṣūl al-Ḥukm.* Cairo, 1925.

Aghnides, Nicolas P. *Mohammedan Theories of Finance.* London and New York, 1916.

Armanāzi, Nagīb. *Les principes Islamiques et les rapports internationaux en temps de paix et de guerre.* Paris, 1929.

Arnold, Thomas W. *The Caliphate.* Oxford, 1924.

———. *The Preaching of Islam.* 3rd. ed. London, 1935.

———, and Alfred Guillaume (eds.) *The Legacy of Islam.* Oxford, 1931.

Becker, C. H. *Islamstudien.* 2 vols. Leipzig, 1924-32.

Caetani, Leone. *Annali dell' Islam.* 10 vols. Milano, 1905-26.

Calverley, Edwin E. "The Fundamental Structure of Islam," *The Moslem World,* Vol. XXIX (1939), pp. 364-84.

Cardahi, Choucri. "La conception et la pratique du droit international privé dans l'Islam," *Académie de Droit International, Recueil des Cours,* 1937 (Paris, 1938), Vol. II, pp. 511-646.

Dennett, Daniel C. *Conversion and Poll Tax in Early Islam.* Cambridge, Mass., 1950.

Fagnan, E. *Le djihad ou guerre sainte selon l'ecole malikite.* Alger, 1908.

Gardner, W. R. W. "Jihad," *The Moslem World,* Vol. II (1912), pp. 347-57.

Gibb, H. A. R. "Al-Māwardī's Theory of the Khilāfah," *Islamic Culture,* Vol. XI (1937), pp. 291-302.

———. "Some Considerations on the Sunnī Theory of the Caliphate," *Archives d'histoire du droit Oriental,* Vol. III (1948), pp. 401-10.

———. (ed.), *Whither Islam.* London, 1933.

Goldziher, Ignaz. *Muhammedanische Studien.* 2 vols. Halle, 1888-90.

———. *Die Zahiriten.* Leipzig, 1884.

———. *Le dogme et la loi de l'Islam,* trans. Felix Arin. Paris, 1920.

Gottheil, Richard J. "Dhimmis and Moslems in Egypt," *Old Testament and Semitic Studies,* Vol. II, pp. 351-414. Chicago, 1908.

Guillaume, Alfred. *The Traditions of Islam.* Oxford, 1924.

Ḥamīdullah, Muḥammad. *Document sur la Diplomatie musulmane à l'époque du Prophète et des Khalifes Orthodoxes.* Paris, 1935.

———. *Muslim Conduct of State.* 3rd. ed. Lahore, 1954.

———. "Administration of Justice in Early Islam," *Islamic Culture,* Vol. XI (1937), pp. 163-71.

Hatschek, Julius. *Der Musta'min.* Berlin, 1920.

Heffening, W. *Das Islamische Fremdendercht.* Hannover, 1925.

Heyd, W. *Histoire du Commerce du levant.* 2 vols. Leipzig, 1885-86.

Hourani, George F. *Arab Seafaring.* Princeton, 1951.

Huart, Clement. "Le droit de la guerre," *Revue du monde musulman,* Vol. II (1907), pp. 331-46.

Hurgronje, C. Snouck. *The Holy War, Made in Germany.* New York, 1915.

Khadduri, Majid. "Nature of the Islamic State," *Islamic Culture,* Vol. XXI (1947), pp. 327-31.

———. "The Juridical Theory of the Islamic State," *The Muslim World,* Vol. (1951), pp. 181-85.

———. "Nature and Sources of Islamic Law," *The George Washington Law Review,* Vol. XXII (1953), pp. 3-23.

———. "From Religious to National Law," in R. N. Anshen, *World Center: Mid-East.* New York, 1955.

Kruse, Hans. *Islamische Völkerrechtslehre.* Göttingen, 1953.

———. "Al-Shaybānī on International Instruments," *Journal of the Pakistan Historical Society,* Vol. I, (1953), pp. 90-100.

———. "Die Begründung der islamischen Völkerrechtslehre," *Saeculum,* Heft 2, pp. 221-39.

Lammens, Henri. *Islam: Beliefs and Institutions,* trans. Dennison Ross. London, 1929.

Lewis, A. R. *Naval Power and Trade in the Mediterranean, A.D. 500-1100.* Princeton, 1951.

Løkkegaard, Frede. *Islamic Taxation in the Classic Period.* Copenhagen, 1950.

Macdonald, Duncan B. *Development of Muslim Theology, Jurisprudence and Constitutional Theory.* New York, 1903.

Maḥmaṣānī, Ṣubḥī. *Falsafat al-Tashrī' fī al-Islām.* Beirut, 1946.

Margoliouth, D. S. *The Early Development of Mohammedanism.* New York, 1914.

Massignon, Louis. "Le respect de la personne humaine en Islam, et la priorite du droit d'asile sur le devoir de juste guerre," *Revue internationale de la Croix-Rouge,* no. 402 (1952), pp. 448-68.

Mez, Adam. *Die Renaissance des Islam.* Heidelberg, 1922.

Mingana, A. *A Charter of Protection Granted to the Nestorian Church in A.D. 1138 by Mustakfī II.* Manchester, 1925.

Nallino, C. A. *Notes on the Nature of the Caliphate in General and on the Alleged Ottoman Caliphate.* Rome, 1919.

Obbink, Herman Theodorus. *De Heilige Oorlog Volgen den Koran.* Leiden, 1901.

Ostrorog, Le Counte Leon. *Traité de droit public musulman.* 2 vols. Paris, 1901-6.

Rechid, Aḥmad. "L'Islam et le droit des gens," *Académie de Droit International, Recueil des Cours,* 1937 (Paris, 1938), Vol. II, pp. 375-504.

Riḍa, Rashīd. *Al-Khilāfa.* Cairo, A.H. 1341. French translation by Henri Laoust, *Le Califat.* Beyrouth, 1938.

Sanhoury, A. *Le Califat.* Paris, 1926.

Sprengling, Martin. "From Persian to Arabic," *American Journal of Semitic Languages and Literatures,* Vol. LVI (1939), pp. 175-224, 325-36.

Taube, le Baron Michel. "Le monde de l'Islam et son influence sur l'Europe Orientale," *Académie de Droit International, Recueil des Cours,* 1926 (Paris, 1927), Vol. I, pp. 380-97.

Tritton, A. S. *The Caliphs and Their Non-Muslim Subjects.* London, 1930.

Tyan, Emile. *Histoire de l'organisation judiciaire en pays d'Islam.* 2 vols. Paris, 1938-43.

———. *Institution du droit public Musulman.* Vol. I. *Le Califat.* Paris, 1954.

Wellhausen, Julius. *Skizzen und Vorarbeiten.* 6 vols. Berlin, 1889.

———. *The Arab Kingdom and its Fall,* trans. M. G. Weir. Calcutta, 1927.

Wensinck, A. J. *A Handbook of Early Muhammadan Tradition.* Leiden, 1927.

Zwemer, Samuel M. *The Law of Apostasy in Islam.* London, 1924.

INDEX

INDEX

'Abbāsids: Army organization of, 90; Mongols and, 143; diplomatic relations of, 216–17, 242, 247–48
'Abd al-Hamīd II, Sultan: constitution of, 287
'Abd al-Malik, Caliph, 216
'Abd al-Rāziq, Shaykh 'Alī, 291–92
Abū Bakr, Caliph: treatment of apostates by, 77; jihād instructions of, 102; on ransoming prisoners, 127; on Arab enslavement, 131
Abū Ḥanīfa, 29–30: on analogy, 29–30; choice of traditions by, 30; school of law of, 36; on definition of a Muslim; commercial experience of, 224
Abū 'Ubayda: treatment of Christians by, 183, 185–86
Abū Ya'la, 108
Abū Yūsuf: on division of spoils, 123; on *musta'min*, 167; on scriptuary compacts, 179–80; on treatment of Christians, 183–85; on taxation, 190, 193; on scripturary commerce, 226
Admiral, 116–17
Ahl al-Kitāb, 176–77
Alberoni, Cardinal, 277–78
'Alī, Caliph: on ownership of spoils, 125; in arbitration, 234–38
Amān: in jihād, 107, 115, 163; Awzā'ī on, 115, 164–65; rules of, 163–65; limitations on Muslims of, 171–72; schools of law on, 164–65; termination of, 168; importance of, 168–69; Muslims in World of War without, 173; dhimmīs under, 177; for merchants, 225; immunity from, 243
Analogy: as a source of law, 29
Apostasy: types of, 76; definition of, 149; punishment of, 149–51, Muḥammad on, 150–52
Arabia: jihād in, 62, 75; Christians in, 75–76, Jews in, 75; arbitration in, 232–33
Arbitration: origins of, 231–33; Muḥammad on, 232–34; between 'Alī and Mu'āwiya, 234–38; al-Shaybāni on, 234; by Abū Mūsa al-Ash'arī, 234–38; by 'Amr Ibn al-'Āṣ, 234–38; frequency of, 238
Army: organization of, 89–91, 136–37; use of foreigners in, 91
al-Ash'arī, Abū Mūsa: on responsibility and position of Caliph, 12–13; on Imām's authority, 78; arbitration by, 234–38
Asylum, right of, 21
al-Awzā'ī: on jihād, 103–108 *passim*, 114, 120, 123, 136; on amān, 115,

Dennett, Daniel C.: on jizya and kharāj, 188–89
Dhāt al-Ṣawārī: naval victory at, 110
Dhimmīs: amān for, 165, 177; definition of, 176; Ahl al-Kitāb as, 176–77, rights of, 177; Sarakhsī on, 177; law enforcement among, 175, 176; disabilities of, 177, 185–87 *passim;* early Islamic position on, 177–87; Islamic Law on, 177, 195–98, 215; taxation on, 191, 193; Islam's relations with, 195; employment in government of, 199; treaties with, 220; European protection of, 287
Diplomacy: in early Islam, 239; Islamic practice of, 239, 240; emissaries in, 240–44; letters of credence, 241; prisoners of war in, 242; Umayyad, 242; amān in, 243; missions in, 245–46; 'Abbāsid, 242–49 *passim;* rivalries in, 246–49; jihād in, 249; Islamic Law on, 249, 250; usefulness of, 250; Ottoman changes in, 271, 272, 286, 287; secularization of, 291, 292, 293; effect of religion on, 295
Diplomatic emissaries: qualifications of, 240–41; Muḥammad's use of, 241–42; immunity of, 243; reception of, 243–44; prohibitions on, 243, 244
Diplomatic missions: functions of, 245–46
Ethiopia: Muslim refugees in, 253–54; Muḥammad on, 253–57; neutrality of, 253–58; Islamic Law on, 257, 258; immunity from jihād of, 258; Mālikī Law on, 258; status difference from Nubia of, 261
Ethiopian hijra, 254
Europe, concert of: Ottoman admission to, 282, 284
al-Fārābī, Abū Naṣr: on Islamic world state, 4, 5, 142
Foreigners: Ottoman treatment of, 272, 273, 274
France: Ottoman treaty with, 272–279 *passim*
Francis I, King of France: Ottoman alliance of, 276
Gentilis, Albericus, 275–76
Ghazzālī: on limits of warfare, 107
God, Grace of: Islamic principle of, 105
Grotius, Hugo, 276
Ḥadīth: on jihād against polytheists, 75; on defensive jihād, 81; on invitation to Islam, 96; sea references in, 113; on treaties, 203
Hall, W. E., 283
Ḥanafī Law: on pre-Islamic rules and practices, 19; attacks on, 31; requirements for jihādists in, 84; invitation to Islam in, 97; property treatment during jihād in, 104; limits on warfare in, 107; on division of spoils, 120–26 *passim;* land transfer in, 126; on cessation of jihād, 135; World of Peace in, 145; on punishment of apostasy, 151; regulation of the harām in, 159; on amān, 164–65; musta' min in, 167; on Muslims in non-Muslim territory, 173; on duration of treaties, 219; Ottoman adoption of, 271–72

220–22; Islamic Law on, 220–21, 273, 274; with Nubia, 259–61; on Cyprus, 262–66; with France, 272, 273, 279
Treaty-making power, 203
Tribute: Qur'ān on, 178; to Byzantium, 215; Muslim payment of, 215, 216; Islamic Law on, 216
Uḥud, battle of, 210
'Umar, Caliph: use of *ra'y* by, 28; treatment of Christians by, 75; sea references by, 112; Cyprus expedition of, 112; on land, 125, 126, 187; on prisoners of war, 128–29; on Arab enslavement, 131, 132; position of scriptuaries under, 182–87 *passim;* Covenant of, 182–83, 193–94
'Umar II, Caliph: uniform jizya rule of, 191
Umayyads: influence on Awzā'ī of, 136; relations with Byzantines of, 136; treaties with Byzantines of, 215, 216; diplomacy of, 242
Umayyad Caliphs: army reorganization of, 89, 90
Unbelief: definition of, 149
Utopia: Islam as, 141–42
Vienna, Congress of, 280, 281
War: Muslim and Christian concepts of, 72, 73; Declaration of, 74; exchange of prisoners in, 101; legal theory of, 102; treatment of non-combatants in, 104, 105, 106; abstention in sacred months from, 105
War, prisoners of: Caliph Abū Bakr on, 127; ransom of, 127, 130, 217, 218; treatment of, 127–30 *passim;* exchange of, 128; Mālikī law on, 128; Muslims as, 129, 130; parole of, 173, 174; obligations of, 174; hostages as, 218; treaties on, 242
War, vessels of, 116
War, World of: nature of, 52, 53; relation to World of Islam of, 53; legal position of, 64, 171; jihād against, 105; Muslim prisoners in, 106; division of spoils in, 120; origins of, 143, 144; non-recognition of, 144; reversion from World of Islam to, 156, 157; territorial divisions of, 157, 158; relations with World of Islam of, 170; authority in, 171; amān in, 171, 172, 173; Muslim residence in, 171–74 *passim;* conduct of Muslims in, 171–74 *passim,* 228; parole of Muslims in, 173, 174; and commerce, 224–28 *passim*
Wellhausen, Julius: on jizya, 188, 189; on kharāj, 188, 189
Wheaton, Henry, 283, 284, 285
World: Islamic concept of, 7–9
World, divisions of: Islamic World State in, 143, 144; Islamic Law on, 144; World of Peace in, 144, 145
Ya'qūbī: on kharāj, 190
Young Turks, 288
Yūḥanna: Muḥammad's compact with, 180, 181
Zāhirī Law: on Muslim commerce, 227

Lightning Source UK Ltd.
Milton Keynes UK
UKOW02f0413200814

237221UK00002B/104/P

9 781616 190484